The History of the Origins of Christianity

Christianity

Book V - The Gospels

By Joseph Ernest Renan

Edited by Anthony Uyl

Devoted Publishing

Woodstock, Ontario, 2017

The History of the Origins of Christianity Book V - The Gospels
By Joseph Ernest Renan
Member of the French Academy.
Edited by Anthony Uyl

Originally Published by:
London: Mathieson & Company New Inn Chambers, 41 Wych Street, W.C.

What kind of philosophies do you have? Let us know!

Contact us at: devotedpub@hotmail.com
Visit us on Facebook: @DevotedPublishing
Get more products via our website: www.devotedpublishing.com

Published in Woodstock, Ontario, Canada 2017

For bulk educational rates, please contact us at the email address above.

ISBN: 978-1-988297-73-6

Table of Contents

INTRODUCTION

CRITICAL OBSERVATIONS ON THE ORIGINAL DOCUMENTS OF THIS HISTORY

I had at first believed that I should be able to finish is one volume this history of the "Origins of Christianity;" but the matter has grown in proportion as I have advanced in my work, and the present volume only the last but two. The reader will find in it the explanation, so far as it is possible to give one, of a fact almost equal in importance to the personal action of Jesus himself--I mean to say, of the manner in which the legend of Jesus was written. The compilation of the Gospels is, next to the life of Jesus, the cardinal chapter of the history of Christian origins. The material circumstances of this compilation are surrounded with mystery; many of the doubts, however, have, in those later years, been dispelled, and it can now he said that the problem of the compilation of the Gospels denominated synoptic, has reached a kind of maturity. The relations of Christianity with the Roman Empire, the first heresies, the disappearance of the last immediate disciples of Jesus, the gradual separation of the Church and the Synagogue, the progress of the ecclesiastical hierarchy, the substitution of the presbytery for the primitive community, the coming in with Trajan of a met of golden age for civil society, these are the great facts which we shall see unfolded to our view. Our sixth volume will embrace the history of Christianity under the reigns of Hadrian and Antoninus; we shall witness the commencement of Gnosticism, the compilation of the pseudo-Johannine writings, the first apologists, the party of St Paul drifting by exaggeration to Marcion, ancient Christianity running into a coarser Millenarism and Montanism. Opposed to all this, the episcopate making rapid strides, Christianity becoming each day more Greek and less Hebrew, a "Catholic Church" beginning to result from the accord of all the individual churches, and to constitute centre of irrefragable authority, which already was established at Rome. We shall see finally the absolute separation of Judaism and Christianity definitively effected, from the time of the revolt of Bar-Coziba, and hatred the most deadly kindled between mother and daughter. From this point it can be said that Christianity is constituted. Its principle of authority exists. The episcopate has entirely replaced the primitive democracy, and the bishops of the different churches are en rapport with one another. The new Bible is complete; it is called the New Testament. The divinity of Jesus Christ is recognised by all the Churches outside of Syria. The Son is not yet the equal of the Father; he is a tend god, a supreme vizier of creation, yet he is in very truth a god. Finally, two or three attacks of maladies, extremely dangerous, which break out in the nascent religion--Gnosticism, Montanism, docetism, the heretical attempt of Marcion--are vanquished by the force of the internal principle of authority. Christianity, moreover, has extended itself everywhere. It has seated itself in the heart of Gaul, it has penetrated into Africa. It is a public affair: the historians speak of it; it has its advocates who defend it officially, its accusers who commence against it a war of criticism. Christianity, in a word, is born, completely born; it is an infant, and will grow a great deal. It has all its organs, it lives in the broad light of day, it is no longer an embryo. The umbilical cord which attached it to its mother is definitely cut; it will receive nothing more from her; it will live its own life.

It is at this moment, about the year 160, that we shall determine this. That which follows belongs to history, and may seem relatively easy to recount. What we have wished to make clear belongs to the embry-organic stage, and must in great part be inferred, sometimes even divined. Minds which only love material certainty, cannot be pleased with such researches. Rarely (for these periods recur) does it happen that one can say with precision how things have taken place; but one may succeed sometimes in picturing to oneself the diverse manners in which they may have taken place, and that is sufficient. If there be a science which can make in our day surprising progress, it is the science of comparative mythology. Now this science has consisted much less in teaching us how each myth has been formed, than in demonstrating to us the diverse categories of formation. Although we cannot say, "Such a demi-god, such a goddess, is surely storm, lightning, the dawn," etc.; but we can say, "The atmospheric phenomena, particularly those which are related to the rising and the setting of the sun, and so forth, have been the fruitful sources of gods and demi-gods." Aristotle has truly said, "There is no science except general science." History herself, history properly speaking, history exposed to the light of day and founded upon documents, does she escape this necessity? Certainly not; we do not know exactly the details of anything. That which is of moment are the general lines, the grand resultant facts which remain true even though all the details may be erroneous.

Hence I have said the most important object of this volume is to explain in a plausible manner the method by which the three Gospels, called synoptic, were formed, which constitute, if we compare them with the fourth Gospel, a family apart. It is certainly true that it is impossible to determine precisely many of the points in this delicate research. It must be confessed, however, that the question has made during the last twenty years veritable progress. As the origin of the fourth Gospel, which is attributed to John, remains enveloped in mystery, so the hypotheses in regard to the compilation of the Gospels called synoptic have attained a high degree of probability. There are in reality three kinds of Gospels: (1) The original Gospels, or Gospels at first hand, composed solely from oral tradition, and without the author having before him any anterior text. (In my opinion, there are two Gospels of this kind, the one written in Hebrew, or rather in Syriac, now lost, but of which many of the fragments have been preserved to us, translated into Greek or into Latin, by Clement of Alexandria, Origen, Eusebius, Epiphanius, St Jerome, etc.; the other written in Greek, which is that of St Mark.) (2) The Gospels, in part original, in part at second hand, formed by combining the anterior texts with the oral traditions (such were the Gospel falsely attributed to the Apostle Matthew and the Gospel composed by Luke). (3) The Gospels at second or third hand, composed deliberately from written documents, without the authors having dipped through any living principle into traditions. (Such was the Gospel of Marcion; such were also these Gospels, called apocryphal, drawn from the canonical Gospels by processes of amplification.) The variety of the Gospels arises from this, that the tradition which is found deposited there was for a long time oral. That variety would not have existed if from the very first the life of Jesus had been written. The idea of modifying arbitrarily the compilation of the texts presents itself less in the East than elsewhere, because the literal reproduction of the anterior accounts, or, if it be preferred, plagiarism is there the rule of the historiographer. The moment when an epic, or a legendary tradition, commences to be put into writing, marks the hour when it ceases to produce divergent branches. Far from subdividing itself, the compilation obeys thenceforward a sort of secret tendency which restores it to unity through the gradual extinction of imperfectly-judged compilations. There existed fewer Gospels at the end of the second century, when Irenæus found mystical reasons to establish that there were four, and that there could not be more, than at the close of the fast, when Luke wrote at the end of his narrative, Eperde per polloi epicheiresan . . . Even in the time of Luke several of the original editions had probably disappeared. The oral form produces a multiplication of variants; but once the written style has been entered upon, this multiplicity is nothing but inconvenience. If logic like that of Marcion's had prevailed, we should have had no more than one Gospel, and the best mark of the sincerity of the Christian conscience is that the necessities of the apologetic have not suppressed the contradictions in the texts by reducing them to one only. This is why, to speak the truth, the want of unity was combated by a contrary desire--that of losing nothing of a tradition which was judged as being equally precious in all its parts. A design like that which is often attributed to St Mark, the idea of making an abridgment of the anteriorily received texts, is more contrary to the spirit of the times than the one in question. People aimed, indeed, rather at completing each text by the heterogeneous additions, as in the case of Matthew, than in discarding from the little book what one possessed of the details which were regarded by all as being penetrated by the Divine Spirit.

The most important documents for the epoch treated of in this volume are, besides the Gospels and the other writings the compilation of which are therein explained, the somewhat numerous epistles which were produced during the last apostolic period--epistles in which almost always the imitation of those of St Paul is discernible. What we shall say in our text will be sufficient to make known our opinion upon each of these writing. A fortuitous accident has willed that the most interesting of these epistles, that of Clemens Romanus, has received, in these later times, considerable elucidation. We should not have before known of this precious document, but for the celebrated manuscript, named Alexandrinus, which was sent, in 1682, by Cyril Lucaris to Charles I. Now, this manuscript contained a considerable omission, not to speak of several places which had been destroyed, or become illegible, which it was necessary to fill up with conjecture. A new manuscript, discovered in the Fanar at Constantinople, contains the work in its entirety. A Syriac manuscript, which formed a portion of the library of the late M. Mohl, and which has been acquired by the library of the University of Cambridge, was found also to include the Syrian translation of the work of which we are speaking. M. Bensley is entrusted with the publication of that text. The collation which Mr Lightfoot has made of it, has produced the most important results which arise from it for criticism.

The question whether the epistle attributed to Clemens Romanus really by that holy personage, has only a mediocre importance, since the writing in question is represented as the collective work of the Roman Church, and since the problem confines itself, consequently, as to who held the pen on this particular occasion. It is not the same as the epistles attributed to St Ignatius. The fragments which compose this collection are either authentic or the work of a forger. In the second hypothesis they were at lead sixty years posterior to the death of St Ignatius, and such is the importance of the change. which operated in those sixty years, that the documentary value of the said fragments is absolutely changed by them. It is hence impossible to treat the history of the origins of Christianity, without taking up a decided position in this regard.

The question of the Epistles of St Ignatius, next to the question of the Johannine writings, is the most difficult of those which belong to the primitive Christian literature. A few of the moat striking features of one of the letters which form a portion of that correspondence, were known and cited from the end of the second century. We have, moreover, here the testimony of a man which we are surprised to see pleaded on a subject of ecclesiastical history--that of Lucian of Samosata. The spirituelle picture of morals which that charming author has entitled "The Death of Peregrinus," contains some almost direct allusions to the triumphal journey of the prisoner Ignatius, and to the circular epistles which he addressed to the Churches. These constitute some strong presumptions in favour of the authenticity of the letters of which we have been speaking. On the other hand, the taste for supposititious writings was at the time so wide-spread amongst Christian society, that we ought always to be on our guard in respect of them, since it is proved that no scruple was made in ascribing some of the letters and other writings to Peter, Paul, and John. There is no prejudicial objection to be raised against the hypothesis which attribute. writings to persona of high authority, such as Ignatius and Polycarpus. It is only the examination of the compositions themselves which will warrant one in expressing an opinion in that regard. Now it is incontestable that the perusal of the writings of St Ignatius inspires the gravest suspicions, and raises objections which no one has as yet satisfactorily answered.

In regard to a personage like St Paul, some of whose longer writings of indubitable authenticity it is universally admitted we possess, and whose biography is well enough known, the discussion of the contested epistles has some foundation. We start with the texts to which no exception can be taken, and from the well-established outlines of the biography; we compare the doubtful writings with them; we see whether they agree with the data admitted by everyone, and, in certain cases, as in those of the Epistles to Titus and Timothy, we reach most satisfactory conclusions. But we know nothing of the private life of St Ignatius; among the writings attributed to him there is not a page of them which is not contestable. We have not their solid criterium to warrant us in saying, "This is or this is not his." That which greatly complicates the question is, that the text of the epistles is extremely variable--the Greek, Latin, Syriac, and Armenian manuscripts of the same epistle differ considerably amongst themselves. These letters, during several centuries, seem to have particularly exercised the forgers and the interpolators. Obstacles and difficulties are encountered in them at each step.

Without taking into account the secondary various readings, as well as some works notoriously spurious, we prossess two collections of unequal length of the epistles attributed to St Ignatius. The one contains seven letters addressed to the Ephesian, the Magnesians, the Trallians, the Romans, the Philadelphians, the Smyrniotes, to Polycarpus. The other consists of thirteen letters, to wit: (1) The seven just mentioned, considerably augmented; (2) Four new letters of Ignatius to the Tarsians, to the Philippians, to the Antiochians, to Heros; (3) and finally, a letter of Maria de Castabala to Ignatius, with the answer of Ignatius. Between those two collections there can be but little possible hesitation. The critics, beginning with Usserius, are nearly agreed in preferring the collection of seven letters to that of the thirteen. There can be no doubt that the added letters in the latter collection are apocryphal. As for the seven letters which are common to the two collections, the actual text must certainly be sought for in the former collection. Many of the particulars in the texts of the second collection betray unmistakably the hand of the interpolator; but this does not necessitate that this second collection may not have a veritable critical value in regard to the construction of the text, for it would appear that the interpolator had in his hands an excellent manuscript, the reading of which ought to be preferred to that of the noninterpolated manuscripts actually existing.

In any case, is the collection of seven letters beyond suspicion? Far from it. The first doubts were raised by the great school of French criticism of the seventeenth century. Saumaise and Blondel raised the moat serious objections against portions of the collection of the seven letters. Daillé, in 1666, published a remarkable dissertation, in which he rejected the collection in its entirety. In spite of the trenchant replies of Pearson, Bishop of Chester, and the resistance of Cotolier, the majority of independent minds--Larroque, Basnage, Casimir Oudin--ranged themselves on the side of Daillé. The school which in our day in Germany has so learnedly applied criticism to the history of the origins of Christianity, has only followed the lines of that of nearly two hundred years ago. Neander and Gieseler remained in doubt; Christian Baur resolutely denied the authenticity of the whole: none of the epistles found grace in his sight. This great critic, it is true, did not rest content with denying, he explained. In his view, the seven Ignatian epistles were a forgery of the second century, fabricated at Rome, with a view of creating a basis for the authority of the episcopate, which was increasing day by day. M. M. Schwegler, Hilgenfeld, Vauchner, Volkmar, and more recently M. M. Scholten and Pfliederer, have adopted the same propositions, with slightly different shades of meaning. Many enlightened theologians, nevertheless, such as Uhlhorn, Hefele, and Dressel, persisted in regarding some portions of the collection of the seven letters as authentic, or even in defending it in its entirety. An important discovery, about the year 1840, ought to have determined the question in an ecclesiastical sense, and furnished an instrument to those who held it to be a difficult operation to separate in the texts, generally little accented, the sincere parts from those interpolated.

Amongst the treasures which the British Museum secured from the convents of Nitria, M. Cureton discovered three Syriac manuscripts, each of which contained the same collection of the Ignatian epistles; but they are much more abridged than the two Greek collections. The Syrian collection found by Cureton contained only three epistles--the epistle to the Ephesians, that to the Romans, that to Polycarpus--and these three epistles were found to be much shorter than in the Greek. It was natural to believe that people would in fine hold Ignatius to be authentic, the text being anterior to all interpolations. The phrases cited as those of Ignatius by Irenæus, by Origen, were found in that Syriac version.

People believed it was possible to show that the suspected passages were not to be found in them. Bunsen, Ritschl, Weiss, and Lipsius displayed an extreme ardour in maintaining that proposition. M. Ewald assumed to advocate it in imperious tone; but very strong objections were raised against it. Baur, Wordsworth, Hefele, Uhlhorn, and Merx set themselves to prove that the small Syriac collection, so far from being the original text, was an abridged and mutilated text. They have not clearly shown, it is true, what motives had guided the abbreviator in this work of making extracts. But in seeking again for the evidences of the knowledge which the Syrians had of the epistles in question, we arrive at the conclusion that not only had the Syrians not possessed an Ignatius more authentic than that of the Greeks, but that even the collection which they have was the collection of thirteen letters from which the abbreviator discovered by Cureton had drawn his extracts. Petermann contributed much to this result in discussing the Armenian translation of the epistles in question. This translation had been made from the Syriac, but it contains the thirteen letters, including the most feeble portions of them. People are to-day so nearly agreed that there is no occasion to consult the Syriac in that which concerns the writings attributed to the Bishop of Antioch, except as to a few details of the various readings.

We see, after what has just been said, that three opinions divide the critics as to the collection of the seven letters, only one of which, however, merits discussion. Some hold that the whole collection is apocryphal, while others maintain that the whole, or nearly so, is authentic. A few seek to distinguish the authentic from the apocryphal portion. The second opinion appears to us indefensible. Without affirming that everything in the correspondence of the Bishop of Antioch is apocryphal, it is allowable to regard as a desperate attempt the pretension of demonstrating that the whole of it is of good alloy.

If we except, in fact, the Epistle to the Romans, which is full of a singular energy, of a kind of sacred fire, and stamped by a character peculiarly original, the six other epistles, excepting two or three passages, are cold, lifeless, and desperately monotonous. There is not one of those striking peculiarities which gave us distinctive a seal to the Epistles of St Paul and even to the Epistles of St James and Clemens Romanus; they consist of vague exhortations, without any special relations to those to whom they are addressed, and always dominated by one fixed idea--the enhancement of the episcopal power, the constitution of the Church into a hierarchy.

Certainly the remarkable evolution which substituted for the collective authority of the ἐκκλησία or συναγωγή the direction of the πρεσβύτεροι or ἐπίσκοποι (two terms at first synonymous), and which, among the πρεσβύτεροι or ἐπίσκοποι, in selecting one out from the circle (?) to be par excellence the ἐπίσκοπος or overseer of the others, began at a very early date. But it is not credible that, about the year 110 or 115, this movement was so advanced as we see it to be in the Ignatian epistles. According to the author of these curious writings, the bishop is the whole Church; it is imperative to follow him in everything, to consult him in everything--he some up the community in himself alone. He is Christ himself. Where the bishop is, there is the Church, just as where Jesus Christ is, there is the Church Catholic. The distinction between the different ecclesiastical orders is not less characteristic. The priests and deacons are in the hands of the bishop like the strings of a lyre; their perfect harmony depends upon the accuracy of the sounds which the Church emits. Above the individual Churches, in fact, there is a Church Universal, ἡ καθολικὴ ἐκκλησία. All this is true enough from the end of the second century, but not so from the early years of that century. The repugnance which our old French critics evinced on this point was well founded, and sprung from the very correct sentiment which they entertained as to the gradual evolution of the Christian dogmas.

The heresies combatted by the author of the Ignatian epistles with so much fury are likewise of an age posterior to that of Trajan. They were wholly attached to a Docetism or a Gnosticism analogous to that of Valentinus. We insist less on this particular, for the pastoral epistles and the Johannine writings combat errors greatly analogous, yet we think these writings belong to the first half of the second century. However, the idea of an orthodoxy outside of which there is only error, appeared in the writings in question, and so fully developed that it seems to approach more nearly the times of St Irenæus than those of the primitive Christian age.

The great feature of the apocryphal writings is the affectation of a leaning in a certain direction: the aim that the forger proposed to himself in their composition always clearly betrays itself in them. This character is observable in the highest degree in the epistles attributed to St Ignatius, the Epistle to the Romans always excepted. The author wishes to strike a great blow in favour of the episcopal hierarchy; he wishes to crush the heretics and the schismatics of his time with the weight of an indisputable authority. But where can we find a higher authority than that of this venerated bishop, whose heroic death was recognised by everyone! What more solemn than the counsels given by this martyr a few days or a few weeks before his appearance in the amphitheatre! St Paul, in like manner, in the epistles supposed to be addressed to Titus and to Timothy, is represented as old, nigh unto death. The last will of a martyr came to be regarded as sacred, and, moreover, the admission of the apocryphal work was so much the more easy, inasmuch as St Ignatius was believed, in fact, to have written different letters on his way to his execution. Let u add to these objections a few material improbabilities. The salutations to the Churches and the relations which these salutations presupposed to exist between the author of the letters and the Churches, are not sufficiently explained. The circumstantial features contain something awkward and stupid just as was also to be remarked in the false epistles of Paul to Titus and to Timothy. The great use which is made in the writings of which we speak, of the fourth Gospel and of the Johannine epistles, the affected way in which the author speaks of the doubtful epistle of St Paul to the Ephesians, likewise excites suspicion. On the other hand, it is very strange that the author, in seeking to exalt the Church at Ephesus, ignores the relations of this Church with St Paul, and says nothing of the sojourn of St John at Ephesus, he who was supposed to be so closely connected with Polycarpus, the disciple of John. It must be confessed, in short, that this correspondence is not often cited by the fathers, and that the estimate which appears to have been put upon it by the Christian authors up to the fourth century, is not in proportion to that which it merited had it been authentic. Let us always put to one side the Epistle to the Romans, which, in our view, does not form a part of the apocryphal collection. The six other epistles have been little read--St John, Chrysostom, and the ecclesiastical writers of Antioch, seem to have been ignorant of them. It is a singular thing that even the author of the Acts, of the Martyrdom of Ignatius, the most authorised of those that Ruinart published from a script of Colbert, possesses only a very vague knowledge concerning them. It is the same with the author of the Acts published by Dressel.

Ought the Epistle to the Romans to be included in the condemnation which the other Ignatian epistles merit? One may read the translation of a part of this writing in our text. There is here certainly a singular fragment, which cuts into the common-places of the other epistles attributed to the Bishop of Antioch. Is the Epistle to the Romans entirely the work of the holy martyrs? This may be doubted, but it appears to cover original ground. Here and there only we acknowledge that which M. Zahn too generously accords to the rest of the Ignatian correspondence--the imprint of a powerful character and of a strong individuality. The style of the Epistle to the Romans is bizarre and enigmatical, whilst that of the rest of the correspondence is plain and insipid enough. The Epistle to the Romans does not include any of those common-places of ecclesiastical discipline by which the intention of the forger is recognised. The strong expressions which we encounter there upon the divinity of Jesus Christ and the eucharist ought not to surprise us too much. Ignatius belonged to the school of Paul, in which the formulas of transcendent theology were much more current than in the severe Judeo-Christian school. Still less must we be astonished at the numerous citations and imitations of Paul which are found in the Epistle of Ignatius of which we speak. There can be no doubt that Ignatius did not make constant use of the authentic epistles of Paul. I have said as much of a citation from St Matthew (sec. 6), which, moreover, is wanting in several of the old translations, as well as a vague allusion to the genealogies of the synoptics (sec. 7). Ignatius doubtless possessed the Λεχθέντα ἢ πραχθέντα of Jesus, such as were read in his times, and, upon the essential points these accounts differed little from those which have come down to us. More serious, undoubtedly, is the objection drawn from the expressions which the author of our epistle appears to have borrowed from the fourth Gospel. It is not certain that this Gospel existed before the year 115. But some expression like ὁ ἄρχων αἰῶνος, some images like hudor zon, may have been mystical expressions employed in certain schools, dating from the first quarter of the second century, and before the fourth Gospel had consecrated them.

These intrinsic arguments are not the only ones which oblige us to place the Epistle to the Romans in a distinct category in the Ignatian correspondence. In some respects this epistle contradicts the other six. At paragraph 4, Ignatius declares to the Romans that he represents them to the Churches as being willing that he should carry off the crown of martyrdom. We find nothing resembling this in the epistles to these Churches. That which is much more serious is that the Epistle to the Romans does not seem to have reached us through the same channel as the other six letters. In the manuscripts which have preserved to us the collection of the suspected letters, the Epistle to the Romans is not to be found. The relatively true text of this epistle has only been transmitted to us by the Acts, called Colbertine, of the martyrdom of St Ignatius. It has been extracted thence, and intercalated in the collection of the thirteen letters. But everything proves that the collection of the letters to the Ephesian, the Magnesian, the Trallians, the Philadelphians, the Smyrniotes, to Polycarpus, did not comprise at first the Epistle to the Romans,--that these six letters in themselves constituted the collection, having a distinct unity, from being the work of a single author; and that it was not until later that the two series of Ignatian correspondence were combined, the one apocryphal, consisting of six letters, the other, probably authentic, consisting of a single letter. It is remarkable that in the collection of the thirteen letters the Epistle to the Romans comes last, although its importance and celebrity ought to have secured it the first place. In short, in the whole of the ecclesiastical tradition, the Epistle to the Romans has a particular design. While the other six letters are very rarely cited, the Epistle to the Romans, beginning with Irenæus, is quoted with extraordinary respect. The energetic sentiments which it contains to express the love of Jesus and the eagerness for martyrdom, constitute in some sort a part of the Christian conscience, and are known of all. Pearson, and, after him, M. Zahn, have likewise proved a singular fact, which is the imitation that is to be found in paragraph 3 of the authentic account of the martyrdom of Polycarpus, written by a Smyrniote in the year 155, of a passage of the Epistle of Ignatius to the Romans. It seems, indeed, that the Smyrniote, the author of these Acts, had in his mind some of the most striking passages of the Epistle to the Romans, above all, the fifth paragraph.

Thus everybody assigns the Epistle to the Romans in the Ignatian literature a distinct place. M. Zahn recognises this peculiar circumstance; he shows clearly in different places that this epistle was never completely incorporated with the other six; but he has failed to point out the consequence of that fact. His desire to discover the collection of the seven authentic letters has led him into an imprudent discussion, to wit, that the collection of the seven letters ought either to be accepted or rejected in its entirety. This is to repeat, in another sense, the fault of Baur, of Helgenfeld, and Volkmar; it is to compromise seriously one of the jewels of the primitive Christian literature, in associating it with these but too often mediocre writings, and which have almost on this point been put out of court.

That which then seems the most probable is that the Ignatian literature contains nothing authentic, except the Epistle to the Romans. Even this epistle has not remained exempt from alterations. The length, the repetitions which are remarked in it, are probably injuries inflicted by an interpolation upon that beautiful monument of Christian antiquity. When we compare the texts preserved by the Colbertin Acts, with the texts of the collection of the thirteen epistles, with the Latin and Syriac translations, with the citations of Eusebius, we find very considerable differences. It seems that the author of the Colbertin Acts, in encasing in his account this precious fragment, has not scrupled to retouch it in many points. In the superscription, for example, Ignatius gives himself the surname of Θεοφόρος. Now neither Irenæus, nor Origen, nor Eusebius, nor St Jerome knew this characteristic surname; it appeared for the first time in the Acts of Martyrdom, which makes the most important part of Trajan's inquiring turn upon the said epithet. The idea of applying it to Ignatius was suggested by passages in the supposititious epistles, such as Ad. Eph., sec. 9. The author of the Acts, finding that name in the tradition, has availed himself of it, and added it to the title of the epistle which he inserted in his narrative, Ἰγνάτιος ὁ καὶ Θεοφόρος. I think that in the original compilation of these six apocryphal epistles, these words, ὁ καὶ Θεοφορος no longer constitute a part of the titles. The post-scriptum to the Epistle of Polycarpus to the Philippians, in which Ignatius is mentioned, and which is by the same hand as the six epistles, as we shall see further on, makes no mention of this epithet.

Is one justified in denying absolutely that in the six suspected epistles there is no portion of them borrowed from the authentic letters of Ignatius? No, certainly not; and the author of the six apocryphal epistles not having known, as it would seem, the Epistle to the Romans, there is no great likelihood that he possessed other authentic letters of the martyr. A single passage in sec. 19 of the Epistle to the Ephesians, appears to me to cut into the dark and vague ground with which the suspected epistles are encompassed, that which concerns the τρία μυστήρια κραυγῆς has much of that mysterious, singular, and obscure style, recalling the fourth Gospel, which we have remarked in the Epistle to the Romans. That passage, like the brilliant sentiments in the Epistle to the Romans, has been much cited. But it occupies too isolated a position there to be insisted on.

A question which is closely connected with that of the epistles ascribed to St Ignatius, is the question of the epistle attributed to Polycarpus. At two different places (sec. 9 and sec. 13), Polycarpus, or the person who has forged the letter, makes formal mention of Ignatius. In a third place (sec. 1), he would seem again to make allusion to it. We read in one of those passages (sec. 13, and last): "You have written to me, you and Ignatius, in order that if there be anyone here who is about to depart for Syria he would bear thence your letters. I shall acquit myself of this task, when I can find a suitable opportunity, either in person, or by a messenger whom I shall send for both of us. As for the epistles that Ignatius has addressed to you, and the others of his which we possess, we send them to you, since you have requested us to do so; they are sent together with this letter. You will be able to extract much profit from them, as they breathe the faith, the patience, the edification of our Lord." The old Latin version adds, "Inform me as to that which you know touching Ignatius, and those who are with him." These lines notoriously correspond with a passage in the letter of Ignatius to Polycarpus (sec. 8), where Ignatius asks the latter to send messengers in different directions. All this is suspicious. As the Epistle of Polycarpus finishes very well with sec. 12, one is led almost necessarily, if one admits the authenticity of this epistle, to suppose that a post-scriptum has been added to the Epistles of Polycarpus by the author of the six apocryphal epistles of Ignatius himself. There is no Greek manuscript of the Epistle of Polycarpus which contains this post-scriptum. We only know it through a citation of Eusebius, and through the Latin version. The same errors are combated in the Epistles to Polycarpus as in the six Ignatian epistles: the order of the ideas is the same. Many manuscripts present the Epistle of Polycarpus joined to the Ignatian collection in the form of a preface or of an epilogue. It would seem, then, either that the epistles of Polycarpus and those of Ignatius are by the same forger, or that the author of the letters of Ignatius had the idea of seeking for a point d'appui in the Epistle of Polycarpus, and in adding to it a post-scriptum,--of creating an interest in his work. This addition harmonises well with the mention of Ignatius which is found in the body of the letter of Polycarpus (sec. 9). It would fit in better still, in appearance, at least, with the first paragraph of this letter in which Polycarpus praises the Philippians for having received in a proper manner some confessors bound in chains who passed some time with them.

From the Epistle of Polycarpus so falsified, and from the six letters ascribed to Ignatius, there was formed a little pseudo-Ignatian Corpus, perfectly homogeneous in style and in colouring, which was a real defence of orthodoxy, and of the episcopate. By the side of this collection there was preserved the more or less authentic Epistle of Ignatius to the Romans. This circumstance induces the belief that the forger was acquainted with this writing, nevertheless it appears that he did not judge it convenient to include it in his collection, the arrangement of which he changed, and demonstrated its non-authenticity.

Irenæus, about the year 180, only knew Ignatius through the energetic sentiments contained in his Epistle to the Romans. "I am the bread of Christ," etc. He had undoubtedly read this epistle, although what he says is sufficiently accounted for by an oral tradition. Irenæus, to all appearance, did not possess the six apocryphal letters, and in all probability he read the true or supposed epistle of his master Polycarpus without the post-scriptum; Επιγράψατέ μοι . . . Origen admitted as authentic the Epistle to the Romans, and the six apocryphal letters. He cited the former in the prologue of his commentary on the Canticle of Canticles, and the pretended Epistle to the Ephesians in his sixth homily upon St Luke. Eusebius knew the Ignatian collection as we have it, that is to say, consisting of seven letters; he did not use the Acts of Martyrdom; he makes no distinction between the Epistle to the Romans and the six others. He read the Epistle of Polycarpus with the post-scriptum. A peculiar fate seemed to designate the name of Ignatius to the fabricators of apocryphas. In the second half of the fourth century, about 375, a new collection of Ignatian epistles was produced: this is the collection of the thirteen letters, to which the collection of the seven letters notoriously served as a nucleus. As these seven letters presented many obscurities, the new forger also set about interpolating them. A multitude of explanatory glosses are introduced into the text, and burden it to no purpose. Six new letters were fabricated from end to end, and, in spite of their shocking improbability, they came to be universally adopted. The retouchings to which they were afterwards subjected, were only abridgments of the two preceding collections. The Syrians, in particular, concocted a small edition, consisting of three abridged letters, in the preparation of which they were guided by no correct sentiment as to the distinction between the authentic and the apocryphal. A few works appeared still later to enlarge the Ignatian works. We possess these only in Latin.

The Acts of the Martyrdom of St Ignatius presents not less diversities than the text itself of the epistles which are ascribed to them. We enumerate as many as eight or nine compilations. We must not attribute much importance to these productions; none of them have any original value; all are posterior to Eusebius, and compiled from the data furnished by Eusebius, data which of themselves have no other foundation than the collection of the epistles, and, in particular, the Epistle to the Romans. These Acts, in their most ancient form, do not go back further than the end of the fourth century. We cannot in any way compare them with the Acts of the Martyrdom of Polycarpus and the martyrs of Lyons, accounts actually authentic and contemporaneous with the fact reported. They are full of impossibilities, of historical errors and mistakes, as to the condition of the Empire at the epoch of Trajan.

In this volume, as in those which precede, we have sought to steer a middle course between the criticism which employs all its resources to defend texts which have for long been stamped with discredit, and the exaggerated scepticism which rejects en bloc and à priori everything which Christianity records of its first origins. One will remark, in particular, the employment of this intermediary method in that which concerns the question of the Clements and that of the Christian Flavii. It is apropos of the Clements that the conjectures of the school called Tübingen have been the worst inspired. The defect of this school, sometimes so fecund, is the rejecting of the traditional systems, often, it is true, built upon fragile materials, and their substituting systems founded upon authorities more fragile still. As regards Ignatius, have not they pretended to correct the traditions of the second century by Jean Malala? As regards Simon Magus, have not some theologians, in other respects sagacious, resisted to the latest the necessity of admitting the real existence of that personage? An regards the Clements, we would be looked upon by certain critics as narrow-minded indeed, if we admitted that Clemens Romanus existed, and if we did not explain all that which relates to him by the certain misunderstandings and confusions with Flavius Clemens. Now it is, on the contrary, the data in regard to Flavius Clemens which are uncertain and contradictory. We do not deny the gleams of Christianity which appear to issue from the obscure rubbish of the Flavian family; but to extract from thence a great historic fact by which to rectify uncertain traditions, is a strange part to take, or rather, this lack of just proportion in induction, which in Germany is so often detrimental to the rarest qualities of diligence and application. They discard solid evidence, and substitute for it feeble hypothesis; they challenge satisfactory texts, and accept, almost without examination, the combinations hazarded by an accommodating archeology. Something new they will have at any cost, and the new they obtained by the exaggeration of ideas, often just and penetrating. From a feeble current proved to exist in some obscure gulf, they conclude the existence of a great oceanic current. The observation was proper enough, but they drew from it false consequences. It is far from my thoughts to deny or to attenuate the services which German science has rendered to our difficult studies, but, in order to profit by those services, we must examine them very closely, and apply to them a thorough spirit of discernment. Above all, we must be most resolute in not taking into account the haughty criticisms of men of system who treat you as ignorant and behind the age because you do not admit at the first onset the latest novelty hatched by the brain of a young doctor, and which, at the best, can only be useful in encouraging research in the circles of the learned.

CHAPTER I

THE JEWS AFTER THE DESTRUCTION OF THE TEMPLE

Never was a people so sadly undeceived as was the Jewish race on the morrow of the day when, contrary to the most formal assurances of the Divine oracles, the Temple which they had supposed to be indestructible collapsed before the assault of the soldiers of Titus. To have been near the realisation of the grandest of visions and to be forced to renounce them, at the very moment when the destroying angel had already partially withdrawn the cloud, to see everything vanish into space; to be committed through having prophesied the Divine apparition, and to receive from the harshness of facts the most cruel contradiction--were not these reasons for doubting the Temple, nay, for doubting God himself? Thus the first years which followed the catastrophe of the year 70 were characterised by an intense feverishness--perhaps the most intense which the Jewish conscience had ever experienced. Edom (the name by which the Jews already distinguished the Roman Empire), the impious Edom, the eternal enemy of God, triumphed. Ideas which had appeared to be unimpeachable were now argued against. Jehovah appeared to have broken his covenant with the sons of Abraham. It was even a question if the faith of Israel--assuredly the most ardent that ever existed--would succeed in executing a complete right-about-face against evidence, and by an unheard-of display of strength continue to hope against all hope.

The hired assassins, the enthusiasts, had almost all been killed: those who had survived passed the rest of their lives in that mournful state of stupefaction which amongst madmen follows attacks of violent mania. The Sadducees had almost disappeared in the year 66 with the priestly aristocracy who lived in the Temple, and drew from it all their prestige. It has been supposed that some survivors of the great families took refuge with the Herodians in the north of Syria, in Armenia, at Palmyra, remained long allied to the little dynasties of those countries, and shed a final brilliancy on that Zenobia who appears to us in effect, in the third century, as a Sadducean Jewess, foreshadowing by a simple monotheism both Arianism and Islam. The theory is a plausible one; but, in any case, such more or less authentic relics of the Sadducean party had become almost strangers to the rest of the Jewish nation: the Pharisees treated them as enemies.

That which survived the Temple and remained almost intact after the disaster at Jerusalem, was Pharisaism: the moderate party in Jewish society, the party less inclined to mingle politics with religion than other sections of the people, narrowing the business of life to the scrupulous accomplishment of the Law. Strange state of things! the Pharisees had passed through the ordeal almost safe and sound; the Revolution had passed over them without injuring them. Absorbed in their sole preoccupation--the exact observance of the Law--almost all of them had fled from Jerusalem before the last convulsions, and had found an asylum in the neutral towns of Jabneh and Lydda. The zealots were only individual enthusiasts; the Sadducees were but a class; the Pharisees were the nation. Essentially pacific, preferring a peaceful and laborious life, contented with the free practice of their family worship, these true Israelites resisted all temptations; they were the corner-stones of Judaism which passed through the Middle Ages and came down to our own days.

The Law was, in truth, all that remained to the Jewish people after the shipwreck of their religious institutions. Public worship, after the destruction of the Temple, had been impossible; prophecy, after the terrible check which it had received, was dumb; holy hymns, music, ceremonies, all had become insipid and objectless, since the Temple, which served as the navel of the entire Hebrew cosmos, had ceased to exist. The Thora, on the contrary, in the non-ritualistic part of it, was always possible. The Thora was not only a religious law, it was a complete system of legislation, a civil code, a personal statute, which made of the people who submitted to it a sort of republic apart from the rest of the world. Such was the object to which the Jewish conscience would henceforward attach itself with a kind of fanaticism. The ritual had to be profoundly modified, but the Canon Law was maintained almost in its entirety. To explain, to practise the Law with minute exactitude, appeared the sole end of life. One science only was held in esteem, that of the Law. Its tradition became the ideal country of the Jew. The subtle discussions which for about a hundred years had filled the schools, were as nothing compared with those which followed. Religious minutiæ and scrupulous devotion were substituted amongst the Jews for all the rest of the worship.

One not less grave consequence springing out of the new conditions under which Israel was henceforward to live was the definitive victory of the teacher (doctor) over the priest. The Temple had perished, but the school of the Law had been spared. The priest, after the destruction of the Temple, saw his functions reduced to very small proportions. The doctor, or, more properly speaking, the judge, the interpreter of the Thora, became, on the contrary, an important personage. The tribunal (Beth-din) was at that time a great Rabbinical school. The Ab-beth-din (president) is a chief at once civil and religious. Every titled rabbin had the right of entry within its limits; its decisions are determined by the majority of votes. The disciples standing behind a barrier heard and learned what was necessary to make them judges and doctors in their turn.

"A tight cistern which did not allow the escape of a drop of water" became henceforward the ideal of Israel. There was as yet no written manual of this traditional law. More than a hundred years had to roll on before the discussions of the schools became crystallised into a body which should be called Mishna, par excellence, but the root of this book really dates from the period of which we speak. Although compiled in Galilee, it was in reality born in Jabneh. Towards the end of the first century it existed only in the form of little pamphlets of notes, in style almost algebraical, and full of abbreviations, which gave the solutions by the most celebrated rabbins of embarrassing cases. The most robust memories already gave way under the weight of tradition and of judicial precedents. Such a state of things made writing necessary. Thus we see at this period mention is made of the Mishna, that is to say, little collections of decisions or halakoth, which bear the names of their authors. Such was that of the Rabbi Eliezer ben Jacob, who about the end of the first century was described as "short but good." The Mishnic treatise Eduïoth, which is distinguished from all others in that it has no special subject and that it is in itself an abridged Mishna, has for central idea the Eduïoth or "testimonies" relative to prior decisions which were collected at Jabneh and submitted to revision after the dismissal of Rabbi Gamaliel the younger. About the same time Rabbi Eliezer ben Jacob composed from memory the description of the sanctuary which forms the basis of the treatise Middoth. Simon of Mispa, at a still earlier date, appears as the author of the first edition of the treatise Ioma, relating to the Feast of the Atonement, and perhaps of the treatise Tamid.

The opposition between these tendencies and those of the nascent Christianity was that of fire and water. Christians detached themselves ever more and more from the Law: the Jews fettered themselves with it frantically. A lively antipathy appears to have existed amongst Christians against the subtle and uncharitable spirit which every day tended to increase in the synagogues. Jesus fifty years before already had chosen this spirit as the object of his severest rebukes. Since then the casuists had only plunged more and more deeply into the abysses of their narrow hair splittings. The misfortunes of the nation had in no way changed their character. Disputatious, vain, jealous, susceptible, given to quarrelling for merely personal motives, they passed their time between Jabneh and Lydda in excommunicating each other for the most puerile reasons. James and the relations of Jesus generally were very strict Pharisees. Paul himself boasted of being a Pharisee and the son of a Pharisee. But after the siege the war was open. In collecting the traditional words of Jesus the change of situation made itself felt. The word "Pharisee" in the Gospels generally, as later the word "Jew" in the Gospel attributed to John, is employed as synonymous with "enemy of Jesus." Derision of the casuist was one of the essential elements of the evangelical literature, and one of the causes of its success. The really good man in truth holds nothing in so much horror as moral pedantry. To clear himself in his own eyes from the suspicion of dupery, he is constrained sometimes to doubt his own works, his own merits. He who pretends to work out his own salvation by infallible receipts, appears to him the chief enemy of God. Pharisaism became thus something worse than vice, since it made virtue ridiculous; and nothing pleases us so much as to see Jesus, the most purely virtuous of men, set a hypocritical bourgeoisie at defiance, and allowing it to be understood that the Law of which he was so proud was perhaps like everything else--vanity.

One consequence of the new situation of the Jewish people was a vast increase of the separatist and exclusive spirit. Hated and despised by the world, Israel withdrew more and more into itself. The perischouth insociability became a law of public salvation. To live apart in a purely Jewish world, to add new requirements to the Law, to render it difficult to fulfil, such was the aim of the doctors, and they attained it very cleverly. Excommunications were multiplied. To observe the Law was so complicated an art that the Jew had no time to think of anything else. Such was the origin of the "eighteen measures," a complete code of sequestration which originally dates from a period anterior to the destruction of the Temple but which did not come into operation until after 70. These eighteen measures were all intended to exaggerate the isolation of Israel. Forbidden to buy the most necessary things amongst Pagans, forbidden to speak their language, to receive their testimony and their offerings, forbidden to offer sacrifices for the Emperor. Many of these prescriptions were at once regretted; some even said that the day on which they were adopted was as sad as that on which the Golden Calf was set up, but they were never abrogated. A legendary dialogue expresses the opposite sentiments of the two parties which divided the Jewish schools in this matter. "To-day," says Rabbi Eliezer, "the measure is filled up." "To-day," says Rabbi Joshua, "it has been made to overflow." "A vessel full of nuts," says Rabbi Eliezer, "may yet contain as much oil or sesame as you wish." "When a jar is full of oil, if you add water you drive out the oil." Notwithstanding all protests, the eighteen measures obtained such authority that some went so far as to say that no power had the right to abolish them. Perhaps certain of these measures were inspired by a sullen opposition to Christianity, and, above all, by the liberal preachings of St Paul. It would seem that the more the Christians laboured to overthrow the legal barriers, the more the Jews laboured to render them impregnable.

It was mainly in what concerned proselytes that the contrast was marked. Not merely did the Jews seek no longer to win them, but they displayed towards these new brethren a scarcely veiled hostility. It had not yet been said that "proselytes are a leprosy for Israel;" but far from encouraging them, they were dissuaded; they were told of the numberless dangers and difficulties to which they exposed themselves by consorting with a despised race. At the same time, the hatred against Rome redoubled. The only thoughts which her name inspired were thoughts of murder and of bloodshed.

But now, as always in the course of its long history there was an admirable minority in Israel who protested against the errors of the majority of the nation. The grand duality which lies at the base of the life of this singular people continued. The calm, the gentleness of the good Jew, was proof against all trials. Shammai and Hillel, though long dead, were as the heads of two opposed families; one representing the narrow, malevolent, subtle, materialistic spirit; the other the broad, benevolent, idealistic side of the religious genius of Israel. The contrast was striking. Humble, polished, affable, putting always the good of others before their own, the Hillelites, like the Christians, had for their principle that God "resisteth the proud but giveth grace to the lowly;" that honours elude those who seek them, and follow after those who fly from them; that he who hurries will obtain nothing, whilst he who knows how to wait has time on his side.

Amongst really pious souls singularly bold ideas sometimes developed themselves. On the one hand the liberal family of Gamaliel, who had for principle in their relations with Pagans to care for their poor, to treat them with politeness even when they worshipped their idols, to pay the last respects to their dead, sought to relax the situation. In business this family already had relations with the Romans, and had no scruple in asking from their conquerors the investiture of a sort of presidency of the Sanhedrim, and, with their permission, the resumption of the title of Nasi. On the other hand, an extremely liberal man, Johanan ben Zakaï, was the soul of the transformation. Long before the destruction of Jerusalem he had enjoyed a preponderating influence in the Sanhedrim. During the Revolution he was one of the chiefs of the moderate party which kept itself aloof from political questions, and did all that was possible to prevent the prolongation of a resistance which must inevitably bring about the destruction of the Temple. Escaped from Jerusalem, he predicted, it is asserted, the Empire of Vespasian; one of the favours which he asked from him was a doctor for the old Zadok, who, in the years before the siege, had ruined his health by fasting. It appears certain that he got into the good graces of the Romans, and that he obtained from them the re-establishment of the Sanhedrim at Jabneh. It is doubtful whether he was ever really a pupil of Hillel, but he was certainly the inheritor of his spirit. To cause peace to reign amongst men was his favourite maxim. It was told of him that no one had ever been able to salute him first, not even a Pagan in the market-place. Though not a Christian, he was a true disciple of Jesus. He even went at times, it is said, so far as to follow the example of the old prophets, denying the efficacy of worship, and recognising the fact that justice accomplishes for Pagans all that sacrifice did for the Jews.

A little consolation came to the frightfully troubled soul of Israel. Fanatics, at the risk of their lives, stole into the silent city and furtively offered sacrifice on the ruins of the Holy of Holies. Some of these madmen spoke on their return of a mysterious voice which had come out from the heaps of rubbish, and had declared acceptance of their sacrifices; but this excess was generally condemned. Certain amongst them forbade all enjoyment, lived in tears and fasting, and drank only water. Johanan ben Zakaï consoled them:--"Be not sad, my son," said he to one of these despairing ones. "If we cannot offer sacrifices, there is still a way of expiating our sins which is quite as efficacious--good works." And he recalled the words of Isaiah, "I love charity better than sacrifice." Rabbi Joshua was of the same opinion. "My friends," said he to those who imposed exaggerated privations upon themselves, "what is the use of abstaining from meat and from wine?" "How," they answered, "should we eat the flesh which is sacrificed on the altar which is now destroyed? should we drink the wine which we ought to pour out as a libation on the same altar?" "Well," replied the Rabbi Joshua, "then eat no bread, since it is no longer possible to make sacrifices of fine flour." "Then we must feed upon fruit." "Nay. Fruits cannot be allowed, since it is no longer possible to offer first-fruits in the Temple." The force of circumstances decided the matter. The eternity of the Law was maintained in theory; it was believed that even Elias himself could not change a single article of it; but the destruction of the Temple suppressed in fact a considerable proportion of the ancient prescriptions; there was no room for anything more than moral casuistry of details or for mysticism. The developed cabbala is surely of a more modern age. But at that time many gave themselves to what were called "the visions of the chariot," that is to say, to speculations on the mysteries concealed in the visions of Ezekiel. The Jewish mind was wrapped up in visions, and created an asylum for itself in the midst of a hated world. The study became a deliverance. Rabbi Nehounia gave currency to the principle that he who takes upon him the yoke of the Law thereby frees himself from the yoke of the world and of politics. When this point of detachment is attained, people cease to be dangerous revolutionaries. Rabbi Hanina was accustomed to say, "Pray for the established government: for without it men would eat each other."

The misery was extreme. A heavy taxation weighed upon all, and the sources of revenue were dried up. The mountains of Judea remained uncultivated and covered with ruins; property itself was very uncertain. When it was cultivated, the cultivator was liable to be evicted by the Romans. As for Jerusalem, it was nothing but a heap of broken stones. Pliny even spoke of it as of a city that had ceased to exist. Without doubt, the Jews who had been tempted to come in considerable numbers to encamp upon the ruins, had been expelled from thence. Yet the historians who insist most strongly on the total destruction of the city, admit that some old men and some women were left. Josephus depicts for us the first sitting and weeping in the dust of the sanctuary, and the second reserved by the conquerors for the last outrages. The 10th Fretensian Legion continued to act as a garrison in a corner of the deserted city. The bricks which have been found with the stamp of that legion, prove that the men of it built it. It is probable that furtive visits to the still visible foundations of the Temple were tolerated or permitted by the soldiers for a money consideration. Christians, in particular, preserved the memory and the worship of certain places, notably of the tabernacle of Mount Sion, where it was believed that the disciples of Jesus met after the Ascension, as well as the tomb of James, the brother of the Lord, near the Temple. Golgotha probably was not forgotten. As nothing was rebuilt in the town or in the suburbs, the enormous stones of the great edifices remained untouched in their places, so that all the monuments were still perfectly recognisable.

Driven thus from their Holy City and from the region which they loved, the Jews spread themselves over the towns and villages of the plain which extends from the foot of the Mountain of Judea to the sea. The Jewish population multiplied there. One locality above all was the scene of that quasi-resurrection of Pharisaism, and became the theological capital of the Jews until the war of Bar Coziba. This was the city--originally Philistine--of Jabneh or Jamnia, four leagues and a half to the south of Jaffa. It was a considerable town, inhabited by Pagans and Jews; but the Jews predominated there, although the town, since the war of Pompey, had ceased to form part of Judea. The struggles between the two populations had been lively. In his campaigns of 67 and 68 Vespasian had had to show himself there to establish his authority. Provisions abounded there. In the earlier days of the blockade many peaceable wise men, such as Johanan ben Zakaï, whom the chimera of natural independence did not lead away, came thither for shelter. There it was that they learned of the burning of the Temple. They wept, rent their garments, put on mourning, but found that it was still worth while to live, that they might see if God had not reserved a future for Israel. It was, it is said, at the entreaty of Johanan that Vespasian spared Jabneh and its savants. The truth is that before the war a Rabbinical school flourished in Jabneh. For unknown reasons, it was a part of the Roman polity to allow it to continue, and after the arrival of Johanan ben Zakaï it assumed a greater importance.

Rabbi Gamaliel the younger put the top stone to the celebrity of Jabneh when he took the direction of the school after Rabbi Johann retired to Berour-Haïl. Jabneh, from this moment, became the first Jewish academy of Palestine. The Jews from various countries assembled there for the feasts, as formerly they had gone up to Jerusalem, and as formerly they profited by the journey to the Holy City to take council with the Sanhedrim and the schools upon doubtful cases, so at Jabneh they submitted difficult questions to the Beth-din. This tribunal was only rarely and improperly called by the name of the ancient Sanhedrim; but it exercised an undisputable authority; the doctors of all Judea sometimes met in it, and so gave to the Beth-din the character of a Supreme Court. The memory was long preserved of the orchard where the sittings of this tribunal were held, and of the dovecote under whose shade the president sat.

Jabneh appeared thus as a sort of resuscitated Jerusalem. As to privileges and religious obligations, it was completely assimilated to Jerusalem; its synagogue was considered the legitimate heiress of that of Jerusalem--as the centre of the now religious authority. The Romans themselves looked at it in this light, and accorded to the Nasi or Ab-beth-din of Jabneh an official authority. This was the commencement of the Jewish patriarchate which developed itself later and became an institution analogous to the Christian patriarchates of the Ottoman Empire of our own days. These magistratures, at once civil and religious, conferred by the political power, have always been in the East the means employed by great Empires to disembarrass themselves of the responsibilities of their satraps. The existence of a personal statute was in no way disquieting to the Romans, above all, in a town partly idolatrous and Roman, where the Jews were restrained by the military force and by the antipathy of the rest of the population. Religious conversations between Jews and non-Jews appear to have been frequent in Jabneh. Tradition shows us Johanan ben Zakaï maintaining frequent controversies with infidels, and furnishing them with explanations of the Bible, on the Jewish festivals. His answers are often evasive, and sometimes alone with his disciples he allows himself to smile at the unsatisfactory solutions he has given to Pagan difficulties.

Lydda had its schools which rivalled those of Jabneh in celebrity, or rather which were a sort of dependency of them. The two towns were about four leagues Apart: when a man had been excommunicated at one he betook himself to the other. All the villages, Danite or Philistine, of the surrounding maritime plain--Berour Haïl, Bakiin, Gibthon, Gimso, Bene Barak, which were all situated to the south of Antipatris, and were until then hardly considered as belonging to the Holy Land at all-- served also as an asylum to celebrated doctors. Finally the Darom, the southern part of Judea, situated between Eleutheropolis and the Dead Sea, received many fugitive Jews. It was a rich country, far from the routes frequented by the Romans, and almost at the limit of their domination.

It thus appears that the current which carried Rabbinism towards Galilee had not yet made itself felt. There were exceptions. Rabbi Eliezer ben Jacob, the editor of one of the first Mishna, appears to have been a Galilean. Towards the year 100 the Mishnic doctors are seen approaching Cæsarea in Galilee. It was, however, only after the war of Hadrian that Tiberias and upper Galilee became par excellence the country of the Talmud.

CHAPTER II

BETHER: THE BOOK OF JUDITH: THE JEWISH CANON

During the first years which followed the war, it appears that a centre of population was formed near to Jerusalem, which fifty or sixty years later was destined to play a very important part. Two leagues and a quarter west-south-west of Jerusalem was a village until then obscure, known as Bether. Many years before the siege a great number of rich and peaceable citizens of Jerusalem, perceiving the storm which was about to break over the capital, had bought lands to which to retire. Bether was in effect situated in a fertile valley outside the important routes which connect Jerusalem with the north and with the sea. An acropolis commanded the village, built near a beautiful spring, and forming a sort of natural fortification; a lower plateau formed a sort of step to the lower town. After the catastrophe of the year 70, a considerable body of fugitives met there. Synagogues, a sanhedrim, and schools were established. Bether became a Holy City, a sort of equivalent to Zion. The little scarped hill was covered with houses, which, supporting themselves by ancient works in the rock and by the natural form of the hill, formed a species of citadel which was completed with steps of great stones. The isolated situation of Bether induces the belief that the Romans did not greatly trouble themselves about these works; perhaps also a part of them dated from before the time of Titus. Supported by the great Jewish communities of Lydda and of Jabneh, Bether thus became a sufficiently large town, and, as it were, the entrenched camp of fanaticism in Judea. We shall there see Judaism offer to the Roman power a last and impotent resistance.

At Bether, a singular book appears to have been composed, a perfect mirror of the conscience of Israel at that date, where may be found the powerful recollection of past defects and a fiery prediction of future revolts. I speak of the book of Judith. The ardent patriot who composed that Agada in Hebrew, copied--according to the custom of the Hebrew Agadas--a well-known history, that of Deborah who saved Israel from her enemies by killing their chief. Every line is full of transparent allusions. The ancient enemy of the people of God, Nebuchadnezzar (a perfect type of the Roman Empire, which, according to the Jews, was but the work of an idolatrous propaganda), desired to subject the whole world to himself, and to cause it to adore him, to the exclusion of every other god. He charges his general Holophernes with this duty. All bow before him save only the Jewish people. Israel is not a military people but a mountaineering race difficult to force. So long as it observes the Law it is invincible.

A sensible Pagan who knows Israel, Achior (brother of the light), tries to stop Holophernes. The one thing necessary, according to him, is to know if Israel fails to keep the Law; in this case, the conquest will be easy; if not, it will be necessary to beware how one attacks her. All is useless; Holophernes marches on Jerusalem. The key of Jerusalem is a place on the north, on the side of Dothaïm, at the entrance of the mountainous region to the south of the plain of Esdraelon. This place is called Beth-eloah (the House of God). The author describes it exactly on the plan of Bether. It is placed at the opening of a Wadi (Fiumara or bed of a watercourse), on a mountain at the foot of which runs a stream indispensable to the people, the cisterns of the upper town being relatively small. Holophernes besieges Beth-eloah, which is soon reduced by thirst to the direst extremity. But it is an attribute of Divine Providence to choose the weakest agents for the greatest works. A widow, a zealot, Judith (the Jewess), arises and prays; she goes forth and presents herself to Holophernes as a rigid devotee who cannot tolerate the breaches of the Law of which she has been witness in the town. She wishes to point out to him a sure means of conquering the Jews. They are dying of hunger and thirst; which induces them to fail with regard to the precepts concerning food, and to eat the first fruits reserved for the priests. They have sent to ask for the authorisation of the Sanhedrim at Jerusalem, but at Jerusalem everything is relaxed, everything is allowed, so that it will be easy to conquer them. "I will pray to God," she adds, "that I may know when they shall sin." Then at the moment when Holophernes thinks himself assured of all her complaisances she cuts off his head. In this expedition she has not once failed to observe the Law. She prays and performs her ablutions at the appointed hours; she eats only of the meats which she has brought with her. Even on the evening when she is about to prostitute herself to Holophernes, she drinks her own wine. Judith lives after all this for a hundred and five years, refusing the most advantageous marriages, happy and honoured. During her life and for a long time after her death no one dares to disquiet the Jewish people. Achior is also well rewarded for having known Israel well. He is circumcised, and becomes a Son of Abraham for ever.

The author, from his singular taste for imagining the conversion of Pagans, from his persuasion that God loves the weak above all, that he is par excellence the God of the hopeless, approaches Christian sentiments. But by his materialistic attachment to the principles of the Law, he shows himself a pure Pharisee. He dreams of an autonomy for the Israelites under the autonomy of the Sanhedrim and their Nasi. His ideal is absolutely that of Jabneh. There is a mechanism of human life which God loves; the Law is the absolute rule of it; Israel is created to accomplish it. It is a people like to no other; a people whom the heathen hate because they know them to be capable of leading the whole world; an invincible people, because they do not sin. To the scruples of the Pharisee are joined the fanaticism of the Zealot, the appeal to the dagger to defend the Law, the apology for the most sanguinary examples of religious violence. The imitation of the book of Esther penetrates the whole work; the author evidently read that book not as it exists in the original Hebrew but with the interpolations which the Greek text offers. The literary execution is weak; the feeble parts--common-places of the Jewish agada, canticles, prayers, etc.--recall at times the tone of the Gospel according to St Luke. The theory of the Messianic claims is, however, little developed. Judith is still rewarded for her virtue by a long life. The book was doubtless read with passion in the circles of Bether and of Jabneh; but it may readily be believed that Josephus knew nothing of it at Rome. It was probably suppressed as being full of dangerous allusions. The success in any case was not lasting amongst the Jews; the original Hebrew was soon lost; but the Greek translation made itself a place in the Christian Canon. We shall see this translation known at Rome towards the year 95. In general it was immediately after their publication that the apocryphal books were welcomed and quoted: those novelties had an ephemeral popularity, then fell into oblivion.

The need of a rigorously limited canon of the sacred books made itself felt more and more. The Thora, the Prophets, the Psalms, were the admitted foundation of all. Ezekiel alone created some difficulties by the passages wherein he is not in accord with the Thora, from which he was extricated only by subtleties. There was some hesitation about Job, whose hardihood was not in accord with the pietism of the times. Proverbs, Ecclesiastes and the Song of Songs were assailed with much greater violence. The picture so freely sketched in the seventh chapter of Proverbs, the altogether profane character of the Canticles, the scepticism of Ecclesiastes, were thought sufficient to deprive those writings of the character of sacred books. Happily, admiration carried them. They were admitted, so to speak, subject to correction and to interpretation. The last lines of Ecclesiastes appeared to extenuate the sceptical crudities of the text. In the Canticles the critics began to seek for mystical profundities. Pseudo-Daniel had conquered his place by dint of audacity and assurance; he failed, however, to force the already impenetrable line of the ancient prophets, and he remained in the last pages of the sacred volume side by side with Esther and the more recent historical compilations. The son of Sirach was stranded simply for having avowed too frankly his modern editing. All this constituted a little sacred library of twenty-four works, the order of which was thenceforward irrevocably fixed. Many variations still existed; the absence of vowel points left many passages in a state of deplorable ambiguity which different parties interpreted in a sense favourable to their own ideas. It was many centuries before the Hebrew Bible formed a volume almost without variants, and the readings of which were settled down to their last details.

As to the Books excluded from the Canon, their reading was forbidden, and it was even sought to destroy them. This it is which explains how books essentially Jewish, and having quite as much right as Daniel and Esther to remain in the Jewish Bible, are only preserved by Greek translations. Thus the Maccabean histories, the book of Tobit, the books of Enoch, the wisdom of the son of Sirach, the book of Baruch, the book called "the third of Esdras," various chapters of which belong to the book of Daniel (the Three Children in the Furnace) Susannah, Bel and the Dragon, the Prayer of Manasseh, the letter of Jeremiah, the Psalter of Solomon, the Assumption of Moses, a whole series of agadic and apocalyptic writings neglected by the Jews of the Talmudic tradition, have been guarded only by Christian hands. The literary community which existed during more than a hundred years between the Jews and the Christians, caused every Jewish book impressed with a pious spirit and imbued with Messianic ideas to be at once accepted by the Churches. At the beginning of the second century the Jewish people, devoted as they were exclusively to the study of the Law, and having no taste save for casuistry, neglected these writings. Many Christian Churches, on the contrary, persisted in placing a high value upon them, and admitted them more or less officially into their Canon. We see, for example, the Apocalypse of Esdras, the work of an enthusiastic Jew like the book of Judith, saved from destruction only through the favour which it enjoyed amongst the disciples of Jesus.

Judaism and Christianity still lived together like those double beings which are joined by one part of their organisation though distinct as regards all the rest. Each of these beings transmitted to the other its sensations and its desires. A book which was the fruit of the most ardent Jewish passions, a book zealous for its first chief, was immediately adopted by Christianity, was preserved by Christianity, introduced itself, thanks to it, into the Canon of the Old Testament. A fraction of the Christian Church, it cannot be doubted, had felt the emotions of the siege, had shared in the grief and anger of the Jews over the destruction of the Temple, had sympathised with the rebels; the author of the Apocalypse, who probably still lived, had surely mourning at his heart, and calculated the days of the great vengeance of Israel. But already the Christian conscience had found other issues; it was not only the school of Paul, it was the family of the Master which passed through the most extraordinary crises, and transformed, according to the necessities of the time, the very memories which it had preserved of Jesus.

CHAPTER III

EBION BEYOND JORDAN

We have seen in 68 the Christian Church of Jerusalem carried on by the relatives of Jesus fly from the city delivered over to terror, and take refuge at Pella on the other side of Jordan. We have seen the author of the Apocalypse some months afterwards employ the most lively and touching images to express the protection which God extended to the fugitive Church, and the repose which it enjoyed in the desert. It is probable that this sojourn was prolonged for many years after the siege. A return to Jerusalem was impossible, and the antipathy between Christianity and the Pharisees was already too strong to allow of the Christians joining the bulk of the nation on the side of Jabneh and Lydda. The saints of Jerusalem dwelt therefore beyond the Jordan. The expectation of the final catastrophe had become extremely vivid. The three years and a half which the Apocalypse fixed for the fulfilment of its predictions, expired about the month of July 72.

The destruction of the Temple had certainly been a surprise for the Christians. They had no more believed in it than had the Jews. Sometimes they had imagined Nero the Anti-Christ returning from amongst the Parthians, marching upon Rome with his allies, sacking it, and then putting himself at the head of the armies of Judea, profaning Jerusalem, and massacring the people of the just on the hill of Zion; but no one had supposed that the Temple itself would disappear. An event so prodigious, when once it occurred, was sufficient to put them beside themselves. The misfortunes of the Jewish nation were regarded as a punishment for the murders of Jesus and of James. In reflecting upon it they endeavoured to find that in all that God had been especially good to his elect. It was because of them that he had deigned to shorten the days which if they had lasted would have seen the extermination of all flesh. The frightful sufferings that they had gone through dwelt in the memory of the Christians of the East, and was for them what the persecutions of Nero were for the Christians of Rome, "the great tribulation," the certain prelude to the days of the Messiah.

One calculation, moreover, appears to have greatly engaged the Christians at this time. They remembered this passage of the Psalm (xcv. 8, et seq.), "To-day if ye will hear his voice harden not your hearts (as at Meriba as in the day of Massa [1]) in the wilderness. . . . Forty years long was I grieved with this generation and said, It is a people that do err in their hearts, for they have not known my ways; unto whom I sware in my wrath that they should not enter into my rest." They applied to the stubborn Jews the words which referred to their rebellion in the desert, and as nearly forty years had gone by since the short but brilliant public career of Jesus, he was believed to address to the unbelieving that pressing appeal, "Forty years have I waited for you, the time is at hand, take care" (cf. Heb. iii. 7, et seq.) All these coincidences, which placed the Apocalyptic year about the year 73, the recent memories of the revolution and of the siege, the strange outbreak of fever, of frenzy, of exaltation, of madness, through which they had passed, and, by way of crowning marvel, the fact that after signs so evident men had still the sad courage to resist the voice of Jesus which called them--all appeared unheard of, and capable of explanation only by a miracle. It was clear that the moment was approaching when Jesus should appear and the mystery of the times should be accomplished.

So great was the influence of that fixed idea that the town of Pella came to be regarded as a temporary asylum where God himself fed his elect and preserved them from the hatred of the wicked (Rev. xii. 14); there was no thought of abandoning a place which they believed to have been pointed out by a revelation from heaven. But when it was clear that they must resign themselves to a longer life, there was a movement in the community. A great number of the brethren, amongst whom were members of the family of Jesus, left Pella and went to establish themselves some leagues off in Batanea, a province which belonged to Herod Agrippa II., but which was falling more and more under the direct sovereignty of the Romans. This country was then very prosperous; it was covered with towns and monuments; the rule of the Herods had been benevolent, and had founded there that brilliant civilisation which lasted from the first century of our era until Islam. The town chosen by preference by the disciples and relations of Jesus was Kokaba near Ashtaroth Carnaïm, a little beyond Adria, and very near the frontier of the kingdom of the Nabathites. Kokaba was only some thirteen or fourteen leagues from Pella, and the Churches of these two localities might long remain in close connection. Without doubt many Christians, from the times of Vespasian and of Titus, returned to Galilee and Samaria; yet it was only after the time of Hadrian that Galilee became the rendezvous of the Jewish population, and that the intellectual activity of the nation concentrated itself there.

The name which these pious guardians of the tradition of Jesus gave themselves was ("Ebionim") or "poor." Faithful to the spirit which had said "Blessed are the poor" ("ebionim") and which had characteristically attributed to the disinherited of this world the Kingdom of Heaven and the inheritance of the Gospel, they gloried in their poverty, and continued, like the primitive Church of Jerusalem, to live upon alms. We have seen St Paul always preoccupied with his poor of Jerusalem, and St James taking the name of "poor" as a title of nobility, (James ii. 5, 6). A crowd of passages from the Old Testament, where the word Ebion is employed to distinguish the pious man, and by extension the whole pietism of Israel, the reunion of the saints of Israel, wretched, gentle, humble, despised of the world but beloved of God, were associated with the sect. The word "poor" implied a shade of tenderness, as when one says, "The poor dear man!" This "poor of God" whose miseries and humiliations the prophets and the psalmists had told of, whose glorious future they had announced, was accepted as the symbolical title of the little Church of Pella and of Kokaba across the Jordan, the continuator of that of Jerusalem. And as in the old Hebrew tongue the word Ebion had received a metaphorical signification to designate the pious part of the people of God, in the same way the saintly little congregation of Batanea, considering itself the only true Israel, the "Israel of God," heir of the heavenly kingdom, called itself the poor, the beloved of God. Ebion was thus often employed in a collective sense, almost as was Israel, or, as amongst ourselves, personifications such as "Jacques Bonhomme." In the remote sections of the Church, to whom the good poor of Batanea were almost strangers, Ebion became a personage, the accepted founder of the sect of the Ebionites.

The name by which the sectaries were known amongst the other populations of Batanea, was that of Nazarenes or Nazoreans. It was known that Jesus, his relations and his first disciples, belonged to Nazareth or its environs; they were described therefore by their place of birth. It is supposed, perhaps not without reason, that the name of Nazarenes was especially applied to the Christians of Galilee, who had taken refuge in Batanea, whilst the name of Ebionim continued to be the title which the mendicant saints of Jerusalem gave themselves. However this may be, "Nazarenes" remained always in the East the generic word by which Christians were designated. Mahomet knew them by no other, and the Mussulmans use it to this day. By a singular contrast, the word "Nazarenes," after a certain date, presented like "Ebionites" an offensive sense in the opinion of Greek and Latin Christians. As in almost all great movements, it came to pass that the founders of the new religion were in the eyes of the foreign crowd which was affiliated to it, simply retrograde persons and heretics; those who had been the corner-stones of the sect found themselves isolated, and, as it were, ostracised. The name of Ebion by which they described themselves, and which conveyed to their minds the loftiest meaning, became an insult, and was, out of Syria, synonymous with "dangerous sectary." Jokes were made about it, and it was ironically interpreted in the sense of "poor-spirited." The ancient name of Nazarenes, after the beginning of the fourth century, served to designate for the orthodox Catholic Church heretics who were scarcely Christians at all.

This singular misunderstanding explains itself when it is remembered that the Ebionim and the Nazarenes remained faithful to the primitive spirit of the Church of Jerusalem, and of the brothers of Jesus, according to whom Jesus was no more than a prophet chosen of God to save Israel, whilst in the Churches founded by Paul, Jesus became more and more the incarnation of God. According to the Greek Christians, Christianity took the place of the religion of Moses, as a superior worship taking the place of an inferior. In the eyes of the Christians of Batanea, this was blasphemy. Not merely did they refuse to consider the Law as abolished, but they observed it with redoubled fervour. They regarded circumcision as obligatory, they observed the Sabbath, as well as the first day of the week, they practised ablutions and all the Jewish ceremonies. They studied Hebrew with care, and read the Bible in Hebrew. Their canon was the Jewish canon; already, perhaps, they began by making arbitrary retrenchments.

Their admiration for Jesus was unbounded: they described him as being in a peculiar degree the Prophet of Truth, the Messiah, the Son of God, the elect of God: they believed in his resurrection, but they never got beyond that Jewish idea according to which a man-God is a monstrosity. Jesus, in their minds, was a mere man, the son of Joseph, born under the ordinary conditions of humanity, without miracle. It was very slowly that they learned to explain his birth by the operation of the Holy Spirit. Some admitted that on the day on which he was adopted by God, the Holy Spirit or the Christ had descended upon him in the visible form of a dove, so that Jesus did not become the Son of God and anointed by the Holy Ghost until after his baptism. Others, approaching more nearly to Buddhist conceptions, held that he attained the dignity of Messiah, and of Son of God, by his perfection, by his continual progress, by his union with God, and, above all, by his extraordinary feat of observing the whole Law. To hear them, Jesus alone had solved this difficult problem. When they were pressed, they admitted that any other man who could do the same thing would obtain the same honour. They were consequently compelled, in their accounts of the life of Jesus, to show him accomplishing the fulfilment

21

of the whole Law; wrongly or rightly applied, they constantly cited these words, "I am not come to destroy, but to fulfil." Many, in short, carried towards gnostic and cabbalist ideas, saw in him a great archangel, the first of those of his order, a created being to whom God had given power over the whole visible creation, and upon whom was laid the especial task of abolishing sacrifices.

Their churches were called "synagogues," their priests "archi-synagogues." They forbade the use of flesh, and practised all the austerities of the hasidim, austerities which, as is well known, made up the greatest part of the sanctity of James, the Lord's brother. Peter also obtained all their respect. It was under the names of these two apostles that they put forth their apocryphal revelations. On the other hand, there was no curse which they did not utter against Paul. They called him "the man of Tarsus," "the Apostate;" they told only the most ridiculous histories of him; they refused him the title of Jew, and pretended that it might be on the side of his father, or it might be on that of his mother, he had had only Pagans for ancestors. A genuine Jew speaking of the abrogation of the Law, appeared to them an absolute impossibility.

We speedily discern a literature springing out of this order of ideas and passions. The good sectaries of Kokaba obstinately turned their backs upon the West, upon the future. Their eyes were for ever turned towards Jerusalem, whose miraculous restoration they confidently anticipated. They called it "the House of God," and as they turned towards it in prayer, it is to be believed that they gave to it a species of adoration. A keen eye might have discovered from that that they were in the way of becoming heretics, and that some day they would be treated as profane in the house which they had founded.

An absolute difference in a word separated the Christianity of the Nazarene--of the Ebionim--of the relatives of Jesus, from the Christianity which triumphed later on. For the immediate successors of Jesus it was a question not of replacing Judaism but of crowning it by the advent of the Messiah. The Christian Church was for them only a re-union of Hasidim, of true Israelites admitting a fact that for a Jew, not a Sadducee, might appear perfectly possible; it was that Jesus put to death and raised again was the Messiah, that after a very brief delay he would come to take possession of the throne of David and accomplish the prophecies. If they had been told that they were deserters from Judaism, they would certainly have cried out, and would have protested that they were true Jews and the heirs of the promises. To renounce the Mosaic Law would have been, from their point of view, an apostasy; they no more dreamed of setting themselves free from it than of liberating others. What they hoped to inaugurate was the complete triumph of Judaism, and not a new religion abrogating that which had been promulgated from Sinai.

Return to the Holy City was forbidden them: but as they hoped that the prohibition would not last long, the important members of the refugee Church continued to associate together, and called themselves always the Church of Jerusalem. From the time of their arrival at Pella, they gave a successor to James, the Lord's brother, and naturally they chose that successor from the family of the Master. Nothing is more obscure than the things which concern the brothers and cousins of Jesus in the Judeo-Christian Church of Syria. Certain indications lead us to believe that Jude, brother of the Lord, and brother of James, was, for some time, head of the Church of Jerusalem, but it is not easy to say when or under what circumstances. He whom all tradition designates as having been the immediate successor of James after the siege of Jerusalem, was Simon, son of Cleophas. All the brothers of Jesus, about the year 75, were probably dead. Jude had left children and grand-children. From motives of which we are ignorant it was not from amongst the descendants of the brothers of Jesus that the head of the Church was taken. The Oriental principle of heredity was followed. Simon, son of Cleophas, was probably the last of the cousins-german of Jesus who was still alive. He might have seen and heard Jesus in his childhood. Although he was beyond Jordan, Simon considered himself as chief of the Church of Jerusalem, and as heir of the singular powers which this title had conferred on James, the Lord's brother.

The greatest uncertainty prevails as to the return of the exiled Church (or rather of a part of that Church) to the city at once so guilty and so holy, which had crucified Jesus and was nevertheless to be the seat of his future glory. The fact of the return is incontestable, but the date of the event is unknown. Strictly we might put back the date to the moment when Hadrian decided on the rebuilding of the city, that is to say, until the year 122. It is more probable, however, that the return of the Christians took place shortly after the complete pacification of Judea. The Romans undoubtedly relaxed their severity towards a people so peaceable as the disciples of Jesus. Some hundreds of saints might well dwell upon Mount Sion in the houses which the destruction had respected, without the city ceasing to be considered a field of ruins and desolation. The 10th Fretensian Legion alone would form around it a certain group of inhabitants. Mount Sion, as we have already said, was an exception to the general appearance of the town. The meeting-place of the Apostles, many other buildings, and particularly seven synagogues, one of which was preserved until the time of Constantine, were almost intact amongst the surrounding ruins, and recalled that verse of Isaiah, "The daughter of Zion is left as a cottage in a vineyard, as a lodge in a garden of cucumbers, as a besieged city." It was there we may believe that the little colony fixed itself which established the continuity of the Church at Jerusalem. We may also believe if we will that it was placed in one of those straggling Jewish villages near Jerusalem, such as Bether, which are ideally identified with the Holy City. In any case, this Church of Mount Sion was, until the time of Hadrian, by no means numerous. The title of chief of the Church of Jerusalem appears to have been only a sort of honorary Pontificate, a presidency of honour, not carrying with it a real cure of souls. The relatives of Jesus especially appear to have remained beyond the Jordan.

The honour of possessing amongst their body persons so distinguished inspired an extraordinary pride amongst the Churches of Batanea. It seems probable that at the moment of the departure of the Church of Jerusalem for Pella, some of "the twelve," that is to say, the Apostles chosen by Jesus--Matthew, for example--were still alive, and were amongst the number of emigrants. Certain of the apostles may have been younger than Jesus, and consequently not very old at the date of which we speak. The data we have to go upon concerning the apostles who remained in the Holy Land and did not follow the example of Peter and John, are so incomplete that it is impossible to be certain on this point. The "Seven," that is to say the Deacons chosen by the first Church of Jerusalem, were also without doubt dead or dispersed. The relatives of Jesus inherited all the importance which the chosen of the first Coenaculum had had. From the year 70 to about the year 110 they really governed the Churches beyond the Jordan, and formed a sort of Christian Senate. The family of Cleophas especially enjoyed in devout circles a universally recognised authority.

The relatives of Jesus were pious people, tranquil, gentle, modest, labouring with their hands, faithful to the rigid principles of Jesus with regard to poverty, but at the same time strict Jews, putting the title of child of Israel before every other advantage. They were much reverenced, and a name was given to them (perhaps maraniin or moranoïe) of which the Greek equivalent was desposynoi. For a long time past, doubtless even during the life-time of Jesus, it had been supposed that he was of the lineage of David, since it was admitted that the Messiah should be of David's race. The admission of such an ancestry for Jesus implied it also for his family. These good people thought much of it, and were not a little proud of it. We see them constantly occupied in constructing genealogies, which rendered probable the little fraud of which the Christian legend had need. When they were too much embarrassed they took refuge behind the persecutions of Herod, which they pretended had destroyed the genealogical books. Nor did they stop here. Sometimes they maintained that the work had been done from memory, sometimes that they had had copies of ancient chronicles whereby to construct it. It was admitted that they had done "the best that they could." Two of these genealogies have come down to us, one in the Gospel attributed to St Matthew, the other in the Gospel of St Luke, and it appears that neither of them satisfied the Ebionim, since their Gospel did not contain them, and the churches of Syria always protested strongly against them.

This movement, inoffensive though it was as a matter of policy, excited suspicion. It appears that the Roman authorities had more than once kept a watch upon these real or pretended descendants of David. Vespasian had heard of the hopes which the Jews founded upon a mysterious representative of their ancient royal race. Fearing that they meant only a pretext for new insurrections, he caused all those who belonged to this line, or who boasted of being of it, to be sought out. This gave rise to much annoyance, which, perhaps, reached the chief of the Church of Jerusalem at Batanea. We shall see these inquiries renewed with much more rigour under Domitian.

The imminent danger which these speculations about genealogy and royal descent implied for the nascent Christianity, needs no elaborate demonstration. A kind of Christian aristocracy was being created In the political world the nobility are almost necessary to the state, politics having to deal with vulgar struggles which make of them a matter--matter is material rather than ideal. A state is strong only when a certain number of families, by traditional privilege, find it alike their duty and their interest to transact its business, to represent it, to defend it. But in the ideal order, birth is nothing; everyone is valued in proportion to what he discerns of the truth, to what he realises of the good. Institutions which have a religious, literary, or moral aim are lost when considerations of family, of caste, of heredity come to prevail amongst them. The nephews and the cousins of Jesus would have been the destruction of Christianity if the Churches of Paul had not been of sufficient strength to act as a counterpoise to that aristocracy, whose tendency had been to proclaim itself alone respectable, and to treat all converts as intruders. Pretensions analogous to those of the sons of Ali in Islam would have been produced. Islamism would certainly have perished under the embarrassments caused by the family of the Prophet, if the result of the struggles of the first century after the Hejira had not been to throw into an inferior rank all these who were too nearly related to the person of the Founder. The true heirs of a great man are those who continue his work, and not his relatives according to the flesh.

Considering the tradition of Jesus as its property, the little coterie of Nazarenes would have surely stifled it. Happily the narrow circle speedily disappeared: the relatives of Jesus were speedily forgotten in the depths of The Hauran. They lost all importance, and left Jesus to his true family, the only one which he would have recognised--those who "hear the word of God and keep it." Many passages from the Gospels where the family of Jesus is seen in an unfavourable light, may spring out of the antipathy which the nobiliary pretensions of the desposynoi could not fail to provoke around them.

Footnotes:
    1. These words are not in either of the English versions.--Trans.

CHAPTER IV

THE RELATIONS OF JEWS AND CHRISTIANS

The relations of these altogether Hebrew Churches of Batanea and of Galilee with the Jews must have been frequent. It is to the Judeo-Christians that an expression frequent in Talmudic traditions, that of minim, corresponding to "heretics," belongs. The minim are represented as a species of wonder-workers and spiritual doctors, curing the sick by the power of the name of Jesus and by the application of holy oil. It will be remembered that this was one of the precepts of St James. Cures of this sort, as well as exorcisms, were the great means of conversion employed by the disciples of Jesus, especially with regard to the Jews. The Jews appropriated to themselves these marvellous receipts, and until the third century we find the doctors curing in the name of Jesus. No one was astonished. The belief in daily miracles was such that the Talmud ordains the prayer that every one must make when "private miracles" happen to him. The best proof that Jesus believed that he could work miracles is, that the members of his family and his most authentic disciples had in some sort the speciality of performing them. It is true that by the same argument we must also believe that Jesus was a strict Jew, which is repugnant to our ideas.

Judaism, besides, included two tendencies which put it into opposite relations with regard to Christianity. The Law and the Prophets continued always the two poles of the Jewish people. The Law gave occasion to that bizarre scholasticism which was called the halaka, out of which the Talmud sprang. The prophets, the psalms, the poetic books inspired an ardent, popular preaching, brilliant dreams, unlimited hopes; what was called the agada, a word which embraces at once passionate fables like that of Judith and the apocryphal apocalypses which agitated the people. Just as the casuists of Jabneh showed themselves contemptuous of the disciples of Jesus, so the agadists sympathised with them. The agadists, in common with the Christians, had a dislike for the Pharisees, a taste for Messianic explanations of the prophetic books, an arbitrary exegesis which recalls the fashion in which the preachers of the Middle Ages played with texts, a belief in the approaching reign of a descendant of David. Like the Christians, the agadists sought to connect the genealogy of the patriarchal family with that of the old dynasty. Like them, they sought to diminish the burden of the Law. Their system of allegorical interpretation which transformed a code of laws into a book of moral precepts was the avowed abandonment of doctrinal rigorism. On the other hand, the halakists treated the agadists (and Christians were agadists in their eyes) as frivolous people, strangers to the only serious study, which was that of the Thora. Talmudism and Christianity became in this way the two antipodes of the moral world, and the hatred between them grew from day to day. The disgust which the subtle researches of the casuists of Jabneh inspired in the minds of the Christians, is written in the Gospels in letters of fire.

The inconvenience of the Talmudic studies was the confidence which they gave and the disdain which they inspired for the profane. "I thank Thee, O Eternal God!" said the student, on coming out of the house of study, "for that by Thy grace I have frequented the school instead of doing as those do who visit the market place. I rose up like them, but it was for the study of the law, and not from frivolous motives. I labour like them, but I shall be rewarded. We both run, but I for life eternal, whilst they can but fall into the pit of destruction." This it was which wounded Jesus and the authors of the Gospels so deeply; this which inspired those beautiful sentences, "Judge not, that ye be not judged," those parables wherein the man who is simple but pure of heart is preferred to the haughty Pharisee. Like St Paul, they saw in the casuists only people who sought to damn the greater part of the world by exaggerating obligations beyond the strength of man. Judaism, having at its basis the fact which was taken for granted that man is treated here below according to his merits, set itself to judge without ceasing, since the justice of God's ways could be proved only under that condition. Pharisaism has its profoundest roots in the theories of the friends of Job and of certain Psalmists. Jesus, by postponing the application of the justice of God to the future, rendered those criticisms of the conduct of others futile. The Kingdom of Heaven would set all things straight: God sleeps until then; but commit yourselves to him. Out of horror of hypocrisy Christianity arrived at even the paradox of preferring a world openly wicked but susceptible of conversion to a bourgeoisie which made a parade of its apparent honesty. Many features of the legend, conceived or developed under the influence of Jesus, arose out of this idea.

Between people of the same race, partakers of the same exile, admitting the same divine revelations and differing only upon a single point of recent history, controversy was inevitable. Sufficiently numerous traces of it are found in the Talmud and in the writings connected with it. The most celebrated doctor whose name appears mixed up in these disputes, is Rabbi Tarphon. Before the siege of Jerusalem he had filled various sacerdotal offices. He loved to recall his memories of the Temple, particularly how he had assisted upon the platform of the priests at the solemn service of the Day of Atonement. The Pontiff had for that day permission to pronounce the ineffable name of the Most High. Tarphon tells how, notwithstanding his efforts, he was unable to hear it, the song of the other officiants having drowned the priest's voice.

After the destruction of the Holy City he was one of the glories of the schools of Jabneh and Lydda. To subtlety he joined what was better--charity. In a year of famine it is said that he married three hundred women so that they might, thanks to their title of future spouses of a priest, have the right to share in the sacred offerings. Naturally, the famine having passed over, nothing more was heard of his espousals. Many sentences of Tarphon recall the Gospel. "The day is short, the work is long; the workmen are idle, the reward is great, the master urges on." "In our time," he adds, "when one says to another, Take the straw out of thine eye,' the answer is, Take the beam out of thine own.'" The Gospel places such a reply in the mouth of Jesus reprimanding the Pharisees, and one is tempted to believe that the ill temper of Rabbi Tarphon came from a response of the same kind which had been made to him by some min. The name of Tarphon, in short, was celebrated in the Church. In the second century Justin, wishing in a dialogue to depict a dispute between a Jew and a Christian, chose our Doctor as the defender of the Jewish thesis, and brought him upon the stage under the name of Tryphon.

The choice of Justin and the malevolent tone in which he makes this Tryphon speak of the Christian faith, are justified by what we read in the Talmud of the sentiments of Tarphon. This Rabbi knew the Gospels and the books of the minim; but, far from admiring them, he wished them to be burned. It was pointed out to him that the name of God constantly appeared in them. "I would rather lose my son," said he, "than that he should not cast these books into the fire, even though they contain the name of God. A man pursued by a murderer, or threatened with the bite of a serpent, had better seek shelter in an idolatrous Temple than in one of the houses of the minim, for these know the truth and deny it, whilst idolators deny God because they do not know him."

If a man relatively moderate like Tarphon could allow himself to be so far carried away, we can imagine how ardent and passionate must have been this hatred in the world of the synagogues, where the fanaticism of the Law was carried to its extremest limit. Orthodox Judaism could not curse the minim with sufficient bitterness. The use of a triple malediction against the partisans of Jesus comprised under the name of Nazarenes was early established, it being said in the synagogue at morning, at mid-day and at evening. This malediction was introduced into the principal prayer of Judaism, the amida or schemoné-esré. The amida is composed first of eighteen benedictions, or rather of eighteen paragraphs. About the time of which we speak, an imprecation in these terms was intercalated between the eleventh and twelfth paragraphs:--

"For the treacherous, no hope! For the malevolent destruction! Let the power of the proud be weakened, broken down, crushed, humiliated, now in these our days. Praised be Thou, O Eternal God who crushest thine enemies and bringest the haughty to the dust"

It is supposed, not without a show of reason, that the enemies of Israel pointed at in this prayer were originally the Judeo-Christians, and that this was a sort of shibboleth to turn the partisans of Jesus out of the synagogues. Conversions of Jews to Christianity were not rare in Syria. The fidelity of the Christians of this country to Mosaic observances afforded great facilities for this kind of thing. Whilst the uncircumcised disciples of St Paul could have no relations with a Jew, the Judeo-Christian might enter the synagogues, approach the teba and the reading-desk where the officials and the preachers presided, and might select the texts which favoured their views. In this way great precautions were taken. The most efficacious, was to compel everyone who wished to pray in the synagogue to recite a prayer which, pronounced by a Christian, would have been a curse upon himself.

To sum up--notwithstanding its appearance of narrowness, this Nazareo-Ebionite Church of Batanea had something mystical and holy about it which is exceedingly striking. The simplicity of the Jewish conceptions of the Divinity preserved it from mythology and from metaphysics, into which Western Christendom was not slow to plunge. Its persistence in maintaining the sublime paradox of Jesus, the nobility and the happiness of poverty was touching in its way. There, perhaps, lay the great truth of Christianity, that by which it has succeeded and by which it will survive. In one sense all of us, such as we are--students, artists, priests, doers of disinterested deeds--have the right to call ourselves Ebionim. The friend of the true, the beautiful, and the good, never admits that he calls for a reward. The things of the soul are beyond price; to the student who illuminates them, to the priest who moralises on them, to the poet and the artist who shed a charm over them, humanity will never give more than alms-- alms wholly out of proportion to what she has received. He who sells the ideal and believes himself paid for what he delivers, is very humble. The proud Ebionite who thinks that the kingdom of Heaven is his, sees that the part which falls to his lot here below is not a salary but the obolus which is dropped into the hand of a beggar.

The Nazarenes of Batanea had thus an inestimable privilege. They held the veritable tradition of the words of Jesus; the Gospel came forth from their midst. Thus those who knew directly the Church beyond the Jordan, such as Hegisippus and Julius Africanus, spoke of it with the greatest admiration. There, principally, it appeared to them, was the true ideal of Christianity to be found; in that Church hidden in the desert, in a profound peace under the wing of God, it appeared to them like a virgin of an absolute purity. The bonds of these scattered communities with Catholicism were broken little by little. Justin hesitates on their account, he knows little of the Judeo-Christian Church; but he knows that it exists, he speaks of it with consideration; at all events he does not break away from communion with it. It is Irenæus who begins the series of these declamations, repeated after him by all the Greek and Latin Fathers, and upon which St Epiphanius puts the topstone by the species of rage which the very names of Nazarene and Ebionite excite in him. It is a law of this world that every originator, every founder, shall speedily become a stranger, then one excommunicated, then an enemy in his own school, and that if he obstinately persists in living, those who go out from him are obliged to take measures against him as against a dangerous man.

CHAPTER V

SETTLEMENT OF THE LEGEND AND OF THE TEACHINGS OF JESUS

When a great apparition of the religious, moral, and literary order is produced, the next generation usually feels the necessity of fixing the memory of the remarkable things which happened at the commencement of the new movement. Those who took part in the first hatching, those who have known according to the flesh, the master whom so many others have been able to adore in the spirit only, have a sort of aversion for the writings which diminish their privilege and appear to deliver to all the world a holy tradition which they keep secretly guarded in their hearts. It is when the last witnesses of the beginning threaten to disappear, that disquietude as to the future sets in, and that attempts are made to trace the image of the founder in durable tints. One circumstance in the case of Jesus, contributed to delay the period when the memoirs of disciples are usually written down, and that was the belief in the approaching end of the world, the assurance that the Apostolic generation would not pass away until the gentle Nazarene had returned as the Eternal Shepherd of his friends.

It has been remarked a thousand times, that the strength of man's memory is in inverse proportion to the habit of writing. We can scarcely imagine what oral tradition might retain, when people did not resort to notes which had been taken or to papers which they possessed. The memory of a man was then as a book; he knew how to report conversation, to which he himself had not listened. "The Clamozenians had heard tell of one Antiphon, who was connected with a certain Pythadorus, friend of Zeno, who remembered the conversations of Socrates with Zeno and Parmenides, in order to repeat them to Pythadorus. Antiphon knew them by heart, and would repeat them to whomsoever would hear them." Such is the opening of the Parmenides of Plato. A host of people who had never seen Jesus, knew him in this way, without the help of any book, almost as well as his disciples themselves. The life of Jesus, although not written, was the food of the Church; his maxims were incessantly repeated; the essentially symbolical parts of his biography were reproduced in the little recitals, in some sort stereotyped and known by heart. This is certain as regards the institution of the Supper. It was probably also the same as regards the essential lines of the story of the Passion; at all events, the agreement of the fourth Gospel with the three others on that essential part of the Life of Jesus, would lead one to suppose so.

The moral sentences which formed the most solid part of the teaching of Jesus were still more easy to retain. They were assiduously recited. "Towards midnight I always awake," Peter is made to say in an Ebionite writing, composed about the year 135, "and then sleep returns to me no more. It is the effect of the habit which I have contracted of recalling to memory the words of my Lord which I have heard, so that I may retain them faithfully." As, however, those who had directly received the divine words were dying day by day, and as many words and anecdotes seemed likely to be lost, the necessity for writing them down made itself felt. On various sides little collections were made. These collections presented, with much in common, strange variants; the order and arrangement especially differed; each author sought to make his copy complete by consulting the papers of others, and naturally every vigorously accentuated word took its origin in the community, provided it conformed to the spirit of Jesus, was greedily seized upon, and inserted in the collections. According to certain appearances, the Apostle Matthew composed one of these memoirs, which has generally been accepted. Doubt is permissible in this matter, however; it is much more probable that all these little collections of the words of Jesus were anonymous, in the condition of personal notes, and were only reproduced by copyists as works possessing an individuality.

One writing which may assist us to form an idea of this first Embryo of the Gospels is the Pirké Aboth, a collection of the sentences of celebrated Rabbis, from the Asmonean times to the second century of our era. Such a book could be formed only by successive accretions. The progress of the Buddhist writings on the life of Saka-Mouni followed a similar course. The Buddhist Sutras corresponded to the collections of the words of Jesus; they are not biographies; they begin simply by indications of this kind:--"At this time Bhagavat sojourned at Sravasti in the Vihara of Jetavana," etc. The narrative part is very limited; the teaching, the parable, is the principal object. Entire parts of Buddhism only possess such Sutras. The Buddhism of the North, and the branches which have issued from it, have more books like the Lalita Vistara, complete biographies of Saka-Mouni, from his birth to the moment of his attaining to perfect intelligence. The Buddhism of the South has no such biographies, not that it ignores them, but because its theological teaching has been able to pass them by, and to hold to the Sutras.

We shall see, in speaking of the Gospel according to Matthew, that the state of these Christian Sutras may readily be imagined. They were a species of pamphlets, of sentences and parables without much order, which the editor of our Matthew inserted into his narrative. The Hebrew genius had always excelled in moral sentences; in the mouth of Jesus that exquisite style attained perfection. Nothing prevents our believing that Jesus himself spoke in this way But the "hedge" which according to the expression of the Talmud, protected the sacred word, was very weak. It is of the essence of such collections to grow by a slow accretion, without the outline of the first stone being ever lost. Thus the treatise Eduïoth, a little Mishna complete, which is the kernel of the great Mishna, and in which the deposits of successive crystallisations of tradition are very visible, is to be found complete in the great Mishna. The Sermon on the Mount may be considered as the Eduïoth of the Gospel, that is to say, as a first artificial grouping which does not prevent later combinations or the maxims thus strung together by a slender thread from shelling off anew.

In what language were those little collections of the sentences of Jesus composed, these Pirké Ieschou, if such an expression may be permitted? In the language of Jesus himself, in the vulgar tongue of Palestine--a sort of mixture of Hebrew and Aramaic which was still called Hebrew, and to which modern savants have given the name of Syro-Chaldaic. Upon this point the Pirké Aboth is perhaps still the book which gives us the best idea of the primitive Gospels, although the Rabbis who figure in this collection, being doctors of the pure Jewish school, speak there a language which is perhaps nearer to Hebrew than was that of Jesus. Naturally the catechists who spoke Greek translated those words as best they could, and in a fashion sufficiently free. It is this that is called the Logia Kyriaca, "the oracles of the Lord," or simply the Logia. The Syro-Chaldaic collections of the sentences of Jesus having never had unity, the Greek collections have even less, and were only written down individually in the manner of notes for the personal use of each one. It was impossible that even in a sketchy fashion Jesus was entirely contained in a gnomic writing; the entire Gospel could not be confined within the narrow limits of a little treatise of morals. A choice of current proverbs or of precepts like the Pirké Aboth would not have changed humanity, even supposing it to have been filled with maxims of the most exalted character.

That which characterises Jesus in the highest degree is that with him teaching was inseparable from action. His lessons were acts, living symbols, bound indissolubly to his parables, and certainly in the most ancient pages which were written to fix his teachings, there are already anecdotes and short narratives. Very soon, however, the first framework became totally insufficient. The sentences of Jesus were nothing without his biography. That biography is the mystery par excellence, the realisation of the Messianic ideal; the texts of the prophets there find their justification. To relate the life of Jesus is to prove his Messiahship, is to make, in the eyes of the Jews, the most complete apology for the new movement.

Thus very early arose a framework which was in some sort the skeleton of all the Gospels, and in which word and action were mingled. In the beginning John the Baptist, forerunner of the Kingdom of God, announcing, welcoming, recommending Jesus; then Jesus preparing himself for his Divine mission by retirement and the fulfilling of the Law; then the brilliant period of his public life, the full sunshine of the Kingdom of God--Jesus in the midst of his disciples beaming with the gentle and tempered radiance of a prophet-son of God. As the disciples had scarcely any save Galilean reminiscences, Galilee was the almost exclusive stage of this exquisite theophany. The part of Jerusalem was almost suppressed. Jesus went there only eight days before his death. His two last days were told almost hour by hour. On the eve of his death he kept the Passover with his disciples and instituted the Divine rite of common communion. One of his disciples betrayed him; the official authorities of Judaism obtained his death from the Roman authority; he died upon Golgotha, he was buried. On the next day but one his tomb was found empty; it was because he had been resuscitated and had ascended to the right hand of the Father. Many disciples were then favoured with appearances of his shade wandering between heaven and earth.

The beginning and the end of the history were, as we see, sufficiently well defined. The interval, on the contrary, was in a state of anecdotic chaos without any chronology. For the whole of this part relative to the public life no order was consecrated; each distributed his matter in his own way. Altogether the compilation became what was called "the good news," in Hebrew Besora, in Greek Evangelion, in allusion to the passage of the second Isaiah: "The spirit of Jehovah is upon me, because Jehovah hath anointed me to preach good tidings unto the meek; he hath sent me to bind up the broken-hearted, to proclaim liberty to the captives, and the opening of the prison to them that are bound; to proclaim the acceptable year of the Lord and the day of vengeance of our God; to comfort all that mourn." The Mebasser or "Evangelist" had as his especial duty to expound this excellent history which has been for eighteen hundred years the great instrument for the conversion of the world, which yet remains the great argument for Christianity in the struggle of the last days.

The matter was traditional: now tradition is in its essence a ductile and extensible matter. Every year sayings more or less apocryphal were mixed with the authentic words of Jesus. Did a new fact, a new tendency, make its appearance in the community, the question was asked what Jesus would have thought of it; and there was no difficulty in attributing it to the Master. The collection, in this way, grew from day to day, and was also purified. Words which were too strongly opposed to the opinions of the moment, or which had been found dangerous, were eliminated. But the basis remained; the foundation was really solid. The evangelical tradition is the tradition of the Church at Jerusalem transported into Perea. The Gospel was born amongst the family of Jesus, and, up to a certain point, is the work of his immediate disciples.

This fact it is which gives us the right to believe that the image of Jesus, as portrayed in the Gospels, resembles the original in all essential particulars. These narratives are at once historical and figurative. Whatever of fable may have mixed itself with them, it would be erring, out of fear of erring, to conclude that nothing in the Gospels is true. If we had known St Francis of Assisi only by the book of the "Conformities," we should have to say that it was a biography like that of Buddha or of Jesus, a biography written à priori to exhibit the realisation of a preconceived type. Still, Francis of Assisi certainly existed. All has become an altogether mythical personage amongst the Shieks. His sons, Hassan and Hosein, have been substituted for the fabulous part of Thammuz. Yet, Ali Hassan and Hosein are real personages. The myth is frequently grafted upon a historical biography. The ideal is sometimes the true. Athens offers the absolutely beautiful in the arts, and Athens exists. Even the personages who may sometimes be taken for symbolical statues, have really at certain times lived in flesh and bone. These histories follow, in fact, certain orderly patterns so closely that there is a certain resemblance amongst all of them. Babism, which is a fact of our days, offers, in its nascent legend, parts that seem drawn from the Life of Jesus; the type of the disciple who denies; the details of the sufferings and the death of Bab, appear to be imitated from the Gospel, which does not imply that these facts did not happen as they are described to have done.

We may add that by the side of these ideal traits, which make up the figure of the hero of the Gospels, there are also characteristics of the time, of the race, and of individual character. This young Jew, at once gentle and terrible, subtle and imperious, childlike and sublime, filled with a disinterested zeal, with a pure morality, and with the ardour of an exalted personality, most certainly existed. He should have his place in one of Bida's pictures, the face encircled with long locks of hair. He was a Jew, and he was himself. The loss of his supernatural aureole has deprived him in no way of his charm. Our race restored to itself and disengaged from all that Jewish influences have introduced into its manner of thought, will continue to love him.

Assuredly in writing concerning such lives, one is perpetually compelled to say, with Quintus Curtius. Equidem plura transcribo quam credo. On the other hand, by an excess of scepticism, one is deprived of many great truths. For our clear and scholastic minds, the distinction between a real and a fictitious history is absolute. The epic poem, the heroic narrative, or the Homerides, the troubadours, the antari, the cantistorie, exhibit themselves with so much ease, are reduced in the poetic of a Lucan or of a Voltaire to the cold puppets of stage machines which deceive nobody. For the success of such narratives, the auditor must accept them; but it is necessary that the author should believe them possible. The legendary, the Agadist, are no more impostors than the authors of the Homeric poems, or than were the Christians of Troyes. One of the essential dispositions of those who create the really fertile fables, is their complete carelessness with regard to material truth. The Agadist would smile if we put a question with all sincerity, "Is what you tell us true?" In such a state of mind no one is uneasy save about the doctrine to be inculcated, the sentiment to be expressed. The spirit is everything; the letter is of no importance. Objective curiosity which proposes to itself no other end than to know as exactly as possible the reality of the facts, is a thing of which there is almost no example in the East.

Just as the life of a Buddha in India was in some sense written in advance, so the life of a Jewish Messiah was traced à priori; it was easy to say what it would be and what it ought to be. His type was as it were sculptured by the prophets, thanks to the exegesis which applied to the Messiah all that belonged to an obscure ideal. Most frequently, however, it was the inverse process which prevailed amongst the Christians. In reading the prophets, especially the prophets of the end of the captivity, the second Isaiah, Jeremiah and Zechariah, they found Jesus in every line. "Rejoice greatly, O daughter of Sion; shout, O daughter of Jerusalem; behold thy King cometh unto thee, he is just and having salvation, lowly and riding upon an ass and a colt the foal of an ass" (Zech. ix. 9). The King of the poor was Jesus, and the circumstance which they recalled was regarded as the fulfilment of that prophecy. "The stone which the builders rejected has become the head of the corner," they read in a psalm. "He shall be a stone of stumbling and a rock of offence," they read in Isaiah, "to both the houses of Israel, a gin and a snare to the inhabitants of Jerusalem. And many among them shall stumble and fall" (Isaiah viii. 14, 15). "There indeed it is!" they said. Above all things, they went ardently over the circumstances of the Passion to find figures. All that passed hour by hour in that terrible drama happened in order to fulfil some prediction, to signify some mystery. It was remembered that he had refused to drink the posca, that his bones bad not been broken, that the soldiers had drawn lots for his garments. The prophets had predicted all. Judas and his pieces of silver (true or supposed) suggested analogous comparisons. All the old history of the people of God became as it were a model which they copied. Moses and Elias, with their luminous apparitions, gave rise to imaginary ascents to glory. All the ancient Theophanies took place on high ground. Jesus revealed himself principally on the mountains; he was transfigured on Tabor. They were not dismayed by apparent contradictions. "Out of Egypt have I called My Son," said Jehovah in Hosea. The words, of course, applied to Israel, but the Christian imagination applied them to Jesus, and made his parents carry him when a child into Egypt. By a yet more strained exegesis they discovered that his birth in Nazareth was the fulfilment of a prophecy.

The whole tissue of the life of Jesus was thus an express fact, a sort of superhuman arrangement intended to realise a series of ancient texts reputed to relate to him. It is a kind of exegesis which the Jews call Midrasch, into which all equivoques, all plays upon words, letters, sense, are admitted. The old biblical texts were for the Jews of this time not as for us an historical and literary whole but a book of gramarye whence were drawn fates, images, inductions of every description. The sense proper for such an exegesis did not exist; the chimeras of the cabbalist were already approached; the sacred text was treated simply as an agglomeration of letters. It is unnecessary to say that all this work was done in an impersonal and in some sense an anonymous fashion. Legends, myths, popular songs, proverbs, historical words, calumnies characteristic of a party--all this is the work of that great impostor who is called the crowd. Assuredly every legend, every proverb, every spiritual word, has its father, but an unknown father. Someone says the word; thousands repeat it, perfect it, refine it, acuminate it; even he who first spoke it has been in saying it only the interpreter of all.

CHAPTER VI

THE HEBREW GOSPEL

This exposition of the Messianic life of Jesus, mixed up with texts of the old prophets, always the same, and capable of being recited in a single sitting, was early settled in almost invariable terms, at least so far as the sense is concerned. Not merely did the narrative unfold itself according to a predetermined plan, but the characteristic words were settled so that the word often guided the thought and survived the modifications of the text. The framework of the Gospel thus existed even before the Gospel itself, almost in the same way as in the Persian dramas of the death of the sons of Ali the order of the action is settled, whilst the dialogue is left to be improvised by the actors. Designed for preaching, for apology, for the conversion of the Jews, the Gospel story found all its individuality before it was written. Had the Galilean disciples, the brothers of the Lord, been consulted as to the necessity for having the sheets containing this narrative worked into a consecrated form, they would have laughed. What necessity is there for a paper to contain our fundamental thoughts, those which we repeat and apply every day? The young catechists might avail themselves, for some time, of such aids to memory; the old masters felt only contempt for those who used them.

Thus it was that until the middle of the second century the words of Jesus continued to be cited from memory often with considerable variations. The texts of the evangelists which we possess, existed; but other texts of the same kind existed by the side of them; and, besides, to quote the words or the symbolical features of the life of Jesus no one felt obliged to have recourse to the written text. The living tradition was the great well from which all alike drew. Hence the explanation of the fact which is in appearance surprising, that the texts which have become the most important part of Christianity were produced obscurely, confusedly, and at first were not received with any consideration.

The same phenomenon makes its appearance furthermore in almost all sacred literatures. The Vedas have been handed down for centuries without having been written; a man who respected himself ought to know them by heart. He who had need of a manuscript to recite these ancient hymns confessed his ignorance; so that the copies have never been held in much esteem. To quote from memory from the Bible, the Koran, is, even in our days, a point of honour amongst Orientals. A part of the Jewish Thora must have been oral before it was written down. It was the same with the Psalms. The Talmud, finally, existed for two hundred years before it was written down. Even after it was written, scholars long preferred the traditional discourses to the MSS. which contained the opinions of the doctors. The glory of the scholar was to be able to cite from memory the greatest possible number of the solutions of the casuists. In presence of these facts, far from being astonished at the contempt of Papias for the Gospel texts existing in his time, amongst which were certainly two of the books which Christianity has since so deeply revered, we find his contempt in perfect harmony with what might be expected from a "man of tradition," an "elder," as those who have spoken of him have called him.

It may be doubted whether before the death of the Apostles, and the destruction of Jerusalem, all that collection of narratives, sentences, parables, and prophetic citations had been reduced to writing. The features of the divine figure before which eighteen centuries of Christians have prostrated themselves, were first sketched about the year 75. Batanea, where the brothers of Jesus lived, and where the remnant of the Church of Jerusalem had taken refuge, appears to have been the country where this important work was executed. The tongue employed was that in which the very words of Jesus had been uttered, that is to say, Syro-Chaldaic, which was abusively called Hebrew. The brothers of Jesus, the fugitive Christians of Jerusalem, spoke that language, little different besides from that of the Batanenas, who had not adopted the Greek tongue. It was in an obscure dialect, and without literary culture, that the first draft of the book which has charmed so many souls was traced. It was in Greek that the Gospel was to attain its perfection, the last form which has made the tour of the world. It must not, however, be forgotten that the Gospel was first a Syrian book, written in a Semitic language. The style of the Gospel--that charming turn of childlike narrative which recalls the most limpid pages of the old Hebrew books--penetrated with a species of idealistic ether that the ancient people did not know, and which has nothing of Greek in it. Hebrew is its basis. A just proportion of materialism and spirituality, or rather an indiscernible confusion of soul and sense, makes that adorable language the very synonym of poetry, the pure vestment of the moral idea, something analogous to Greek sculpture, where the ideal allows itself to be touched and loved.

Thus was sketched out by an unconscious genius that masterpiece of spontaneous art, the Gospel, not such and such a gospel, but this species of unfixed poem, this unrevised masterpiece where every defect is a beauty, and the indefiniteness of which has been the chief cause of its success. A portrait of Jesus, finished, revised, classic, would not have had so great a charm. The Agada, the parable, do not require hard outlines. They require the floating chronology, the light transition, careless of reality. It is by the Gospel that the Jewish agada has been universally accepted. The air of candour is fascinating. He who knows how to tell a tale can catch the crowd. Now, to know how to tell stories is a rare privilege; a naïveté, an absence of pedantry of which a solemn doctor is hardly capable, are absolutely necessary. The Buddhists and the Jewish Agadists (the evangelists are true Agadists) have alone possessed this art in the degree of perfection which makes the entire universe accept a story. All the stories, all the parables which are repeated from one end of the world to the other, have but two origins, one Buddhist and the other Christian, because Buddhists and the founders of Christianity alone had the care of the popular preaching. The situation of the Buddhists with regard to the Brahmans was in a sense analogous to that of the Agadists with regard to the Talmudists. The latter have nothing which resembles the Gospel parable, any more than the Brahmans would have arrived by themselves at a turn so light, so agile, and so flowing as the Buddhist narrative. Two great lives well told, that of Buddha and that of Jesus--there lies the secret of the two vastest religious propaganda that humanity has ever seen.

The Halaka has converted no one; the Epistles of St Paul alone would not have won a hundred disciples to Jesus. That which has conquered the hearts of man is the Gospel, that delicious mixture of poetry and the moral sense, that narrative floating between dreams and reality in a Paradise where no note is taken of time. In all that there is assuredly a little literary surprise. The success of the Gospel was due on the one hand to the astonishment caused amongst our heavy races by the delicious strangeness of the Semitic narrative, by the skilful arrangement of these sentences and discourses, by these cadences, so happy, so serene, so balanced. Strangers to the artifices of the agada, our good ancestors were so charmed with them that even in the present day we can scarcely persuade ourselves that this species of narrative may be devoid of objective truth. But to explain how it has happened that the Gospel may have become amongst all nations what it is, the old family book whose worn pages have been moistened with tears, and on which the finger of generations has been impressed, more is required. The literary success of the Gospel is due to Jesus himself. Jesus was, if we may so express ourselves, the author of his own biography. One experience proves the fact. There have been many Lives of Jesus in the past. Now the life of Jesus will always obtain a great success when the writer has the necessary degree of ability, of boldness, and of naïveté to translate the Gospel into the style of his time. A thousand reasons for this success may be looked for, but there is never more than one, and that is the incomparable intrinsic beauty of the Gospel itself. When the same writer later on attempts a translation of St Paul, the public will not be attracted. So true it is that the eminent person of Jesus trenching vigorously on the mediocrity of his disciples was pre-eminently the soul of the new apparition, and gave to it all its originality.

The Hebrew Protavangel was preserved in the original amongst the Nazarenes of Syria until the fifth century. There are besides Greek translations of it. A specimen was found in the library of the priest Pamphilus of Cæsarea; St Jerome is said to have copied the Hebrew text at Aleppo, and even to have translated it. All the Fathers of the Church have found that this Hebrew Gospel is much like the Greek Gospel which bears the name of St Matthew. They usually assume that the Greek Gospel attributed to St Matthew was translated from the Hebrew, but the deduction is erroneous. The generation of our Gospel of St Matthew was a much more complicated matter. The resemblance of the Gospel with the Gospel of the Hebrews does not go so far as identity. Our St Matthew is anything but a translation. We will explain later on why of all the Gospel texts the latter approaches most nearly to the Hebrew prototype.

The destruction of the Judeo-Christians of Syria brought about the disappearance of the Hebrew text. The Greek and Latin translations, which created a disagreeable discord by the side of the canonical Gospels, also perished. The numerous quotations made from it by the Fathers, allow us to imagine the original up to a certain point. The Fathers had reason to connect it with the first of our Gospels. This Gospel of the Hebrews, of the Nazarenes, resembled in truth much of that which bears the name of Matthew, both in plan and in arrangement. As to length, it holds the middle place between Mark and Matthew. It is impossible sufficiently to regret the loss of such a text, though it is certain that even supposing we still possessed the Gospel of the Hebrews seen by St Jerome, our Matthew would be preferred to it. Our Matthew, in a word, has been preserved intact since its final revision in the last years of the first century, whilst the Gospel of the Hebrews, through the absence of an orthodoxy (the jealous guardian of the text) amongst the Judaising Churches of Syria, has been revised from century to century, so that at the last it was no better than one of the apocryphal Gospels.

In its origin it appears to have possessed the characteristics which one expects to find in a primitive work. The plan of the narrative was like that of Mark, simpler than that of Matthew and Luke.

The virginal birth of Jesus does not figure in it at all. The struggle about the genealogies was lively, and the great battle of Ebionism took place on this point. Some admitted the genealogical tables into their copies, while others rejected them. Compared with the Gospel which bears the name of Matthew, the Gospel of the Hebrews, so far as we can judge by the fragments which remain to us, was less refined in its symbolism, more logical, less subject to certain objections of exegesis, but of a stranger, coarser supernaturalism, more like that of Mark. Thus the fable that the Jordan took fire at the Baptism of Jesus--a fable dear to popular tradition in the earlier ages of the Church--is to be found there. The form under which it was supposed that the Holy Spirit entered into Jesus at that moment, as a force wholly distinct from himself, appears also to have been the oldest Nazarene conception. For the transfiguration, the Spirit, which was the Mother of Jesus, takes her Son by a hair, according to an imagination of Ezekiel (Ezek. viii. 3), and in the additions to the book of Daniel, and transports him to Mount Tabor. Some material details are shocking, but are altogether in the style of Mark. Finally some features which had remained sporadic in the Greek tradition, such as the anecdote of the woman taken in adultery, which is thrust rightly or wrongly into the fourth Gospel, had their place in the Gospel of the Hebrews.

The stories of the appearances of Jesus after his resurrection, presented evidently in that Gospel a character apart. Whilst the Galilean tradition represented by Matthew will have it that Jesus appointed a meeting with his disciples in Galilee, the Gospel of the Hebrews--without doubt because it represented the tradition of the Church of Jerusalem--supposed that all the appearances took place in that city, and attributed the first vision to James. The endings of the Gospels of St Mark and St Luke place, in the same way, all the apparitions at Jerusalem. St Paul followed an analogous tradition.

One very remarkable fact is that James, the man of Jerusalem, played in the Gospel of the Hebrews a more important part than in the evangelical tradition which has survived. It appears that there was amongst the Greek evangelists a sort of agreement to efface the brother of Jesus, or even to allow it to be supposed that he played an odious part. In the Nazarene Gospel, on the contrary, James is honoured with an appearance of Jesus after his resurrection; that apparition is the first of all; it is for him alone; it is the reward of the vow, full of lively faith, that James had made, that he would neither eat nor drink until he had seen his brother raised from the dead. We might be tempted to regard this narrative as a sufficiently modern resetting of the legend, without a single important circumstance. St Paul in the year 57 also tells us that, according to the tradition which he had received, James had had his vision. Here, then, is an important fact which the Greek evangelists suppressed, and which the Gospel of the Hebrews related. On the other hand, it appears that the first Hebrew edition embodies more than one hostile allusion to Paul. People have prophesied, and cast out devils in the name of Jesus: Jesus openly repulses them because they have "practised illegality." The parable of the tares is still more characteristic. A man has sown in his field only good seed; but whilst he slept an enemy came, sowed tares in the field, and departed. "Master," said the servants, "didst thou not sow good seed in thy field? from whence then hath it tares?" And he said unto them, "An enemy hath done this." The servants said unto him, "Wilt thou that we go and gather them up?" But he said unto them, "Nay, lest while ye gather up the tares ye root up also the wheat with them. Let both grow together until the harvest, and in the time of harvest I will say to the reapers, gather ye together first the tares, and bind them in bundles to burn them, but gather the wheat into my barn." It must be remembered that the expression "the enemy" was the name habitually given by the Ebionites to Paul.

Was the Gospel of the Hebrews considered by the Christians of Syria, who made use of it, as the work of the Apostle Matthew? There is no valid reason for such a belief. The witness of the fathers of the Church proves nothing about the matter. Considering the extreme inexactitude of the ecclesiastical writers, when Hebrew affairs are in question, this perfectly accurate proposition, "The Gospel of the Hebrews of the Syrian Christians resembles the Greek Gospel known by the name of St Matthew," transforms itself into this, with which it is by no means synonymous:--"The Christians of Syria possessed the Gospel of St Matthew in Hebrew," or rather, "St Matthew wrote his Gospel in Hebrew." We believe that the name of St Matthew was not applied to one of the versions of the Gospel until the Greek version which now bears his name was composed, which will be much later. If the Hebrew Gospel never bore an author's name, or rather a title of traditional guarantee, it was the title of "the Gospel of the Twelve Apostles," sometimes also that of "the Gospel of Peter." Still, we believe that these names were given later, when Gospels bearing the names of the Apostles came into use. A decisive method of preserving to the original Gospel its high authority, was to cover it with the authority of the entire Apostolic College.

As we have already said, the Gospel of the Hebrews was ill preserved. Every Judaising sect of Syria added to it, and suppressed parts of it, so that the orthodox sometimes presented it as swollen by interpolation to a greater size than St Matthew, and sometimes as mutilated. It was especially in the hands of the Ebionites of the second century that the Gospel of the Hebrews arrived at the lowest point of corruption. These heretics issued a Greek version the style of which appears to have been awkward, heavy, overloaded, and in which, moreover, the writer did not fail to imitate Luke and the other Greek evangelists. The so-called Gospels of Peter and of the Egyptians came from the same source, and presented equally an apocryphal character and a mediocre standard.

CHAPTER VII

THE GREEK GOSPEL--MARK

The Christianity of the Greek countries had still greater need than those of Syria for a written version of the life and teaching of Jesus. It appears at the first glance that it would have been very simple, for the satisfaction of that demand, to translate the Hebrew Gospel, which shortly after the fall of Jerusalem had taken a definite form. But translation pure and simple was not the fashion of those times: no text had sufficient authority to cause it to be preferred over others; it is, moreover, doubtful if the little Hebrew pamphlets of the Nazarenes could have passed the sea and gone out of Syria. The Apostolic men who were in communication with the Western Churches trusted to their memories, and without doubt did not carry with them works which would have been unintelligible to the faithful. When the necessity for a Gospel in Greek made itself felt, it was composed of fragments. But, as we have already said, the plan, the skeleton, the book almost in its entirety, were sketched out in advance. There was at bottom but one way of telling the life of Jesus, and two disciples, working separately, one at Rome, the other at Kokaba, the one in Greek, the other in Syro-Chaldaic, could not but produce two works very much like each other.

The general lines, the order of the narrative, had already been settled. What had to be created were the Greek style and the choice of the necessary words. The man who accomplished this important work was John-Mark, the disciple and interpreter of Peter. Mark, it appears, had seen when a child something of the facts of the Gospel; it may even be believed that he was at Gethsemane. He had personally known those who had played a part in the drama of the last days of Jesus. Having accompanied Peter to Rome, he probably remained there after the death of the Apostle, and passed through the terrible crisis which followed the event in that town. It was there that, according to all appearances, he put together the little book of forty or fifty pages which was the corner stone of the Greek Gospels.

The document, although composed after the death of Peter, was in a sense his work; it was the way in which he had been accustomed to relate the life of Jesus. Peter knew scarcely any Greek; Mark served him as dragoman; hundreds of times he had been the channel through which this marvellous history had passed. Peter did not follow a very rigid order in his preaching; he cited facts and parables as the exigencies of his teaching required. This licence of composition is also found in the book of Mark. The distribution of the subject is often logically at fault; in some respects the work is very incomplete, since entire parts of the Life of Jesus are wanting, of which complaint was made even in the second century. On the other hand, the clearness, the precision of detail, the originality, the picturesqueness, the life of this first narrative were not afterwards equalled. A sort of realism renders the form heavy and hard; the ideality of the character of Jesus suffers from it; there are incoherencies, inexplicable whimsicalities. The first and the third Gospels greatly surpass that of Mark in the beauty of the discourses, the happy application of the anecdotes; a crowd of touching details have disappeared, but as an historical document the Gospel of Mark is greatly superior. The strong impression left by Jesus is there found almost entire. We see him really living and acting.

The part which Mark took in so singularly abridging the great discourses of Jesus is astonishing. These discourses could not have been unknown to him: if he has omitted them, he must have had some motive for doing so. The somewhat narrow and dry spirit of Peter is perhaps the cause of this suppression. This spirit is certainly also the explanation of the puerile importance which Mark attaches to the miracles. The working of wonders in his Gospel has a singular character of heavy materialism, which for the moment recalls the reveries of the magnetizers. The miracles are painfully accomplished by successive steps. Jesus works them by means of Aramaic formulae, which have a Cabbalistic air. There is a struggle between the natural and supernatural forces: the evil yields only step by step, and under reiterated injunctions. Add to this a sort of secret character, Jesus always forbidding those who are the recipients of his favours, to speak of them It is not to be denied that Jesus comes out of this Gospel not as the delightful moralist whom we love, but as a terrible magician. The sentiment with which he inspires the majority of those about him is fear; the people, terrified by his miracles, pray him to depart out of their coasts.

It is not to be concluded from this that the Gospel of Mark is less historic than the others; quite the contrary. Things which offend us in the highest degree were of the first importance to Jesus and his immediate disciples. The Roman world was even more than the Jewish world the dupe of these illusions. The miracles of Vespasian are conceived on exactly the same lines as those of Jesus in the Gospel of Mark. A blind man, a lame man, stop him on the public road, and beg him to cure them. He cures the first by spitting on his eyes; the second by treading upon his leg. Peter appears to have been principally struck by these prodigies, and we may readily believe that he insisted much upon them in his preaching. Hence the work which he inspired has a physiognomy peculiar to itself. The Gospel of Mark is less a legend than a memoir written by a credulous person. The characters of the legend, the vagueness of the details, the softness of the outlines, strike one in Matthew and Luke. Here, on the contrary, everything is taken from life; we feel that we are in the presence of memories.

The spirit which rules in this little book is certainly that of Peter. In the first place, Cephas plays there an eminent part, and appears always at the head of the apostles. The author is in no way of the school of Paul, yet in various ways he approaches him much more nearly than in the direction of James by his indifference with regard to Judaism, his hatred for Pharisaism, his lively opposition to the principles of the Jewish theocracy. The story of the Syro-Phoenician woman (Mark vii. 24, et seq.), which evidently signifies that the Pagan may obtain grace, provided he have faith, is humble and recognises the precedence of the son of the house, is in perfect harmony with the part which is played by Peter in the history of the centurion Cornelius. Peter, it is true, appears much later to Paul as a timid man, but he was none the less, in his day, the first to recognise the calling of the Gentiles.

We shall see later what kind of modifications it was thought necessary to introduce into the first Greek version, in order to make it acceptable to the faithful, and how, from that revision, emerged the Gospels attributed to Matthew and Luke. One cardinal fact of primitive Christian literature is that these connected, and in a sense more complete texts, did not cause the primitive text to disappear, The little work of Mark was preserved, and soon, thanks to the convenient but altogether erroneous hypothesis which makes of him "a divine abbreviator," he took his place amongst the mysterious four evangelists. Is it certain that the text of Mark can have remained pure from all interpolations,--that the text which we read to-day is purely and simply the first Greek Gospel? It would be a bold thing to affirm that it is. At the very time that it was found necessary to compose, other Gospels bearing other names, taking Mark for the foundation, it is very possible that Mark himself may have been retouched, whilst his name was still left at the head of the book. Many particulars appear to suppose a sort of retroactive influence upon the text of Mark, exercised by the Gospels composed after Mark. But these are complicated hypotheses of which there is no absolute proof. The Gospel of Mark presents a perfect unity and, except for certain matters of detail where the manuscripts differ, apart from those little retouchings, from which the Christian writings have, almost without exception, suffered, it does not appear to have received any considerable addition since it was composed.

The characteristic feature of the Gospel of Mark was, from the first, the absence of the genealogies and of the legends relating to the infancy of Jesus. If there was a gap which ought to be filled up for the benefit of Catholic readers, it was to be found there. And yet no attempt was made to fill it. Many other particulars, inconvenient from the apologist's point of view, were not erased. The story of the Resurrection alone presents itself in Mark with evident traces of violence. The best manuscripts stop after the words ephobountogar (xvi. 8). It is scarcely probable that the primitive text should have finished so abruptly. On the other hand, it is very likely that something followed which was shocking to received ideas, and it was cut out, but the conclusion ephobountogar being very unsatisfactory, various little clauses were invented, not one of which possessed sufficient authority to exclude the others from the manuscripts.

When Matthew, and, above all, Luke, omit certain passages which are actually in Mark, are we forced to conclude that these passages were not in the proto-Mark? We are not. The authors of the second version selected and omitted, guided by the sentiment of an instinctive art and by the unity of their work. It has been said, for example, that the Passion was wanting in the primitive Mark, because Luke, who has followed him up to that point, does not follow him in the narrative of the last hours of Jesus. The truth is that Luke has taken for the Passion another guide more symbolical, more touching than Mark, and Luke was too great an artist to muddle his colours. The Passion of Mark, on the contrary, is the truest, the most ancient, the most historical. The second version in any case is always blunter, more governed by a priori, reasons than those which have preceded it. Precise details are matters of indifference to generations which have not known the primitive actors. What is pre-eminently required is an account with clear outlines and significant in all its parts.

There is everything to lead us to believe that Mark did not write down his Gospel until after the death of Peter. Papias assumes this when he tells us that Mark wrote "from memory" what he had from Peter. Finally the fact that the Gospel of Mark contains evident allusion to the catastrophe of the year 70 is decisive when we admit the unity and integrity of the work. The author puts into the mouth of Jesus in Chapter xiii. a species of apocalypse wherein are intermingled predictions relative to the capture of Jerusalem and the approaching end of time. We believe that this little apocalypse, in part designed to induce the faithful to retire to Pella, was spread amongst the community of Jerusalem about the year 68.

It certainly did not then contain the prediction of the destruction of the Temple. The author of the Johanine apocalypse, however well he may have understood the Christian conscience, did not yet believe, in the later days of 68 or the early days of 69, that the Temple would be destroyed. Naturally all the collections of the life and words of Jesus which adopted this fragment as prophetic would modify it in the light of accomplished facts, and would see in it a clear prediction of the ruin of the Temple. It is probable that the Gospel of the Hebrews in its first form contained the apocalyptic discourse in question. The Hebrew Gospel, indeed, certainly contained the passage relating to the murder of Zecharias, son of Barachias, a feature which took its rise about the time of the apocalyptic discourse in question. Mark would scarcely venture to neglect a matter so striking. He supposes that Jesus in the last days of his life clearly foresaw the ruin of the Jewish nation, and took that ruin as the measure of the time which must elapse before his second appearing. "In those days after that tribulation . . . they shall see the Son of Man coming in the clouds with great power and glory." Such a formula notoriously assumes that at the moment when the author wrote the ruin of Jerusalem was accomplished, but accomplished very lately.

On the other hand, the Gospel of St Mark was composed before all the eye-witnesses of the life of Jesus were dead. Hence we may see within what narrow limits the possible date of the compilation of the book is restricted. In all ways we are brought to the first years of calm which followed the war of Judea. Mark could not have been more than fifty-five years old.

According to all appearances, it was at Rome that Mark composed this first attempt at a Greek gospel, which, imperfect though it is, contains the essential outlines of the subject. Such is the old tradition, and there is nothing improbable in it. Rome was, after Syria, the headquarters of Christianity. Latinisms are more frequent in the little work of Mark than in any other of the New Testament writings. The biblical texts to which reference is made recall the Septuagint. Many details lead to the belief that the writer had in view readers who knew little of Palestine and Jewish customs. The express citations from the Old Testament made by the author himself may be reduced to one; the exegetical reasonings which characterise Matthew and even Luke are wanting in Mark; the name of the Law never drops from his pen. Nothing, in fact, obliges us to believe that this may be a work sensibly different from that of which the Presbyter Joannes in the first years of the second century said to Papias:--"The Presbyters still say this: Mark, become the interpreter of Peter, wrote exactly but without order all that he remembered of the words and actions of Christ. For he did not hear or follow the Lord; but later, as I have said, he followed Peter, who made his didascalies according to the necessities of the moment, and not as if he wished to prepare a methodical statement of the discourses of the Lord; hence Mark is in no way to be blamed if he has thus written down but a small number of details, such as he remembered them. He had but one concern, to omit nothing that he had heard, and to let nothing pass that was false."

CHAPTER VIII

CHRISTIANITY AND THE EMPIRE UNDER FLAVIUS

Far from diminishing the importance of the Jews at Rome, the war of Judea had in a sense contributed to increase it. Rome was by far the greatest Jewish city in the world: she had inherited all the importance of Jerusalem. The war of Judea had cast into Italy thousands of Jewish slaves. From 65 to 72 all prisoners made during the war had been sold wholesale. The places of prostitution were filled with Jews and Jewesses of the most distinguished families. Legend has pleased itself by building a most romantic structure on this foundation.

Except for the heavy poll tax which oppressed the Jews, and which was for Christians more than an exaction, the reign of Vespasian was not remarkable for any special severities towards the two branches of the House of Israel. We have seen that the new dynasty, far from drawing down upon itself the contempt of Judaism in the beginning, had been compelled by the fact of the war of Judea, inseparable from its approach, to contract obligations towards a great number of Jews. It must be remembered that Vespasian and Titus, before attaining to power, had remained about four years in Syria, and had there formed many connections. Tiberius Alexander was the man to whom the Flavii owed the most. He continued to occupy one of the chief positions in the state; his statue was one of those which adorned the Forum. Nec meiere fas est! said the old Romans in their wrath, irritated by that intrusion of the Orientals. Herod Agrippa II., whilst continuing to reign and to coin money at Tiberias and Paneas, lived at Rome surrounded by his co-religionists, keeping up a great state, astonishing the Romans by the pomp and ostentation with which he celebrated the Jewish feasts. He displayed in his relations a certain largeness, since he had for his secretary the radical Justus of Tiberias, who had no scruple in eating the bread of a man whom he had certainly more than once accused of treason. Agrippa was decorated with the ornaments of the priesthood, and received from the Emperor an augmentation of fiefs on the side of Hermon.

His sisters Drusilla and Berenice also lived at Rome. Berenice, notwithstanding her already ripe age, exercised over the heart of Titus such an empire, that she had the design of marrying him, and Titus it was said had promised her, and was only deterred by political considerations. Berenice inhabited the palace, and, pious as she was, lived openly with the destroyer of her country. The jealousy of Titus was active, and it appears to have contributed, not less than policy, to the murder of Caecina. The Jewish favourite enjoyed to the full her royal rights. Legal cases were taken under her jurisdiction, and Quintilian relates that he pleaded before her in a case in which she was both judge and party. Her luxury astonished the Romans; she ruled the fashions; a ring which she had worn on her finger sold for an insane price; but the serious world despised her, and openly described her relations with her brother Agrippa as incestuous. Other Herodians still lived in Italy, perhaps at Naples, in particular that Agrippa, son of Agrippa and Felix, who perished in the eruption of Vesuvius. In a word, all these dynasties of Syria and Armenia which had embraced Judaism, remained with the new Imperial family in daily relations of intimacy.

Around this aristocratic world the subtle and prudent Josephus hovered, like a complaisant servant. Since his entry into the household of Vespasian and of Titus, he had taken the name of Flavius, and in the usual manner of a common-place soul, he reconciled contradictory characters--he was obsequious to the executioners of his country, he was a boaster concerning his national memories. His domestic life, until then by no means correct, now began to become orderly. After his defection, he had been weak enough to accept from Vespasian a young prisoner from Cesarea, who left him as soon as she could. At Alexandria he took another wife, by whom he had three children. Two of them died young, and he repudiated his wife, he says, on the ground of incompatability of temper, about the year 74. He then married a Jewess of Crete, in whom he found all perfections, and who bore him two children. His Judaism had always been lax, and became more and more so; it was very easy to believe that even at the period of the greatest Galilean fanaticism he was a liberal, preventing the forcible circumcision of people, and protesting that everyone ought to worship God in his own way. This idea that everyone should choose his own form of worship gained the day, and lent powerful help to the propagation of a religion founded on a rational idea of the divinity.

Josephus had undoubtedly a superficial Greek education, of which, like a clever man, he knew how to make the most. He read the Greek historians; that reading provoked him to emulation; he saw the possibility of writing in the same way the history of the last misfortunes of his country. Too little of an artist to understand the temerity of his undertaking, he plunged into it, as happens sometimes with Jews who begin in literature in a foreign tongue, like one who fears nothing. He was not yet accustomed to write in Greek, and it was in Syro-Chaldaic that he made the first version of his work; later he put forward the Greek version which has come down to our own times. Notwithstanding his protestations, Josephus is not a truthful man. He has the Jewish defect--the defect most opposed to a healthy manner of writing history--an extreme personality. A thousand preoccupations govern him; first the necessity for pleasing his new masters, Titus and Herod Agrippa; then the desire of proving his own importance, and of showing to those of his compatriots who looked askance at him, that he had acted only from the purest inspirations of patriotism; then an honest sentiment in many respects which induces him to present the character of his nation in the light which would compromise them least in the eyes of the Romans. The rebellion, he pretends, was the work of a handful of madmen; Judaism is a pure doctrine elevated in philosophy, inoffensive in policy; the Jews moderate, and, far from making common cause with sectaries, have usually been their first victims. How could they be the enemies of the Romans? they who had asked from the Romans aid and protection against the revolutionaries? These systematic views contradict on every page the pretended impartiality of the historian.

The work was submitted (at least Josephus wishes us to believe so) to the criticism of Agrippa and of Titus, who appear to have approved it. Titus would have gone further; he would have signed with his own hand the copy which was intended to serve as a type, to show that it was according to this volume that he desired that the history of the siege of Jerusalem should be told. The exaggeration here is palpable. What is clearly evident is the existence around Titus of a Jewish coterie which flattered him, which desired to persuade him that, far from having been the cruel destroyer of Judaism, he had wished to save the Temple; that Judaism had killed itself, and that, in any case, a superior decree of the Divine will, of which Titus had been but the instrument, hovered over all. Titus was evidently pleased to hear this theory maintained. He willingly forgot his cruelties, and the decree that he had to all appearance pronounced against the Temple, when the vanquished themselves came to offer such apologies. Titus had a great fund of humanity; he affected an extreme moderation; he was without doubt very well pleased that this version should be circulated throughout the Jewish world; but he was also well pleased when in the Roman world the story was told in quite a different way, and represented him upon the walls of Jerusalem as the haughty conqueror breathing only fire and death.

The sentiment of sympathy for the Jews, which is thus implied on the part of Titus, might be expected to extend itself to the Christians. Judaism, as Josephus understood it, approached Christianity on many sides, especially the Christianity of St Paul. Like Josephus, the majority of the Christians had condemned the insurrection, and cursed the zealots. They loudly professed submission to the Romans. Like Josephus they held the ritual part of the Law as secondary, and understood the sonship of Abraham in a moral sense. Josephus himself appears to have been favourable to the Christians, and to have spoken of the chiefs of the sect with sympathy. Berenice, on her side, and her brother Agrippa, had had for St Paul a sentiment of benevolent curiosity. The private friends of Titus were rather favourable than unfavourable to the disciples of Jesus, by which circumstance may be explained the fact, which appears incontestable, that there were Christians in the very household of Flavius. Let it be remembered that this family did not belong to the great Roman aristocracy; that it formed part of what may be called the provincial middle class; that it had not, consequently, against the Jews and Orientals in general, the prejudices of the Roman nobility, prejudices which we shall soon see regain all their power under Nerva, and bring about a century of almost continuous persecution of the Christians. That dynasty fully admitted popular charlatanism. Vespasian had no scruple about his miracles of Alexandria, and when he remembered that juggleries had had much to do with his fortune, he no doubt felt merely an increase of that sceptical gaiety which was habitual to him.

The conversions which brought the faith in Jesus so near to the throne, were probably not effected until the reign of Domitian. The Church of Rome was reformed but slowly. The inclination which Christians had felt about the year 68 to flee from a town upon which they expected every moment the wrath of God to descend, had grown weak. The generation mown down by the massacres of 64 was replaced by the continual immigration which Rome received from other parts of the Empire. The survivors of the massacres of Nero breathed at last, they considered themselves as in a little provisional Paradise, and compared themselves with the Israelites after they had passed the Red Sea. The persecution of 64 presented itself to them as a sea of blood, where all had only not been drowned. God had inverted the parts, and as to Pharaoh, he had given to their executioners blood to drink: it was the blood of the civil wars, which from 68 to 70 had poured out in torrents.

The exact list of the ancient presbyteri or episcopi of the Roman Church is unknown. Peter, if he went to Rome, as we believe, occupied there an exceptional place, and would certainly have had no successor properly so-called. It was not until a hundred years afterwards, when the episcopate was regularly constituted, that any attempt was made to present a consecutive list of the successors of Peter as bishops of Rome. There are no accurate memorials until after the time of Xystus, who died about 125. The interval between Xystus and St Peter is filled with the names of Roman presbyters who had left some reputation. After Peter we come upon a certain Linus, of whom nothing certain is known; then Anenclet, whose name was disfigured afterwards, and of whom two person ages were compounded, Clet and Anaclet.

One phenomenon which is manifested more and more is that the Church of Rome became the heiress of that of Jerusalem, and was in some sort substituted for it. There was the same spirit, the same traditional and hierarchical authority, the same taste for command. Judeo-Christianity reigned at Rome as at Jerusalem. Alexandria was not yet a great Christian centre. Ephesus, even Antioch, could not struggle against the preponderance which the capital of the Empire, by the very nature of things, tended more and more to arrogate to itself.

Vespasian arrived at an advanced old age, esteemed by the serious part of the Empire, repairing, in the bosom of a profound peace, with the aid of an active and intelligent son, the evils which Nero and the civil war had created. The high aristocracy, without having much sympathy for a family of parvenus--men of capacity but without distinction, and of manners sufficiently common--sustained and seconded it. They were at last delivered from the detestable school of Nero,--a school of wicked, immoral, and frivolous men, wretched soldiers and administrators. The honest party which, after the cruel trial of the reign of Domitian was to arrive definitely at power with Nerva, breathed at last, and already was almost triumphant. Only the madmen and the debauchees of Rome who had loved Nero laughed at the parsimony of the old General, without dreaming that that economy was perfectly simple and altogether praiseworthy. The treasury of the Emperor was not clearly distinguished from his private fortune; but the treasury of Nero had been sadly dilapidated. The situation of a family without fortune, like that of Flavius, borne to power under such circumstances, became very embarrassing. Galba, who was of the great nobility, but of serious habits, was lost because one day at the theatre he offered to a player on the flute who had been much applauded, five denarii, which he drew from his purse. The crowd received it with a song:

"Onesimus comes from the village,"

the burden of which the spectators repeated in chorus. There was no way of pleasing these impertinents save by magnificence and cavalier manners. Vespasian would have found it much more easy to obtain pardon for crimes than for his rather vulgar good sense, and that species of awkwardness which the poor officer usually retains who has risen from the ranks by his merits. The human race is so little disposed to encourage goodness and devotion in its sovereigns, that it is sometimes surprising that the offices of king and of emperor still find conscientious men to discharge them.

A more importunate opposition than that of the idlers of the amphitheatre and the worshippers of the memory of Nero, was that of the philosophers, or, to be more correct, of the republican party. This party, which had reigned for thirty-six hours after the death of Caligula, gained, on the death of Nero, and during the civil war which followed that event, an unexpected importance. Men highly considered, like Helvidius Priscus, with his wife Fannia (daughter of Thrasea), were seen to refuse the most simple fictions of imperial etiquette, to affect with regard to Vespasian an air at once cavilling and full of effrontery. We must do Vespasian the justice to remember that it was with great regret that he treated the grossest provocations with rigour, provocations which were the simple result of the goodness and simplicity of this excellent sovereign. The philosophers imagined, with the best faith in the world, that they defended the dignity of man with their little literary allusions; they did not see that in reality they defended only the privileges of an aristocracy, and that they were preparing for the ferocious reign of Domitian. They hoped for the impossible,--a municipal republic governing the world,--public spirit in an immense Empire composed of the most diverse and unequal races. Their madness was almost as great as that of the lunatics whom we have seen in our own days dreaming that the Commune of Paris could be the monarchy of France. Thus the good spirits of the time, Tacitus, the two Plinies, Quintilian, saw clearly the vanity of this political school. Whilst full of respect for Helvidius Priscus, the Rusticus, the Senecion, they abandoned the republican chimera. Seeking no more than to ameliorate the princely power, they drew from it the finest fruits for about a century.

Alas! that power had the cardinal defect of floating between the elective dictatorship and the hereditary monarchy. Every monarchy aspires to be hereditary, not merely because of what the democracies call the egotism of the family, but because monarchy is advantageous for the people only when it is hereditary. Heredity, on the other hand, is impossible without the Germanic principle of fidelity. All the Roman Emperors aimed at heredity; but heredity could never extend beyond the second generation, and it scarcely ever produced any but fatal consequences. The world only breathes when through particular circumstances adoption (the system best adapted to Cæsarism) prevails; there was in it only a happy chance; Marcus Aurelius had a son, and lost everything.

Vespasian was exclusively preoccupied with this cardinal question. Titus, his eldest son, at the age of thirty-nine, had no male issue, nor had Domitian at twenty-seven a son. The ambition of Domitian ought to have been satisfied with such hopes. Titus openly announced him as his successor, and contented himself with desiring that he should marry his daughter Julia Sabina. But in spite of so many favourable conditions, Nature gave herself up in that family to an atrocious complication. Domitian was a scoundrel before whom Caligula and Nero might pass for harmless jesters. He did not hide his intention of dispossessing his father and his brother. Vespasian and Mucianus had a thousand difficulties in preventing him from spoiling all.

As happens with good-hearted men, Vespasian improved every day as he grew older. Even his pleasantry, which was often, from want of education, of a coarse description, became just and fine. He was told that a comet had shown itself in the sky. "It is the King of the Parthians whom that concerns," said he, "he wears long hair." Then his health growing worse,--"I think I am about to become a god," said he, smiling. He occupied himself with business to the last, and feeling himself dying, "an Emperor should die standing," said he. He expired, in fact, in the arms of those who supported him, a grand example of manly attitude and firm bearing in the midst of troubled times, which seemed almost desperate. The Jews alone preserved his memory as that of a monster who had made the entire earth groan under the weight of his tyranny. There was without doubt some Rabbinical legend concerning his death; he died in his bed they admitted, but he could not escape the torments which he merited.

Titus succeeded him without difficulty. His virtue was not a profound virtue like that of Antoninus or of Marcus Aurelius. He forced himself to be virtuous, and sometimes nature got the upper hand. Nevertheless, a good reign was hoped for. As rarely happens, Titus improved after his accession to power. He had great powers of self-control, and he began by making the most difficult of all sacrifices to public opinion. Berenice was less than ever disposed to renounce her hope of being married. She behaved in all respects as if she were. Her quality of Jewess, of foreigner, of "Queen"--a title which, like that of King, sounded ill in the ears of a true Roman, and recalled the East--created an insurmountable obstacle to that fortune. Nothing else was spoken of in Rome, and more than one impertinence was daringly uttered aloud. One day in the full theatre a cynic named Diogenes, who had introduced himself into Rome, notwithstanding the decrees of expulsion issued against the philosophers, rose, and in the presence of all the people poured forth a torrent of insults. He was beaten. Heras, another cynic, who thought to enjoy the same liberty at the same price, had his head cut off. Titus yielded, not without pain, to the murmurs of the people. The separation was all the more cruel, since Berenice resisted. It was necessary to send her away. The relations of the Emperor with Josephus, and probably with Herod Agrippa, remained what they had been before the rupture. Berenice herself returned to Rome, but Titus had no further communication with her.

Honest folks felt their hopes revive. With the spectacles, and a little charlatanism, it was easy to content the people, and they remained quiet. Latin literature, which, since the death of Augustus, had undergone so great an eclipse, was in the way of recovery. Vespasian seriously encouraged science, literature, and the arts. He established the first professors paid by the state, and was thus the creator of the teaching body, at the head of which illustrious fraternity shines the name of Quintilian. The sickly poetry of the epopoeias and the artificial tragedies continued piteously. Bohemians of talent, like Martial and Statius, both excellent in little verses, did not come out from a low and barren literature. But Juvenal attained, in the truly Latin species of satire, an uncontested mastery for force and originality. A haughty Roman spirit, narrow, if you will, closed, exclusive, but full of tradition, patriotic, opposed to foreign corruptions, breathes through his verses. The courageous Sulpicia dared to defend the philosophers against Domitian. Great prose writers, above all, sprang up, rejected all that was excessive in the declamation of the time of Nero, preserving that part of it which did not shock the taste, animated the whole with an exalted moral sentiment, prepared, in a word, that noble generation which discovered and surrounded Nerva, which brought about the philosophical reigns of Trajan, of Antoninus, and of Marcus Aurelius. Pliny the younger, who so greatly resembles the cultivated wits of our eighteenth century; Quintilian, the illustrious pedagogue, who traced the code of public instruction, the master of our great masters in the art of education; Tacitus, the incomparable historian; others, like the author of the Dialogue of the Orators, who equalled them, but whose names are ignored or whose writings are lost, increased the labours which had already begun to bear fruit. A gravity full of elevation, respect for the moral laws and for the laws of humanity, replaced the gross debauchery of Petronius and the excessive philosophy of Seneca. The language is less pure than that of the writers of the time of Cæsar and of Augustus, but it has character, audacity, something which ought to cause it to be appreciated and imitated in modern times, which have conceived the middle tone of their prose in a more declamatory key than that of the Greeks.

Under this wise and moderate rule Christians lived in peace. The memory which Titus left in the Church was not that of a persecutor. One event of his reign made a lively impression. This was the eruption of Vesuvius. The year 79 witnessed this, perhaps the most striking phenomenon in the volcanic history of the earth. The entire world was moved. Since humanity had a conscience, nothing so remarkable had ever been seen. An old crater, extinct from time immemorial, broke into activity with an unequalled violence, just as if in our days the volcanoes of Auvergne should recommence their most furious manifestations. We have seen since the year 68 the preoccupation of the volcanic phenomena fill the Christian imagination and leave its traces in the Apocalypse. The event of the year 79 was equally celebrated by the Judeo-Christian seers, and provoked a species of recrudescence of the Apocalyptic spirit. The Judaising sects especially considered the catastrophe of the Italian towns thus swallowed up as the punishment for the destruction of Jerusalem. The blows which continued to rain upon the world were, to a certain point, the justification for such imaginings. The terror produced by these phenomena was extraordinary. Half of the pages of Dion Cassius which remain to us are consecrated to prophecies. The year 80 witnessed the greatest fire Rome had ever seen, save that of the year 64. It lasted for three days and three nights: the whole district of the Capitol and the Pantheon was destroyed. A frightful pestilence ravaged the world about the same time; it was believed to be the most terrible epidemic ever known. The tremblings of the earth spread terror everywhere; famine oppressed the nations.

Would Titus keep to the end his promise of goodness? That was the question. Many pretended that the part of "delight of the human race" is difficult to maintain, and that the new Cæsar would follow in the footsteps of Tiberius, of Caligula, and of the Neros, who after having begun well finished most badly. Souls absolutely given over to the stoic philosophy, like those of Antoninus and Marcus Aurelius, were required by those who would not succumb to the temptations of a boundless power. The character of Titus was of a rare quality; his attempt to reign by goodness, his noble illusions as to the humanity of his times, were something liberal and touching; his morality was not, however, of a perfect solidity; it was forced. He repressed his vanity and forced himself to propose purely objective aims in life. But a philosophical and virtuous temperament is of more value than a ready-made morality. The temperament does not change; morality of that kind may do so. It might be that the goodness of Titus was only the effect of an arrested development; it was asked if in the course of years he was not likely to become such another as Domitian.

These, however, were only retrospective apprehensions. Death came to withdraw Titus from a trial which might have been fatal had it been too prolonged. His health failed visibly. At every instant he wept as if, after having attained the highest rank in the world, he saw the frivolity of all things in spite of appearances. Once especially, at the end of the ceremony of the inauguration of the Coliseum, he burst into tears before the people. In his last journey to Rhætum he was overwhelmed with sadness. At one moment he was seen to draw back the curtains of his litter, to look at the sky, and to swear that he had not deserved death. Perhaps it was the wasting, the enervation produced by the part which he chose to play, the life of debauchery which he had lived at various times before attaining to the Empire, that was the cause of this. Perhaps also it was the protest which a noble soul had in such a time the right to raise against destiny. His nature was sentimental and amiable. The frightful wickedness of his brother killed him. He saw clearly that if he did not take the initiative, Domitian would. To have dreamed of the empire of the world, to make himself adored by it, to see his dream accomplished, and then to see its vanity, and to recognise that in politics good nature is a mistake; to see evil rise before him in the form of a monster, saying, "Kill me or I will kill you!" What a trial for a good heart! Titus had not the hardness of a Tiberius, or the resignation of a Marcus Aurelius. Let it be remembered also that his hygenic régime was the worst conceivable. At all times, and especially in his house near Rhætum, where the waters were very cold, Titus took baths sufficient to kill the most robust of men. All this assuredly renders it unnecessary to suppose that his premature death was the effect of poison. Domitian was not a fratricide in the material sense; he became one through his hatred, his jealousy, his undisguised desires. His attitude after the death of his father was a perpetual conspiracy. Titus had scarcely given up the ghost when Domitian obliged all those about him to abandon him as dead, and, mounting his horse, hurried to the camp of the Prætorian Guard.

The world mourned but Israel triumphed. That unexplained death from exhaustion and philosophical melancholy, was it not a manifest judgment from heaven upon the destroyer of the Temple--the guiltiest man the world had yet seen? The rabbinical legend on this subject took as usual a puerile turn which, however, was not wholly without justice. "Titus the wicked," said the Agadists, "died through the bite of a fly which introduced itself into his brain and killed him amidst atrocious tortures." Always the dupes of popular reports, the Jews and the Christians of the time generally believed in the fratricide. According to them, the cruel Domitian, the murderer of Clemens, the persecutor of the saints, was more than the assassin of his brother, and that foundation, like the parricide of Nero, became one of the bases of a new apocalyptic symbolism, as we shall see somewhat later on.

CHAPTER IX

PROPAGATION OF CHRISTIANITY--EGYPT--SIBYLLISIM

The tolerance which Christianity enjoyed under the reign of the Flavii was eminently favourable to its development. Antioch, Ephesus, Corinth, Rome, especially, were the active centres where the name of Jesus became every day more and more important, and from which the new faith shone out. If we except the exclusive Ebionites of Batanea, the relations between the Judeo-Christians and the converted Pagans became every day more easy; prejudices were set aside; a fusion was wrought. In many important towns there were two Presbyteries and two Episcopi, one for Christians of Jewish extraction, the other for the faithful of Pagan origin. It is supposed that the Episcopos of the converted Pagans had been instituted by St Paul, and the other by some apostle of Jerusalem. It is true that in the third and fourth centuries this hypothesis was abused, in order that the Churches might escape from the difficulty in which they found themselves when they sought to found a regular succession of bishops with antagonistic elements of tradition. Nevertheless, the double character of the two Churches appears to have been a real fact. Such was the diversity of education of the two sections of the Christian community, that the same pastor could scarcely give to both the teaching of which they stood in need.

Matters fell out thus especially when, as at Antioch, the difference of origin was joined with difference of language, where one of the groups spoke Syriac and the other Greek. Antioch appears to have had two successions of Presbyteri, one belonging in theory to St Peter, the other to St Paul. The constitution of the two lists was managed in the same way as the lists of the Bishops of Rome. They took the oldest names of the Presbyteri whom they remembered, that of a certain Evhode much respected--that of Ignatius who was greatly celebrated--and put them at the heads of the files of the two series. Ignatius died only under the reign of Trajan; St Paul saw Antioch for the last time in 54. The same thing then happened for Ignatius as for Clement, for Papias and for a great number of personages of the second and third Christian generations--the dates were garbled, so that they might be supposed to have received from the Apostles their institution or their teaching.

Egypt, which for a long time was much behind-hand in the matter of Christianity, probably received the germ of the new faith under the Flavii. The tradition of the preaching of St Mark at Alexandria is one of those tardy inventions by which the great Churches sought to give themselves an Apostolic antiquity. The general outline of the life of St Mark is well known; it is in Rome and not in Alexandria that it must be sought. When all the great Churches pretended to an Apostolic foundation, the Church of Alexandria, already very considerable, wished to supply titles of nobility which it did not possess. Mark was almost the only one amongst the personages of Apostolic history who had not yet been appropriated. In reality the cause of the absence of the name of Egypt from the narrative of the Acts of the Apostles and from the Epistles of St Paul is that Egypt had a sort of pre-Christianity which long held it closed against Christianity properly so called. She had Philo, she had the Therapeutes, that is to say, doctrines so like those which grew up in Judea and Galilee that it was unnecessary for her to lend an attentive ear to the latter. Later, it was maintained that the Therapeutes were nothing else than the Christians of St Mark, whose kind of life Philo had described. It was a strange hallucination. In a certain sense, however, this bizarre confusion was not altogether so devoid of truth as might be imagined at the first glance.

Christianity appears indeed to have had a very undecided character in Egypt for a long time. The members of the old Therapeutic communities of Lake Narcotis, if their existence must be admitted, ought to appear like saints to the disciples of Jesus, the Exegetas of the school of Philo, like Apollos, marched side by side with Christianity, entered into it even without staying there; the other Alexandrine Jewish authors of the apocryphal books shared largely, it is said, in the ideas which prevailed in the Council of Jerusalem. When the Jews, animated, it is said, by like sentiments, heard Jesus spoken of, it was unnecessary that they should be converted in order to sympathise with his disciples. The confraternity established itself. A curious monument of the spirit, peculiar to Egypt, has been preserved in one of the Sibylline poems--a poem dated with great precision from the reign of Titus or one of the first years of Domitian, which the critics have been able, with almost equal reason, to accept as Christian on the one hand and Essenian or Therapeutic on the other. The truth is that the author was a Jewish sectary, floating between Christianity, Baptism, Essenism, and inspired, before all things, by the dominant idea of the Sibyllists, who were the first preachers of monotheism to the Pagans, and of morality, under cover of a simplified Judaism.

Sibyllism was born in Alexandria about the time when apocalypticism came into existence in Palestine. The two parallel theories owed their existence to analogous spiritual conditions. One of the laws of every apocalypse is the attribution of the work to some celebrity of past times. The opinion of the present day is that the list of great prophets is closed, and that no modern can pretend to equal the ancient inspired ones. What then was a man to do who was possessed with the idea of producing his thought and giving to it the authority which would be lacking if he published it as his own? He takes the mantle of an ancient man of God and boldly puts forth his book under the shelter of a venerated name. The forger who, to expound an idea which he thinks just, abnegates his own personality in this way, has not a shadow of scruple. Far from believing that he injures the antique sage whose name he takes, he thinks he does him honour by attributing to him good and beautiful thoughts. And as to the public to whom these writings were addressed, the complete absence of criticism prevented anyone from raising a shadow of objection. In Palestine the authorities chosen to serve as name-lenders to these new revelations were real or fictitious personages whose holiness was known to and admitted by all--Daniel, Enoch, Moses, Solomon, Baruch, Esdras. At Alexandria, where the Jews were initiated into the Greek literature, and where they aspired to exercise an intellectual and moral influence over the Pagans, the forgers chose renowned Greek philosophers or moralists. It is thus that we see Aristobalus alleging false quotations from Homer, Hesiod, and Linus, and that there was soon a pseudo-Orpheus, a pseudo-Pythagoras, an aprocryphal correspondence of Heraclites, a moral poem attributed to Phocylides. The object of all these works was the same; they preached deism to idolators and the precepts known as Noachian, that is to say, Judaism mitigated for their use or reduced almost to the proportions of the natural law. Two or three observances only were retained which in the eyes of the most liberal Jews passed almost as forming part of the natural law.

The Sibyls present themselves to the mind as forgers in search of incontestable authorities under cover of whom they may present themselves to the Greeks the ideas which were dear to them. They already circulated little poems, pretended Cumæans, Erythæans, full of threats, prophesying calamities to different countries. These dicta, which had a great effect on the popular imagination, especially when fortuitous coincidences appeared to justify them, were conceived in the old epic hexameter, in a language which affected a resemblance to that of Homer. The Jewish forgers adopted the same rhythm, and, the better to deceive credulous people, they served in their text some of those threats which they thought in harmony with the character of the ancient prophetic virgins.

Sibyllism was thus the form of the Alexandrine Apocalypse. When a Jew--a friend of the good and of the true in that tolerant and sympathetic school--wished to address warnings or counsels to the Pagans, he made one of the prophetesses of the Pagan world to speak, to give to his utterances a force which they would not otherwise have had. He took the tone of the Erythæan oracles, forced himself to imitate the traditional style of the prophetic poetry of the Greeks, provided himself with some of these versified threats which made a great impression on the people, and framed the whole in pious utterances. Let us repeat it--such frauds with a good object were in no way repugnant to anybody. By the side of the Jewish manufactory of false classics, the art of which consisted in putting into the mouths of Greek philosophers and moralists the maxims which they were desirous of inculcating, there was established in the second century before Christ a pseudo-Sibyllism in the interest of the same ideas. In the time of the Flavii, an Alexandrine looked up the long interrupted tradition and added some new pages to the former oracles. These pages are of a remarkable beauty.

Happy is he who worships the Great God, him whom human hands have not made, who hath no temple, whom mortal eye cannot see nor haul measure. Happy are those who pray before they eat, and before they drink; who, at sight of the temples make a sign of protestation, and who turn away with horror from the altars bedabbled with blood. Murder, shameful gain, adultery, the crimes against nature, do they hold in horror. Other men given over to their perverse desires run after these holy men with laughter and with insult; in their madness they charge them with the crimes of which they themselves have been guilty; but the judgment of God shall be accomplished. The impious shall be cast into darkness, but the godly shall dwell in a fertile land, and the Spirit of God shall give to them light and grace.

After this exordium came the essential parts of every apocalypse; first a theory concerning the succession of empires--a species of philosophy of history imitated from Daniel; then signs in heaven, tremblings of the earth, islands emerging from the depths of the sea, wars, famines, and all the preparations which announce the coming of God's judgment. The author particularly mentions the earthquake at Laodicaea in 60; that of Myra; the invasions of the sea at Lycia, which took place in 68. The sufferings of Jerusalem then appeared to him. A powerful king, the murderer of his mother, flees from Italy, ignored, unknown, under the disguise of a slave, and takes refuge beyond the Euphrates. There he waits in hiding whilst the candidates for the Empire make bloody war. A Roman chief will deliver the Temple to the flames and will destroy the Jewish nation. The bowels of Italy will be torn; a flame will come out of her and will mount to heaven, destroying the cities, consuming thousands of men; a black dust will fill the air; lapilli like vermillion red will fall from heaven. Then it may be hoped men will recognise the wrath of God Most High, the wrath which has fallen on them because they have destroyed the innocent tribe of pious men. As the topstone of misfortune, the fugitive king, hidden behind the Euphrates, will draw his great sword and will recross the Euphrates with myriads of men.

It will be remarked how immediately this work follows the Apocalypse of St John. Taking up the ideas of the seer of 68 or 69, the Sibyllist of 81 or 82, confirmed in his dark previsions by the eruption of Vesuvius, revives the popular belief of Nero living beyond the Euphrates, and announces his immediate return. Some indications exist that there was a false Nero under Titus. A more serious attempt was made in 88, and nearly brought about a war with the Parthians. The prophecy of our Sibyllist is without doubt prior to that date. He announces in effect a terrible war; now the affair of the false Nero under Titus, if it ever occurred, was not serious, and as to the false Nero of 88, he created nothing more than a false alarm.

When piety, faith, and justice shall have entirely disappeared, when no one will care for pious men, when all will seek to kill them, taking pleasure in insulting them, plunging their hands in their blood, then will be seen an end to the Divine patience; trembling with wrath, God will annihilate the human race with fire.

Ah! wretched mortals! change your conduct; do not force the great God to the last outbreak of his wrath; leaving your swords, your quarrels, your murders, your violence, wash your whole bodies in running water, and, lifting up your hands to Heaven, ask pardon for your sins that are past, and with your prayers heal yourselves of your dreadful impieties. Then will God repent him of his threat, and will not destroy you. His wrath shall be appeased if you cultivate this precious piety in your hearts. But if you persist in your evil mind; if you do not obey me, and if, nursing your madness, you receive these warnings ill, fire shall spread itself upon the earth, and these shall be the signs of it. At the rising of the sun there shall be sounds in the heavens and the noise of trumpets; the whole earth shall hear bellowings and a terrible uproar. Fire shall burn the earth; the whole race of man shall perish, and the world shall be reduced to small dust.

When all shall be in ashes, and God shall have put out the great fire which he had kindled, then shall the Almighty restore form to the dust and bones of men, and restore man as he was before. Then shall cone the Judgment, when God himself shall judge the world. Those who remain hardened in their wickedness, the earth spread upon their heads shall recover them; they shall be cast into the abysses of Tartarus and of Jehannum, sister of Styx. But those who have lived a pious and godly life shall live again in the world of the Great and Eternal God, in the bosom of imperishable happiness, and God shall give them, to reward their piety, spirit, life, and grace. Then all shall see themselves, and their eyes shall behold the undying light of a sun that shall never go down. Blessed is the man who shall see those days!

Was the author of this poem a Christian? He certainly was one at heart, but he was one also by his style. The critics who see in this fragment the work of a disciple of Jesus, support their view principally upon the invitation to the Gentiles to be converted and to wash their whole bodies in the rivers. But baptism was not an exclusively Christian rite. There were by the side of Christianity sects of Baptists, of Hemero-Baptists, with whom the Sibylline verse would agree better, since Christian baptism can be administered but once, whilst the baptism mentioned in the poem would seem to have been like the prayer which accompanied it, a pious practice for the washing away of sin, a sacrament which might be renewed, and which the penitent administered to himself. What would be altogether inconceivable is that in a Christian apocalypse of nearly two hundred verses written at the beginning of the age of Domitian there was not a single word about the resurrection of Jesus or of the coming of the Son of Man in the clouds to judge the quick and the dead. If we add to that the employment of mythological expressions, of which there is no example in the first century, an artificial style which is a pasticcio of the old Homeric style which takes for granted a study of the profane poets and a long stay in the schools of the grammarians of Alexandria, our case is complete.

The Sibylline literature appears then to have originated amongst the Essenian or Therapeutic communities; now the Therapeutists, the Essenians, the Baptists, the Sibyllists, lived in an order of ideas very like that of the Christians, and differing from them only on the point of the worship of the person of Jesus. Later on, without doubt, all these sects were merged in the Church. More and more but two classes of Jews came to be left; on the one hand, the Jew who was a strict observer of the Law-- Talmudist, Casuist, Pharisee, in a word; on the other, the liberal Jew who reduced Judaism to a sort of natural religion open to virtuous Pagans. About the year 80 there were, especially in Egypt, sects which took up this position without, however, adhering to Jesus. Soon there will be more, and the Christian Church will include all those who wish to withdraw themselves from the excessive demands of the Law, without ceasing to belong to the spiritual family of Abraham.

The book numbered fourth in the Sibylline collection is not the only one of its class which the period of Domitian may have produced. The fragment which serves as the preface to the entire collection, and which has been preserved for us by Theophilus, Bishop of Antioch (end of second century), greatly resembles the fourth book, and ends in the same way: "A torrent of fire will fall upon you; burning torches will scorch you through all eternity; but those who have worshipped the true and infinite God, shall inherit life for ever, dwelling in the free and laughing garden of Paradise, and eating the sweet bread which shall fall from the starry skies." This fragment appears at first sight to present in some expressions indications of Christianity, but expressions altogether analogous may be found in Philo. The nascent Christianity had outside the divine aspect lent to it by the person of Jesus so few features specially proper to it, that the rigid distinction between what is Christian and what is not, becomes at times extremely delicate.

A characteristic detail of the Sibylline Apocalypses is that, according to them, the world will finish by a conflagration. Many passages in the Bible lead to this idea. Nevertheless, it is not found in the great Christian Apocalypse attributed to John. The first trace of it, found amongst the Christians, is in the Second Epistle of Peter, written, it is supposed, at a very late date. The belief thus appears to have sprung up in Alexandrian centres, and we are justified in believing that it came in part from the Greek philosophy; many schools, particularly the Stoics, held it as a principle that the world would be consumed by fire. The Essenes had adopted the same opinion; it became, in some sort, the basis of all the writings attributed to the Sibyl, so long as that literary fiction continued to serve as a skeleton for the dreams of unquiet minds as to the future. It is there and in the writings of the psuedo Hytasper that the Christian doctors found it. Such was the authority of these supposed oracles, that they were accepted as inspired, with the utmost simplicity. The imagination of the Pagan crowd was haunted by terrors of the same kind, utilised by more than one impostor.

Ananias, Avilius, Cerdon, Primus, who are described as the successors of St Mark, were without doubt old presbyters whose names had been preserved and of whom bishops were made when the divine origin of the episcopate was recognised, and when every see was expected to show an unbroken succession of presidents up to the apostolic personage who was accredited with its foundation. Whatever it may have been, the Church of Alexandria appears to have been from the first of a very isolated character. It was exceedingly anti-Jewish; it is from its bosom that we shall see emerge, in the course of the next fourteen or fifteen years, the most energetic manifesto of separation between Judaism and Christianity, the treatise known by the name of "the Epistle of Barnabas." It will be a different matter in fifty years, when gnosticism shall be born there proclaiming that Judaism was the work of an evil God, and that the essential mission of Jesus was to dethrone Jehovah. The importance of Alexandria, or, if you choose, of Egypt, in the development of Christian theology, will then clearly describe itself. A new Christ will appear resembling the Christ whom we know, just as the parables of Galilee resemble the myths of Osiris or the symbolism of the mother of Apis.

CHAPTER X

THE GREEK GOSPEL IS CORRECTED AND COMPLETED (MATTHEW)

The defects and omissions in the Gospel of Mark became every day more obnoxious. Those who knew the beautiful addresses of Jesus as they appeared in the Syro-Chaldaic Scriptures, regretted the dryness of the narrative based on the tradition of Peter. Not only did the most beautiful of his preachings appear in a truncated form, but parts of the life of Jesus, which had come to be recognised as essential, were altogether omitted. Peter, faithful to the old ideas of the first Christian century, attached little importance to the story of the childhood and to the genealogies. Now it was especially with respect to those things that the Christian imagination laboured. A crowd of new narratives sprang up; a complete Gospel was demanded, which to all that Mark embodied should be added all that the best traditionists of the East knew, or believed they knew.

Such was the origin of our text "according to Matthew." The author has taken as the foundation of his work the Gospel of Mark. He follows him in his order, in his general plan, in his characteristic forms of expression, in a way which does not leave it open to doubt that he had beneath his eyes, or in his memory, the work of his predecessor. The coincidences in the smallest details throughout entire pages are so literal, that one is tempted at times to declare that the author possessed a manuscript of Mark. On the other hand, certain changes of words, numerous transpositions, certain omissions, the reason for which it is not easy to explain, lead rather to the belief that the work was done from memory. The matter is of small consequence. What is important is that the text said to be of Matthew supposes that of Mark as pre-existing, and requiring only to be completed. He completes it in two ways, first by inserting in it the long discourses which make the Hebrew Gospels precious, then by adding to it traditions of more modern origin, fruits of the successive development of the legend, and to which the Christian conscience already attached an infinite value. The last version has, besides, much unity of style; a single hand has presided over the very various fragments which have entered into its composition. This unity leads to the belief that for the parts engrafted upon Mark the editor worked from the Hebrew; if he had made a translation, we should feel the differences of style between the foundation and the intercalated parts. Besides, the taste of the times was rather towards new versions than to translations properly so called. The biblical citations of the pseudo-Matthew suppose at once the use of a Hebrew text, or of an Aramaic Targum, and of the version of the Seventy (the Septuagint): a part of his exegesis has no meaning save in Hebrew.

The fashion in which the author managed the intercalation of the great discourses of Jesus is singular. Whether he takes them from the collections of sentences which may have existed at a certain period of the evangelic tradition, or whether he takes them ready made from the Gospel of the Hebrews, these discourses are inserted by him like great parentheses in the narrative of Mark, into which he cuts as it were grooves. The chief of these discourses, the Sermon on the Mount, is evidently composed of parts which have no natural connection, and which have been only artificially brought together. The twenty-third chapter contains all that tradition has preserved of the reproaches which Jesus on various occasions addressed to the Pharisees. The seven parables of the thirteenth chapter were certainly never uttered by Jesus on the same day, and one after another. Let us take a familiar illustration, which alone renders our meaning. There were, before the issue of the first Gospel, bundles of discourses and parables where the words of Jesus were classified for purely external reasons. The author of the first Gospel found those bundles ready made up, and inserted them into the text of Mark, which served him as a canvas all tied up together without breaking the thread which bound them. Sometimes the text of Mark, brief though the discourses have been made, contains some parts of the sermons which the new editor took bodily from the collection of the Logia, hence some repetitions. Generally the new editor cares little about those repetitions; sometimes he avoids them by retrenchments, transpositions, and certain little niceties of style.

The insertion of traditions unknown to the old Mark is done by the pseudo-Matthew by yet more violent processes. In possession of some accounts of miracles or of healings of which he does not perceive the identity with those which are already told by Mark, the author prefers telling the story twice over, to omitting any particular. He desires, before all things, to be complete, and he does not disquiet himself lest he should stumble in thus arranging portions of various productions with contradictions and the difficulties of narration. Hence these circumstances, obscure at the moment when they are introduced, which are only explained by the course of the work; these allusions to events of which nothing is said in the historical part. Hence the singular doublets which characterise the first Gospel: two cures of two blind men; two cures of a dumb demoniac; two multiplications of bread; two demands for a sign from heaven; two invectives against scandals; two sentences on divorce. Hence, also, perhaps, that method of proceeding by couples which produces the effect of a sort of duplicate narrative; two blind men of Jericho and two other blind men; two demoniacs of the Gergesenes; two disciples of John; two disciples of Jesus; two brothers. The harmonistic exegesis produces hence its usual results of redundance and heaviness. At other times the cut is seen to be quite fresh, the operation of the grafting by which the addition is made. Thus the miracle of Peter--a story which Mark does not give--is intercalated between Mark vi. 50 and 51 in such a way that the edges of the wound are still raw. It is the same with the miracle of the tribute money; with Judas pointing himself out and questioned by Jesus; with Jesus rebuking the stroke of Peter's sword; with the suicide of Judas; with the dream of Pilate's wife, etc. If we cut out all these details, the fruits of a later development of the legend of Jesus, the very text of Mark remains.

In this way a crowd of legends were introduced into the Gospel text which are wanting in Mark-- the genealogy; the supernatural birth; the visit of the Magi; the flight into Egypt; the massacre of Bethlehem; Peter walking upon the water; the prerogatives of Peter; the miracle of the money found in the fish's mouth; the eunuchs of the kingdom of God; the emotion of Jerusalem at the entrance of Jesus; the Jerusalem miracles and the triumph of the children various legendary details about Judas, particularly his suicide; the order to put the sword back into its sheath; the intervention of Pilate's wife; Pilate washing his hands and the Jewish people taking all the responsibility for the death of Jesus; the tearing of the curtain of the Temple; the earthquake and the rising of the saints at the moment of the death of Jesus; the guard set over the tomb, and the corruption of the soldiers. In all these places the quotations are from the Septuagint. The Editor for his personal use avails himself of the Greek version, but when he translates the Hebrew Gospel he conforms to the exegesis of that original which often had no basis in the Septuagint.

A sort of competition in the use of the marvellous; the taste for more and more startling miracles; a tendency to present the Church as already organised and disciplined from the days of Jesus; an ever-increasing repulsion for the Jews, dictated the majority of these additions to the primitive narrative. As has already been said, there are moments in the growth of a dogma when days are worth centuries. A week after his death, Jesus was the hero of a vast legend of his life, the majority of the details to which we have just referred were already written in advance.

One of the great factors in the creation of the Jewish Agada are the analogies drawn from Biblical texts. These things serve to fill up a host of gaps in the souvenirs. The most contradictory reports were current, for example, about the death of Judas. One version soon prevailed: Achitophel, the betrayer of David, served as his prototype. It was admitted that Judas hanged himself as he did. A passage of Zechariah furnished the thirty pieces of silver, the fact of his having cast them down in the Temple, as well as the potter's field--nothing is wanting to the story.

The apologetic intention was another fertile source of anecdotes and intercalations. Already objections to the Messiahship of Jesus had been raised, and required answering. John the Baptist, said the misbelievers, had not believed in him or had ceased to believe in him; the towns where his miracles were said to have been performed were not converted; the wise men and the sages of the nation despised him; if he had driven out devils, it was through Beelzebub; he had promised signs in the heavens which he had not given. There was an answer to all this which flattered the democratic instincts of the crowd. It was not the nation which had repulsed Jesus, said the Christians, it was the superior classes, always egotists, who would none of him. Simple people would have been for him, and the priests took him with subtlety, for they feared the people. "It was the fault of the Government"--here is an explanation which in all ages has been readily accepted.

The birth of Jesus and his resurrection were the cause of endless objections from low minds and ill-prepared hearts. The resurrection no one had seen; the Jews declared that the friends of Jesus had carried his corpse away into Galilee. It was answered by the fable of the guardians to whom the Jews had given money to say that the disciples had carried away the body. As to the birth, two contradictory currents of opinion may be traced; but as both responded to the needs of the Christian conscience, they were reconciled as well as they might be. On the one hand, it was necessary that Jesus should be the descendant of David; on the other, he might not be conceived under the ordinary conditions of humanity. It was not natural that he who had never lived as other men lived should be born as other men were born. The descent from David was established by a genealogy which showed Joseph as of the stock of David. That was scarcely satisfactory, in view of the hypothesis of the supernatural conception, according to which Joseph and his supposed ancestors had nothing to do with the birth of Jesus. It was Mary whom it was necessary to attach to the royal family. Now no attempt was made in the first century to do this, doubtless because the genealogies had been fixed before it was seriously pretended that Jesus was born otherwise than as the result of the lawful union of the two sexes, and no one denied to Joseph his rights to a real paternity. The Gospel of the Hebrews--at least at the period at which we now are--always described Jesus as the son of Joseph and Mary the Holy Spirit in the conception of this Gospel was for Jesus the Messiah (a distinct personage from the man Jesus) a mother, not a father. The Gospel of Matthew, on the contrary, propounds an altogether contradictory combination. Jesus, with him, is the son of David through Joseph, who is not his father. The author evades this difficulty with an extreme naïveté. An angel comes to relieve the mind of Joseph from suspicions which in a case so peculiar he had a right to entertain.

The genealogy which we read in the Gospel ascribed to Matthew is certainly not the work of the author of that Gospel. He has taken it from some previous document. Was it in the Gospel of the Hebrews itself? It is doubtful. A large proportion of the Hebrews of Syria kept always a text in which such genealogies did not figure; but also certain Nazarene manuscripts of very ancient date presented by way of preface a sepher toledoth. The turn of the genealogy of Matthew is Hebrew; the transcriptions of the proper names are not those of the Septuagint. We have seen, besides, that the genealogies were probably the work of the kinsmen of Jesus, retired to Batanea and speaking Hebrew. What is certain is that the work of the genealogies was not executed with much unity or much authority, for two altogether discordant systems of connecting Joseph with the last known persons of the line of David have come down to us. It is not impossible that the names of the father and grandfather of Joseph were known. After that, from Zerubbabel to Joseph, all has been fabricated. As after the captivity the Biblical writings give no more genealogies, the author imagines the period to have been shorter than it really was, and puts in too few generations. From Zerubbabel to David, Paralipomenes are made use of, not without sundry inaccuracies and failures of memory. Genesis, the Book of Ruth, the Paralipomenes, have furnished the body as far as David. A singular preoccupation of the author of the genealogy contained in Matthew has been to mention, by exceptional privilege, or even to introduce by force, in the ascending line of Jesus, four women who were sinners, faithless to a point which a Pharisee might well criticise--Tamar, Rahab, Ruth, and Bathsheba. It was an invitation to sinners never to despair of entering into the family of the elect. The genealogy of Matthew gives also to Jesus as ancestors the kings of Judah, descendants of David, beginning with Solomon, but soon, not wishing that that genealogy should borrow too much from profane glory, Jesus is connected with David by a little known son, Nathan, and by a line parallel to that of the kings of Judah.

For the rest, the supernatural connexion gained every day so much in importance, that the question of the father and of the ancestors of Jesus after the flesh, became in some sort a secondary matter. It was believed to have been prophesied by Isaiah in a passage which is ill-rendered in the Septuagint, that Christ should be born of a Virgin. The Holy Spirit, the Spirit of God, had done all. Joseph in reality appears to have been an old man when Jesus was born. Mary, who appears to have been his second wife, might be very young. This contrast rendered the idea of the miracle easy. Certainly the legend would not have come into existence without that; as, moreover, the myth was elaborated in the midst of a people who had known the family of Jesus, such a circumstance as an old man taking a young wife was not indifferent. A common feature of the Hebrew histories, is the magnifying of the Divine power by the very weakness of the instruments which he employed. Thus came the habit of describing great men as the offspring of parents old or long childless. The legend of Samuel begot that of John the Baptist, that of Jesus and that of Mary herself. On the other hand, this provoked the objections of ill-wishers. The coarse fable invented by the opponents of Christianity, which made Jesus the fruit of a scandalous adventure with the soldier Pantheris, arose out of the Christian narrative without much difficulty--that narrative presenting to the imagination the shocking picture of a birth where the father had only a false part to play. The fable shows itself clearly only in the second century; in the first, however, the Jews appear to have malignantly represented the birth of Jesus as illegitimate. Perhaps they so argued from the species of ostentation with which at the head of the book of the toledoth of Jesus the names of Tamar, of Rahab, and of Bathsheba were placed, whilst omitting those of Sarah, Rebecca, and Leah.

The stories of the childhood, ignored by Mark, are confined by Matthew to the episode of the magi, linked with the persecution by Herod, and the Massacre of the Innocents. All this development appears to be of Syrian origin; the odious part which Herod plays, was, without doubt, the invention of the family of Jesus, refugees in Batanea. The little group appears, in a word, to have been a source of hateful calumnies against Herod. The fable about the infamous origin of his father, contradicted by Josephus and Nicholas of Damascus, appears to have come from thence. Herod became the scapegoat of all Christian grievances. As for the dangers with which the childhood of Jesus is supposed to have been surrounded, they are simply an imitation of the childhood of Moses, whom a king also desired to slay, and who was obliged to escape to foreign parts. It happened to Jesus as to all great men. We know nothing of their childhood, for the simple reason that no one can predict the future of a child; we supplement our imperfect knowledge by anecdotes invented after the event. Imagination, besides, likes to figure to itself that the men of Providence have grown in spite of perils, as the effect of a special protection of Heaven. A popular story relative to the birth of Augustus, and various features of Herod's cruelty, might give rise to the legend of the massacre of the children of Bethlehem.

Mark, in his singularly naïve narrative, has eccentricities, rudenesses, passages not very easy of explanation and open to much objection. Matthew proceeds by retouchings and extenuations of detail. Compare, for example, Mark iii. 31-35 with Matthew xii. 46-50. The second editor gets rid of the idea that the relations of Jesus thought him mad, and wished to put him under restraint. The astonishing simplicity of Mark vi. 5, "He could do there no mighty work, save that he laid his hands upon a few sick folk, and healed them," is softened in Matthew xiii. 58, "And he did not many mighty works there, because of their unbelief." The strange paradox of Mark, "Verily I say unto you, There is no man that hath left house, or brethren, or sisters, or father, or mother, or wife, or children or lands, for my sake, and the gospel's, but he shall receive an hundredfold now in this time, houses, and brethren, and sisters, and mothers, and children, and lands, with persecutions; and in the world to come eternal life," becomes in Matthew, "And everyone that hath forsaken houses, or brethren, or sisters, or father, or mother, or wife, or children, or lands, for my name's sake, shall receive an hundredfold, and shall inherit everlasting life." The motive assigned for the visit of the women to the sepulchre, implying clearly that they did not expect the resurrection, is replaced in Matthew by an insignificant expression. The scribe who interrogates Jesus on the great commandment does so in Mark with a good intention. In the two other Evangelists he does it to tempt Jesus. The times have advanced: it is no longer to be admitted that a scribe could possibly act without malice. The episode when the young rich man calls Jesus "Good Master," and where Jesus reproves him with the words, "there is none good but God," appeared scandalous a little later. Matthew settles it in a less shocking manner. The fashion in which the disciples are sacrificed in Mark is equally extenuated in Matthew. Finally, this last is guilty of some inaccuracies, in order to obtain pathetic effects: thus the wine of the condemned, the institution of which was really humane, becomes with him a refinement of cruelty to bring about the fulfilment of a prophecy.

The two lively sallies of Mark are thus effaced; the lines of the new Gospel are larger, more correct, more ideal. The marvellous features are multiplied, but we should say that there is an attempt to make the marvellous more credible. Miracles are less clumsily told; certain prolixities are omitted. Thaumaturgic materialism, the use of natural means to produce miracles --characteristic features of Mark's narrative--have almost wholly disappeared in Matthew. Compared with the Gospel of Mark, that attributed to Matthew presents corrections of taste and tact. Various inaccuracies are rectified; details æsthetically weak or inexplicable are suppressed or cleared up. Mark has often been considered as the abbreviator of Matthew. The very reverse is the truth; only the addition of the discourses has the effect of extending the abridgment considerably beyond the limits of the original. When we compare the accounts of the demoniac of the Gergesenes, the paralytic of Capernaum, the daughter of Jairus, the woman with the issue of blood, the epileptic boy, the correctness of our view is apparent. Often, also, Matthew gathers together, into a single group, circumstances which in Mark constitute two episodes. Some stories, which appear at first sight to be his especial property, are really stripped and impoverished copies of the longer accounts of Mark.

It is especially with regard to poverty that we discover in the text of Matthew precautions and uneasiness. Jesus had boldly placed poverty at the head of the heavenly beatitudes. "Blessed are ye poor," was probably the first word which came out of the Divine mouth, when he began to speak with authority. The majority of the sentences of Jesus (as happens always when we wish to give a living form to thought) lent themselves to misunderstanding; the pure Ebionites drew from them subversive consequences. The editor of our Gospel adds a word to prevent certain excesses. The poor in the ordinary sense become the "poor in spirit"--that is to say, pious Israelites who play a humble part in the world, which contrasts with the haughty air of the great men of the day. In another beatitude, those who are hungry become those who "hunger and thirst after righteousness."

The progress of thought is then very visible in Matthew; we catch glimpses in him of a crowd of after thoughts, the intention of parrying certain objections; an exaggeration of the symbolical pretensions. The story of the Temptation in the Wilderness has developed itself and has changed its character; the passion is enriched with some beautiful details; Jesus speaks of his "Church" as of a body already constituted and founded under the primacy of Peter. The formula of baptism is enlarged, and comprehends, under a form sufficiently syncretic, the three sacramental words of the theology of the time, the Father, the Son, and the Holy Ghost. The germ of the doctrine of the Trinity is thus deposited in a corner of the sacred page, and will become fertile. The Apocalyptic discourse attributed to Jesus, with reference to the war in Judea, is rather strengthened and particularised than weakened. We shall soon see Luke employing all his art to extenuate whatever was embarrassing in these daring predictions of an end that had not come.

CHAPTER XI

SECRET OF THE BEAUTIES OF THE GOSPEL

What is chiefly remarkable in the new Gospel is an immense literary progress. The general effect is that of a fairy palace constructed wholly of luminous stones. An exquisite vagueness in the transitions and the chronological relations gives to this divine composition the light attractiveness of a child's story. "At that hour," "at that time," "that day," "it happened that," and a crowd of other formulæ which look precise, but which are nothing of the kind, hold the narrative as it were in suspense between earth and heaven. Thanks to the uncertainty of the time, the Gospel story only touches the reality. An airy genius whom one touches, one embraces, but who never strikes against the pebbles in the road, speaks to us and enchants us. We do not stop to ask if he is certain of what he tells us. He doubts nothing, and he knows nothing. There is an analogous charm in the affirmation of a woman who subjugates us while she makes us smile. It is in literature what a picture of a child by Correggio or a Virgin of sixteen by Raphael is in art.

The language is of the same character and perfectly appropriate to the subject. By a veritable tour de force the clear and childlike method of the Hebrew narrative, the fine and exquisite stamp of the Hebrew proverbs, have been translated into a Hellenic dialect, correct enough as far as grammatical forms are concerned, but in which the old learned syntax is completely cast aside. It has been remarked that the Gospels were the first books written in the Greek of everyday life. The Greek of antiquity is there, in effect, modified in the analytical sense of modern languages. The Hellenist cannot but admit that the language is commonplace and weak; he is certain that from the classical point of view the Gospel has neither style, nor plan, nor beauty; but it is the masterpiece of popular literature, and in one sense the most ancient popular book that has been written. That half-articulate language has the additional advantage of preserving its character in different versions, so that for such writings the translation is as valuable as the original.

This simplicity of form ought to give rise to no illusion. The word "truth" has not the same significance for the Oriental as for ourselves. The Oriental tells with a bewitching candour and with the accent of a witness, a crowd of things which he has not seen and about which he is by no means certain. The fantastic tales of the Exodus from Egypt, which are told in Jewish families during the Feast of the Passover, deceive nobody, yet none the less they enchant those who listen to them. Every year the scenic representations by which they commemorate the martyrdom of the sons of Ali in Persia, are enriched with some new invention designed to render the victims more interesting and their murderers more hateful. There is more passion in these episodes than anyone might think possible. It is the especial quality of the Oriental agada to touch most profoundly those who best know how fictitious it is. It is its triumph to have created such a masterpiece that all the world is deceived by it, and for want of knowing laws of this kind the credulous West has accepted as infallible truth the recital of facts which no human eye has ever seen.

The especial quality of a literature of logia, of hadith, is to go on increasing. After the death of Mohammed the number of words which "the people of the Bench" attributed to him was not to be counted. It was the same with Jesus. To the charming apologues which he had really pronounced, others were added conceived in the same style, which it is very difficult to distinguish from the genuine. The ideas of the time expressed themselves especially in those seven admirable parables of the kingdom of God, where all the innocent rivalries of the golden age of Christianity have left their traces. Some persons were aggrieved by the low rank of those who entered the Church; the doors of the churches of St Paul opening with both leaves, appeared to them a scandal; they wanted a selection, a preliminary examination, a censorship. The Shamaites in like manner desired that no man should be admitted to Jewish teaching unless he were intelligent, modest, of good family, and rich. To these exigent persons an answer was given in the shape of a parable of a man who prepared a dinner, and who, in the absence of the regularly invited guests, invited the lame, the vagabonds, and the beggars; or of a fisherman whose net gathered of every kind, both bad and good, the choice being made afterwards. The eminent place which Paul, once one of the enemies of Jesus, one of the last comers to the Gospel work, occupied amongst the faithful of these early days, excited murmurs. This was the occasion of the workers who were engaged at the eleventh hour, and were rewarded equally with those who had borne the burden and heat of the day. A statement of Jesus, "the last shall be first and the first shall be last," had furnished the text. The owner of a vineyard goes out at various hours of the day to hire labourers. He takes all that he can find, and in the evening the last comers who had worked but a single hour, are paid exactly as those who had toiled the whole day through. The struggle of two generations of Christians is seen here very clearly. When the converted appeared to say with sadness that the places were taken, and that they had to fill a secondary part, this beautiful parable was quoted to them, from which it was evident that they had no reason to envy the ancients.

The parable of the tares also signifies in its way the mixed composition of the kingdom, wherein Satan himself has sometimes power to cast in a few grains. The mustard seed expresses its future greatness; the leaven its fermentative force; the hidden treasure and the pearl of great price; the thread, its success, mixed with perils in the future. "The first shall be last," "many are called but few chosen," such were the maxims which they especially loved to repeat. The expectation of Jesus above all inspired living and strong comparisons. The image of the thief in the night, the lightning which shines from the east to the west, of the fig tree whose young shoots announce the approach of summer, filled all minds. They repeated the charming fable of the wise and the foolish virgins, masterpieces of simplicity, of art, of wit, of subtlety. Both awaited the bridegroom, but as he was long in coming, they all slumbered. Then in the middle of the night was heard the cry, "Behold him! Behold him:" The wise virgins, who had carried oil in their flasks, soon lighted their lamps, but the foolish were confounded. There was no place for them at the banquet.

We do not say that these exquisite fragments are not the work of Jesus. The great difficulty of a history of the origins of Christianity is to distinguish in the Gospels between the part that comes directly from Jesus, and the part which is inspired by his spirit. Jesus having written nothing, and the editors of the Gospels having handed down to us pell-mell his own authentic words and those which have been attributed to him, there is no critic sufficiently subtle to work in such a case with absolute certainty. The life of Jesus, and the history of the compilation of the Gospels, are two subjects which are so interwoven that the boundary between them must be left undefined, at the risk of appearing to contradict oneself. In reality, this contradiction is of small consequence. Jesus is the veritable creator of the Gospel; Jesus did all, even what has been only attributed to him; his legend and himself are inseparable; he was so identified with his idea that his idea became himself, absorbed him, made his biography what it ought to be. There was in him what theologians call "communication of the idioms." The same communication exists between the first and last book but one of this history. If that is a defect, it is a defect springing out of the nature of the subject, and we have thought it would be a mark of truth not to seek to avoid it. What is striking in any case is the original physiognomy of these narratives. Whatever may be the date of their compilation, they are truly Galilean flowers blossoming beneath the sacred feet of the divine dreamer.

The Apostolic instructions, such as our Gospel presents them, appear in some respects to proceed from the ideal of the Apostle formed upon the model of Paul. The impression left by the life of the great missionary had been profound. Many apostles had already suffered martyrdom for having carried to the people the appeals of Jesus. The Christian preacher was imagined as appearing before kings, before the highest tribunals, and proclaiming Christ. The first principle of this apostolic eloquence was not to prepare the discourses. The Holy Ghost would at the moment put into the mind of the preacher what he ought to say. In travelling, no provision, no money, not even a scrip, not even a change of garments, not even a staff. The workman deserved his daily bread. When the apostolic missionary entered into a house he might remain there without scruple, eating and drinking what was given to him, without feeling himself obliged to give in return anything but the word and wishes for health. This was the principle of Paul, but he did not put it in practice except amongst people of whom he was altogether sure, as for example with the woman of Philippi. Like Paul, the apostolic traveller was guarded in the dangers of the way by a Divine protection; he played with serpents, poisons did not affect him. His lot will be the hatred of the world, persecution. . . . Tradition always exaggerates the primitive feature. It is in some sort a necessity of the memory, the mind retaining better strongly accented and hyperbolical words than measured sentences. Jesus had too profound a knowledge of the souls of men not to know that rigour and exigence are the best means of gaining them and keeping them under the yoke. We do not, however, believe that he ever went to the excess which has been attributed to him, and the sombre fire which animates the apostolic instructions, appears to us, in part, a reflection of the feverish ardour of Paul.

The author of the Gospel according to Matthew takes no decisive aide in the great questions which divided the Church. He is neither an exclusive Jew after the manner of James, nor a lax Jew after the fashion of Paul. He feels the necessity for attaching the Church to Peter, and insists upon the prerogative of this last. On the other hand, he allows certain shades of ill will to appear against the family of Jesus and against the first Christian generation. He suppresses, in particular, in the list of the appearances of Jesus after the Resurrection, the part played by James, whom the disciples of Paul held as an avowed enemy. Opposite theories may find equally valuable support from him from time to time. At times he speaks of faith almost in the tone of St Paul's Epistles. The author accepts from tradition sayings, parables, miracles, decisions in the most contrary senses, provided they are edifying, without any effort to reconcile them. Here there is a question of evangelising Israel; there the world. The Canaanitish woman, received at first with hard words, is then saved, and a history is begun to prove that Jesus has only been sent to the house of Israel, which finishes up with an exaltation of the faith of a Pagan woman. The centurion of Capernaum finds from the first both grace and favour. The legal chiefs of the nation have been more opposed to the Messiah than Pagans such as the magi, Pilate and Pilate's wife. The Jewish people pronounce their own curse upon themselves. They have not chosen to enter the feast of the Kingdom of God prepared for them; the people of the highway--the Gentiles--will take their place. The formula, "Ye have heard that it was said by them of old time . . . but I tell you," is placed repeatedly in the mouth of Jesus. The society to which the author addresses himself is a society of converted Jews. The polemic against the unconverted Jews occupies him much. His quotations of the prophetic texts, as well as of a certain number of circumstances related by him, refer to the assaults which the faithful had to submit to on the part of the orthodox majority, and especially to the great objection of these official representatives of the nation to believe in the Messianic character of Jesus.

The Gospel of St Matthew, like almost all fine compositions, was the work of a conscience in some sort double. The author is at once Jew and Christian; the new faith has not killed the old, nor has it taken any of its poetry from it. He loves two things at the same moment. The spectator enjoys the struggle without discomfort. Charming state to be in, without as yet anything being determined. Exquisite transition, excellent for art, where a conscience is a peaceable field of battle upon which opposing parties contend without either being overthrown! Although the pretended Matthew speaks of the Jews in the third person and as though they were strangers, his spirit, his apology, his Messianism, his exegesis, his piety, are essentially those of a Jew. Jerusalem is for him essentially "the holy city," "the holy place." Missions are in his eyes the appanage of the Twelve; he does not associate St Paul with them, and he certainly does not accord to this last a special vocation, although the apostolic instructions such as he gives them contain more than one feature drawn from the life of the great preacher of the Gentiles. His aversion to the Pharisees does not prevent him from admitting the authority of Judaism. Christianity is with him like a newly-blown flower, which still bears the envelope of the bud from which it has escaped.

In this lay one of his strong points. The supreme ability in the work of conciliation is to deny and affirm at the same moment, to practise the Ama tanquam osurus of the sage of antiquity. Paul suppresses all Judaism, and even all religion, to replace everything by Jesus. The Gospels hesitate, and remain in a much more delicate half-light? Does the Law still exist? Yes, and no. Jesus fulfilled it and destroyed it. The Sabbath? He suppressed and maintained it. The Jewish ceremonies? He observes them, and will not allow of their being held to. Every religious reformer has to observe this rule; men are not discharged from a burden impossible to be borne, except he takes it for himself without reserve or softening. The contraction was everywhere. When the Talmud has quoted on the same line opinions which exclude each other absolutely, it finishes by this formula:--"And all these opinions are the word of life." The anecdote of the Canaanitish woman is the true image at this moment of Christianity. She prays. "I am not sent but to the lost sheep of the house of Israel," Jesus answers to her. She approaches, and worships him. "It is not meet to take the children's bread and to cast it to the dogs." "Truth, Lord, but the dogs eat of the crumbs which fall from the Master's table." "Oh, woman, great is thy faith; be it unto thee even as thou wilt." The converted Pagan finished by carrying off, by force of humility, and on condition of submitting first to the ill reception of an aristocracy which wished to be flattered and solicited, all that she desired.

Such a state of mind, to say the truth, agreed only with a single kind of hatred--the hatred of the Pharisee, the official Jew. The Pharisee, or, more properly, the hypocrite (for the word was now used in an abusive sense, just as with us the name of Jesuit is applied to a host of people who form no part of the society founded by Loyola), had to appear especially guilty, opposed in everything to Jesus. Our Gospel groups into a single invective, full of virulence, all the discourses which Jesus pronounced at various times against the Pharisees. The author undoubtedly took this fragment from some previous collection which had not the ordinary form. Jesus is there accredited with having made numerous journeys to Jerusalem; the punishment of the Pharisees is predicted in a vague fashion, which carries us back to the date before the revolution in Judea.

From all this results a Gospel infinitely superior in beauty to that of Mark, but of a much smaller historical value. Mark remains, as far as facts are concerned, the only authentic record of the life of Jesus. The narratives which the pseudo-Matthew adds to those of Mark are only legends; the modifications which he applies to the tales of Mark are only methods of hiding certain difficulties. The assimilation of the elements which the author takes from Mark is effected in the roughest way; the digestion--if such an expression may be permitted--is not completed; the morsels are left whole, so that they may still be recognised. In this connection Luke will introduce great improvements. But what gives value to the work attributed to Matthew, are the discourses attributed to Jesus, preserved with an extreme fidelity, and probably in the relative order in which they were first written.

This was more important than biographical exactitude, and the Gospel of Matthew, all things considered, is the most important book of Christianity--the most important book that has ever been written. It was not without reason that in the classification of the writings of the new Bible it received the first place. The biography of a great man is a part of his work. St Louis would not be what he is in the conscience of humanity, without Joinville. The life of Spinoza, by Colerus, is the finest of Spinoza's works. Epictetus owes almost as much to Arrian, Socrates to Plato and to Xenophon. Jesus in the same way is in part made by the Gospel. In this sense, the compilation of the Gospels is, next to the personal action of Jesus, the leading fact of the history of the origins of Christianity; I will even add of the history of humanity. The habitual reading of the world is a book where the priest is always in fault, where respectable people are always hypocrites, where the lay authorities are always scoundrels, and where all the rich are damned. This book--the most revolutionary and dangerous ever written--the Roman Church has prudently put aside; but it has not been able to prevent it from bearing fruit. Malevolent towards the priesthood, contemptuous of austerity, indulgent towards the loose liver of good heart, the Gospels have been the perpetual nightmare of the hypocrite. The man of the Gospel has been an opponent of pedantic theology, of hierarchical haughtiness, of the ecclesiastical spirit such as the centuries have made it. The Middle Ages burned it. In our days, the great invective of the twenty-third chapter of St Matthew against the Pharisees is still a sanguinary satire on those who cover themselves with the name of Jesus, and whom Jesus, if he were to return to this world, would drive out with scourges.

Where was the Gospel of St Matthew written? Everything appears to indicate that it was in Syria, for a Jewish circle which knew scarcely anything but Greek, but which had some idea of Hebrew. The author makes use of the original Gospels written in Hebrew; yet it is doubtful whether the original Hebrew of the Gospel texts ever went out of Syria. In five or six cases, Mark had preserved little Aramaic phrases uttered by Jesus; the pseudo-Matthew effaces all of them with but one exception. The character of the traditions proper to our evangelist is exclusively Galilean. According to him, all the appearances of Jesus after the Resurrection took place in Galilee. His first readers appear to have been Syrians. He gives none of those explanations of customs and those topographical notes which are to be found in Mark. On the contrary, there are details which, meaningless at Rome, were interesting in the East. A Greek Gospel appeared a precious thing; but the gaps in that of Mark were striking, and they were filled up. The Gospel which resulted from these additions came in time to Rome. Hence the explanation of Luke's ignorance of it in that city about 95.

Hence, also, the explanation of the reasons why to exalt the new work and to oppose to the name of Mark that of a superior authority, the text was attributed to the Apostle Matthew. Matthew was a Judeo-Christian apostle, living an ascetic life like that of James, abstaining from flesh, and living only upon vegetables and the shoots of trees. Perhaps his former occupation of publican gave rise to the idea that, accustomed to writing, he more than anyone else was likely to record the facts of which he was credited with having been a witness. Certainly Matthew was not the editor of the work which bears his name. The Apostle had long been dead when the Gospel was composed, and the book, besides, absolutely could not have been the work of such an author. Never was book so little that of an eye-witness. How, if our Gospel were the work of an apostle, could it possibly have been so defective in all that concerns the public life of Jesus? Perhaps the Hebrew Gospel with which the author completed that of Mark, bore the name of Matthew. Perhaps the collection of Logia bore that name. The addition of the Logia being what gave character to the new Gospel, the name of the apostle guaranteeing these Logia may have been preserved to designate the author of the work which drew its chief value from these additions. All that is doubtful. Papias believes the work to be really that of Matthew, but after fifty or sixty years the means of solving so complicated a question must have been wanting.

What is certain, in any case, is that the work attributed to Matthew had not the authority which its title would lead one to suppose, and was not accepted as final. There have been many similar attempts which are no longer in existence. The mere name of an apostle was not enough to recommend a work of this kind. Luke, who was not an apostle, and whom we shall soon see resuming the attempt at a Gospel embodying and superseding the others, was, in all probability, ignorant of the existence of that said to be according to Matthew.

CHAPTER XII

THE CHRISTIANS OF THE FLAVIA FAMILY--FLAVIUS JOSEPHUS

The fatal law of Cæsarism fulfilled itself. The legitimate king improves as his reign grows older: the Cæsar begins well, and finishes ill. Every year was marked in Domitian by the progress of evil passions. The man had always been perverse. His ingratitude towards his father and his eldest brother was something abominable, but his first government was not that of a bad sovereign. It was only by degrees that the sombre jealousy of all merit, the refined perfidy, the black malice which were ingrained in his nature, disclosed themselves. Tiberius had been very cruel, but this was through a sort of philosophic rage against humanity which was not without its grandeur, and which did not prevent him from being in some respects the most intelligent man of his time. Caligula was a melancholy buffoon, at once grotesque and terrible, but amusing, and not very dangerous to those who did not approach him. Under the reign of that incarnation of satanic irony who called himself Nero, a sort of stupor held the world in suspense; people had the consciousness of assisting at an unprecedented crisis, at the definitive struggle between good and evil. After his death there was a breathing space; evil appeared to be chained up; the perversity of the century seemed to be softened. It is easy to imagine the horror which seized on all honest minds when they saw "the Beast" revived; when they recognised that the abnegation of all the honourable men in the Empire had served only to hand over the world to a sovereign much more worthy of execration than the monsters whom they believed relegated to the souvenirs of the past.

Domitian was probably the wickedest man who over lived. Commodus is more odious, for he was the son of an admirable father; but Commodus is a sort of brute; Domitian is a man of strong sense, and of a calculating wickedness. He had not the excuse of madness; his head was perfectly sound, cold, and clear. He was a serious and logical politician. He had no imagination, and if at a certain period of his life he dabbled somewhat in literature, and made fairly good verses, it was out of affectation, and in order to appear a stranger to business; soon he renounced it and thought no more of it. He did not love the arts; music found him and left him indifferent; his melancholy temperament rejoiced only in solitude. He was seen walking alone for hours; his followers were then sure to see the breaking out of some perverse scheme. Cruel without disguise, he smiled almost in the act of murder. His base extraction constantly reappeared. The Cæsars of the House of Augustus, prodigal and greedy of glory, are bad, often absurd, rarely vulgar. Domitian is the tradesman of crime: he makes a profit of it. Not rich, he makes money everywhere, and pushes taxation to its last limits. His sinister face never knew the mad laugh of Caligula. Nero, a very literary tyrant, always engaged in making the world love and admire him, heard raillery and provoked it. Domitian had nothing burlesque about him. He did not lend himself to ridicule; he was too tragic. His manners were no better than those of the son of Agrippina, but to infamy he joined a sly egotism, a hypocritical affectation of severity, the air of a rigid censor (sanctissimus censor)--all which things were only pretexts for destroying the innocent. The tone of austere virtue which his flatterers assume is nauseous in the extreme. Martial, Statius, Quintilian, when they wished to give him the title which he coveted the most, bestowed on him that of Saviour of the gods, and Restorer of morals.

Nero's vanity was not less than that which impelled him to so many pitiable freaks, and it was much less innocent. His false triumphs, his pretended victories, his monuments full of lying adulation, his accumulated consulates, were something sickening, much more irritating than the eighteen hundred crowns of Nero.

The other tyrannies which had afflicted Rome were much less wise. His was administrative, meticulous, organised. The tyrant himself played the part of chief of the police and prosecuting counsel. It was a juridical reign of terror. The proceedings were conducted with the burlesque legality of the Revolutionary Tribunal. Flavius Sabinus, cousin of the Emperor, was put to death because of a mistake of the crier who proclaimed him Emperor instead of Consul; a Greek historian, for certain images which appeared obscure: all the copyists were crucified. A distinguished Roman was killed because he loved to recite the harangues of Livy, possessed certain maps, and had given to two slaves the names of Mago and of Hannibal; a highly-esteemed soldier, Sallustius Lucullus, perished for having suffered his name to be given to some lances of a new model which he had invented. Never had the trade of informer thriven so greatly; tempters and spies abounded everywhere. The mad faith of the Emperor in astrologers doubled the danger. The instruments of Caligula and Nero had been vile Orientals, strangers to Roman society, and satisfied when they were rich. The informers of Domitian--men like Tonquier Tinville, sinister and ghostly--struck a sure blow. The Emperor concerted with the accusers and the false witnesses what they were to say; he then was himself present at the tortures, diverting himself with the pallor painted in all faces, and appearing to count the groans extorted by suffering. Nero spared himself the sight of the crimes he commanded; Domitian insisted on seeing everything. He had nameless refinements of cruelty. His mind was so perverse that he was offended equally by flattery and by its absence; his suspicion and jealousy were unbounded. Every worthy man, every benevolent man, had him for a rival. Nero at least found them only amongst the singers, and did not regard every statesman, every military superior, as an enemy.

The silence during this time was frightful. The Senate passed some years in a mournful stupor. What was most terrible was that there seemed to be no way out. The Emperor was thirty-six. The feverish outburst of evil which had been observed up to that time had been short; it was felt that they were crises and that they could not last. This time there was no reason for their coming to an end. The army was content; the people were indifferent. Domitian, it is true, never attained the popularity of Nero; and in the year 88 an impostor thought he saw a chance of dethroning him, by presenting himself as the adored master who had given the people such days of enjoyment. Nevertheless, too much had not been lost. The spectacles were as monstrous as they had ever been. The Flavian amphitheatre (the Coliseum) inaugurated under Titus, had even made progress in the ignoble art of amusing the people. No danger then on that side. He, however, read only the Memoirs of Tiberius. He despised the familiarity which his father Vespasian had encouraged; he treated as childishness the good nature of his brother Titus, and the delusion of governing humanity by making himself beloved, under which he laboured. He pretended to know better than anybody the requirements of a power without constitution, obliged to defend itself, to refound itself every day.

It was felt, in short, that there was a political reason for these horrors, which was not the mere caprice of a lunatic. The hideous image of the new sovereignty such as the necessities of the times had made it, suspicious, fearing everything from everybody, head of Medusa which froze with terror, appeared in this odious mask all splashed with blood, with which the cunning terrorist seemed to have shielded his face against all modesty.

It was principally upon his own house that his fury was spent. Almost all his cousins or nephews perished. Everything that recalled Titus to him exasperated him. That singular family which had none of the prejudice, aristocratic coolness, profound scepticism of the high Roman aristocracy, offered strange contrasts. Frightful tragedies were played in it. What a fate, for example, was that of Julia Sabina, the daughter of Titus, sinking from crime to crime, until she finished, like the heroine of a vulgar romance, in the anguish of an abortion. So much perversity provoked strange reactions. The tender and sentimental parts of the nature of Titus reappeared amongst some members of the family, especially in the branch of Flavius Sabinus, the brother of Vespasian. Flavius Sabinus, who was long Prefect of Rome, and particularly in 64, might already know the Christians; he was a gentle, humane man, and one who was already reproached with "poor spiritedness." For Roman ferocity such a word was equivalent to humanity. The numerous Jews who were familiar with the Flavian family, found, especially on this side, an audience already prepared and attentive.

It is, in short, not to be denied that Christian or Judeo-Christian ideas penetrated the Imperial family, especially in its collateral branch. Flavius Clemens, son of Flavius Sabinus, and consequently cousin-german to Domitian, had married Flavia Domitilla, his second cousin, daughter of another Flavia Domitilla, herself the daughter of Vespasian, who had died before the accession of her father to the Empire. By means which are unknown to us, but probably arising out of the relations of the Flavian family with the Jews, Clemens and Domitilla adopted Jewish customs, that is to say, of course, that mitigated form of Judaism which differed from Christianity only by the importance attached to the part of Jesus. The Judaism of the proselytes, confined to the Noachian precepts, was precisely that preached by Josephus, the client of the Flavian family. That it was which was represented as having been settled by the agreement of all the apostles at Jerusalem. Clemens allowed himself to be seduced by it. Perhaps Domitilla went further, and merited the name of Christian. Nothing, however, ought to be exaggerated. Flavius Clemens and Flavia Domitilla do not appear to have been veritable members of the Church of Rome. Like so many other distinguished Romans, they felt the emptiness of the official worship, the insufficiency of the moral law which sprang out of Paganism, the repulsive hideousness of the manners and the society of the times. The charm of the Judeo-Christian ideas wrought upon them. They recognised from that side life and the future; but, without doubt, they were not ostensibly Christians. We shall see later Flavia Domitilla acting rather as a Roman matron than as a Christian woman, and not hesitating at the assassination of a tyrant. The single fact of accepting the consulate was for Clemens to accept the obligation of essentially idolatrous sacrifices and ceremonies. Clemens was the second person in the State. He had two sons whom Domitian had named as his successors, and to whom he had already given the names of Vespasian and Domitian. The education of these boys was entrusted to one of the most upright men of the time, Quintilian the rhetorician, to whom Clemens accorded the honorary insignia of the consulate. Now Quintilian regarded with equal horror the ideas of the Jews and those of the Republicans. Side by side with the Gracchi he placed "the author of the Jewish superstition" amongst the most fatal revolutionaries. Was Quintilian thinking of Moses or of Jesus? Perhaps he scarcely knew himself. "Jewish superstition" was still the generic title which comprehended both Jews and Christians. Christians were not furthermore the only people who lived the Jewish life without submitting to circumcision. Many of those who were attracted by Mosaism confined themselves to the observance of the Sabbath. A similar purity of life, a similar horror of polytheism, united all these groups of pious men upon whom the verdict of superficial Pagans was, "they live the Jewish life."

If the family of Clemens were Christians, it must be owned that they were Christians of a very undecided kind. What the public saw of the conversion of these two illustrious personages was a very small matter. The distracted world which surrounded them could not well say whether they were Jews or Christians. Changes of this kind are recognised only by two symptoms, first, an ill-concealed aversion from the national religion, an estrangement from all apparent rites, on the part of those who are supposed to hold to the secret worship of an intangible, unnameable God; in the second place, an apparent indolence, a total abandonment of the duties and honours of civic life inseparable from idolatry. A taste for solitude, a search after a peaceable and retired life, an aversion for the theatres, for the shows and for the cruel scenes which Roman life offered at every step, fraternal relations with persons of humble station, by no means inclined to the military life (for which the Romans despised them), indifference to public business, as frivolous matters to those who looked for the speedy coming of Christ, meditative habits, a spirit of detachment--all this the Romans described by the single word ignavia. According to the ideas of the time, everyone ought to have as much ambition as comported with his birth and fortune. The man of high rank who ceased to take an interest in the struggle of life, who feared bloodshed, who assumed a gentle and humane air, was an idle and degraded man incapable of any enterprise. Impious and cowardly--such were the adjectives applied to him, which in a still vigorous state of society must infallibly result in destroying him.

Clemens and Domitilla were not, moreover, the only ones whom the blast of the reign of Domitian inclined towards Christianity. The terror and the sadness of the times crushed souls. Many persons of the Roman aristocracy lent an ear to teaching, and which, in the midst of the night through which they were passing, showed the pure heaven of an ideal kingdom. The world was so dark, so wicked! Never, besides, had the Jewish propaganda been so active. Perhaps we must refer to the time of the conversion of a Roman lady, Veturia Paulla, who, being converted at the age of 70, took the name of Sara, and was mother of the synagogues of the Campus Martius and of Volumnus, for sixteen years longer. A great part of the movement in these immense suburbs of Rome, where seethed an immense population, far greater in number than the aristocratic society enclosed in the circuit of Servius Tullius, came from the sons of Israel. Confined to a spot near the Capenian Gate by the side of the unwholesome stream of the fountain of Egeria, they lived there, begging, carrying on disreputable trades, the art of the gipsies, telling fortunes, levying contributions on visitors to the wood of Egeria, which they rented. The impression produced upon the public mind by that strange race was more lively than ever. "He to whom fate has given for father an observer of the Sabbath, not contented with adoring the God of heaven, and with putting on the same level the flesh of pigs and the flesh of human beings, soon hurries to get rid of his foreskin. Accustomed to despise the Roman law, he studies and observes, with trembling, the Jewish law which Moses has deposited in a mysterious volume. There he learns not to show the way save to him who practises the same religion with himself, and when one asks him, where is the fountain? to point out the road to the circumcised only. The fault is ih the father who adopted the seventh day of rest, and forbade on that day all the acts of life." (Juv. xiv.)

Saturday, in fact, notwithstanding all the bad temper of the true Romans, was not in Rome in the least like other days. The world of little tradesmen who on other days filled the public places, seemed to have sunk into the earth. That irregularity, yet more than their easily recognisable type, drew attention, and made those eccentric foreigners the object of the gossip of the idle.

The Jews suffered like the rest of the world from the hardness of the times. The greed of Domitian made all taxation excessive, especially the poll tax, called the fiscus Judaïcus, to which the Jews were subject. Until this time the tribute was exacted only from those who avowed themselves to be Jews. Many disguised their origin and did not pay. To prevent that tolerance, the truth was sought in the most odious way. Suetonius remembers having seen in his youth an old man of ninety stripped before a numerous audience to see if he were not circumcised. These rigours brought about, as a consequence, the practice, in a great number of instances, of the operation of blistering; the number of recutiti at this date is very considerable. Such inquiries, on the other hand, brought the Roman authorities to a discovery which astonished them: it was that there were people who were living the Jewish life in all ways who were not circumcised. The treasury decided that that class of persons, the improfessi, as they were called, should pay the poll-tax like the circumcised. "The Jewish life," and not the circumcision, was thus taxed, and the Christians saw themselves subjected to the impost. The complaints which this abuse called forth moved even those statesman who had least sympathy with Jews and Christians; the liberal were shocked by these corporeal visitations, these distinctions made by the state as to the meaning of certain religious denominations, and saw in the suppression of this abuse their programme for the future.

The vexations introduced by Domitian contributed greatly to deprive Christianity of its previously undecided character. By the side of the severe orthodoxy of the Jewish doctors, and afterwards of those of Jabneh, there had been until that time in Judaism schools analogous to Christianity, without being identical with it. Apollos, in the bosom of the Church, was an example of those inquiring Jews who tried many sects without adhering resolutely to any one. Josephus when he wrote for the Romans, reduced his Judaism to a kind of Deism, owning that circumcision and the Jewish practices were good for Jews by race, whilst the true worship is that which each adopts in full liberty. Was Flavius Clemens a Christian in the strict sense of the word? It may be doubted if he were. He loved the Jewish life, he practised Jewish customs, and it was that fact which struck his contemporaries. He went no further, and perhaps he himself would have been puzzled to say to what class of Jews he belonged. The matter was not cleared up when the treasury took it in hand. The circumcision received on that day a fatal blow. The greed of Domitian extended the tax on the Jews, the fiscus Judaïcus, who without being Jews by race, and without being circumcised, practised Jewish customs. Then the categories were marked out: there was the pure Jew, whose quality was established by physical inquiry, and the quasi-Jew, the improfessus, who took nothing from Judaism besides its honest morality and its purified worship.

The penalties ordained by a special law against the circumcision of non-Jews contributed to the same result. The precise date of that law is unknown, but it certainly appears to be of the period of Flavius. Every Roman citizen who allowed himself to be circumcised was punished with perpetual exile, and the loss of all his goods. A master rendered himself liable to the same penalty if he permitted his slaves to submit to the operation; the doctor who performed it was punished with death. The Jews who circumcised their slaves were equally liable to death. That was thoroughly conformable to the Roman policy,--tolerant towards foreign religions when they kept themselves within the limits of their own nationalities; severe when those religions entered upon the work of the propaganda. But it is easy to understand how decisive such measures were in the struggle between the circumcised Jews and the uncircumcised or improfessi. These last alone could carry on a serious proselytism. By the law of the Empire, the circumcision was condemned to go no further than the narrow limits of the house of Israel.

Agrippa II., and probably Berenice, died about this time. Their death was an immense loss to the Jewish colony, which these exalted personages covered by their credit with Flavius. Josephus, in the midst of this ardent struggle, doubled his activity. He had the superficial facility characteristic of the Jew transported into a civilisation which is foreign to him, of placing himself with marvellous quickness abreast of the ideas in the midst of which he finds himself thrown, and of seeing in what way he can profit by them. Domitian protected him, but was probably indifferent to his writings. The Empress Domitia heaped favours on him. He was, besides, the client of a certain Epaphroditus, a considerable personage, supposed to be identical with the Epaphroditus of Nero, whom Domitian had taken into his service. This Epaphroditus was a man of a singularly liberal mind, who encouraged historical studies, and who interested himself in Judaism. Not knowing Hebrew, and probably not understanding the Greek version of the Bible very well, he engaged Josephus to compose a history of the Jewish people. Josephus received the commission with eagerness. It fully accorded with the suggestions of his literary vanity and of his liberal Judaism. The objection which the Jews made to learned persons imbued with the beauties of Greek and Roman history, was that the Jewish people had no history, that the Greeks had not cared to know it, that good authors never mentioned its name, that it had never had any connection with the noble races, and that in its past there were to be found no such heroic histories as those of Cynegirus and of the Scævola. To prove that the Jewish people were also of a high antiquity, that they possessed the memory of heroes comparable to those of Greece, that they had had in the course of ages the finest relations of people to people, that many learned Greeks had spoken of them, such was the aim that the protege of Epaphroditus sought to realise in a vast composition divided into twenty books and entitled "Antiquities of the Jews." The Bible naturally formed the basis: Josephus made additions to it, without value as to the ancient times, since there were no Hebrew documents relating to those times other than those which we ourselves possess, but which for more modern times are of the highest interest, since they fill up a gap in sacred history.

Josephus added to this curious work, in the form of an appendix, an autobiography, or rather an apology for his own conduct. His ancient enemies of Galilee who, rightly or wrongly, called him a traitor, were still alive and left him no repose. Justus of Tiberius, writing, from his point of view, the history of the catastrophe of his country, accused him of falsehood, and presented his conduct in Galilee in the most odious light. We must do Josephus the justice of saying that he did nothing to injure this dangerous rival, as would have been easy to him, in view of the favour which he enjoyed in high places. Josephus, on the other hand, is weak enough, when he defends himself against the accusations of Justus, by invoking the official approbation of Titus and Agrippa. It is impossible to regret too much that a writing which would have given us the history of the war in Judea, from the revolutionary point of view, should be totally lost to us.

The fecundity of Josephus was inexhaustible. As many persons raised doubts as to what he said in his "Antiquities," and objected that if the Jewish nation had been as ancient as he represented, the Greek historians would have spoken of it, he undertook on this subject a justificatory memoir, which may be regarded as the first monument of the Jewish and Christian apology. Already towards the middle of the second century B.C. Aristobalus, the Jewish peripatician, had maintained that the Greek poets and philosophers had known the Hebrew writings, and had borrowed from them all those parts of their writings which have a monotheistic appearance. To prove his theory, he forged without scruple passages from profane authors--Homer, Hesiod, Linus--which he pretended were borrowed from the Bible. Josephus took up the task with more honesty, but as little critical ability. It was necessary to refute the learned men who, like Lysimachus of Alexandria, Apollonius Molon (about a hundred years B.C.), expressed themselves unfavourably with regard to the Jews. It was especially necessary to destroy the authority of the Egyptian scholar Apion, who fifty years before had, it may be in his history of Egypt, or else in a distinct work, exhibited an immense amount of learning in disputing the antiquity of the Jewish religion. In the eyes of an Egyptian, or of a Greek, that was quite sufficient to deprive it of all nobility. Apion had relations with the imperial world of Rome, Tiberius called him "the cymbal of the world"; Pliny thought he had better have been called the tom-tom. His book might still be read in Rome under the Flavii.

The science of Apion was that of a vain and frivolous pedant; but that which Josephus opposed to it was scarcely better. Greek erudition was for him an improvised speciality, since his early education had been Jewish, and altogether confined to the law. His book is not, and could not be, anything but a pleading without criticism; one feels in every page the presence of the advocate who cuts his arrow in any wood. Josephus does not manufacture his texts, but he takes anything that comes; the false historians, the garbled classics of the Alexandrian school; the valueless documents accumulated in the book "on the Jews" which circulated under the name of Alexander Polyhiston, all are greedily accepted by him; through him that suspected literature of the Eupolemes, the Cleodemes, the so-called Hecatea of Abvera, Demetrius of Phalera, etc., makes its entrance into science, and troubles it seriously. The apologists, and the Christian historians--Justin, Clement of Alexandria, Eusebius, Moses of Khorone-- followed him in this bad path. The public to whom Josephus addressed himself was superficial in point of erudition; it was easily contented; the rational culture of the time of the Cæsars had disappeared; the human mind was rapidly lowering its standard, and offered to all charlatanisms an easy prey.

Such was the literature of the cultivated and liberal Jews grouped around the principal representatives of a dynasty liberal in itself and in its origin, but for the moment devoured by a madman. Josephus formed endless projects of work. He was fifty-six. With his style, artificial and chequered with a patchwork heterogeneous of rags, he seriously thought himself a great writer; he thought he knew Greek, with which he had only a second-hand acquaintance. He wished to take the "Wars of the Jews" in hand again; to abridge it, to make it the continuation of his "Antiquities," and to tell all that had happened to the Jews from the end of the war to the moment of his writing. He meditated, above all, a philosophical work in four books upon God and his essence, according to Jewish ideas, and upon the Mosaic laws, with the object of rendering account of the prohibitions which they contain, and which greatly astonished the Pagans. Death doubtless prevented him from carrying out these new designs. It is probable that if he had composed these writings they would have come down to us as the others have done. Josephus in effect had a very strange literary destiny. He remained unknown to the Jewish Talmudic tradition; but he was adopted by Christians as one of themselves, and almost as a sacred writer. His writings complete the holy history which, reduced to the Biblical documents, offers only a blank page for many centuries. They form a sort of commentary on the Gospels, of which the historical sequence would have been unintelligible without the information which the Jewish historian furnishes as to the history of the Herods. They flattered especially one of the favourite theories of the Christians, and furnished one of the bases of the Christian apology, by the account of the siege of Jerusalem.

One of these ideas, to which Christians held most strongly, was that Jesus had predicted the ruin of the rebellious city. What could more strongly prove the literal accomplishment of that prophecy than the history, told by a Jew, of the unheard-of atrocities which accompanied the destruction of the Temple? Josephus became thus a fundamental witness and a supplement to the Bible. He was read and copied assiduously by Christians. He made of it, if I may so say, a Christian edition, wherein certain corrections may be permitted in passages which offended the copyists. These passages, above all, present in this connection doubts which criticism has not even yet allayed. These are the passages relative to John the Baptist, to Jesus, and to James. Certainly it is possible that these passages, at least that relating to Jesus, may be interpolations made by the Christians in a book which they had in some sort appropriated. We prefer, however, to believe that in the three places in question he spoke in effect of John the Baptist, of Jesus, and of James, and that the labour of the Christian editor, if he may be so called, was confined to pruning away from the passage upon Jesus certain clauses, and modifying some expressions offensive to an orthodox reader.

The reduced circle of aristocratic proselytes of a mediocre literary taste, for whom Josephus composed his book, were doubtless entirely satisfied with it. The difficulties of the old texts were ably disguised. Jewish history became as attractive as Greek, sown with harangues conducted according to the rules of profane rhetoric. Thanks to a charlatanesque display of erudition, and to a choice of doubtful or slightly falsified situations, there was an answer to all objectors. A discreet rationalism threw a veil over the too naive wonders of the ancient Hebrew books; after having read the accounts of the greatest miracles, you might believe them or not at will. For non-Jews never an insulting word; provided one is willing to recognise the historic nobility of the race, Josephus is satisfied. On every page a gentle philosophy, sympathetic with all virtue, treating the ritual precepts of the Law as binding upon Jews only, and proclaiming aloud that every just man has the essential qualities necessary for becoming a son of Abraham. A simple metaphysical and rationalistic Deism, a purely natural morality, replaces the sombre theology of Jehovah. The Bible thus rendered altogether human, appeared to the deserter of Jotapata to become more acceptable. He deceived himself. His book, precious as it is to the student, rises no higher in point of value in the eyes of the man of taste than one of those insipid Bibles of the seventeenth century where the most awful of the old texts are translated into academic language and decorated with vignettes in rococo style.

CHAPTER XIII

THE GOSPEL OF LUKE

As we have already several times had occasion to remark, the Gospel writings at the period at which we have arrived, were numerous. The majority of those writings did not bear the names of Apostles; they were second-hand attempts founded upon oral tradition, which they did not pretend to exhaust. The Gospel of Matthew alone presented itself as having the privilege of an apostolic origin; but that Gospel was not widely diffused; written for the Jews of Syria, it had not yet, to all appearance, penetrated to Rome. It was under these conditions that one of the most conspicuous members of the Church at Rome undertook--"himself also" (Luke i. 3)--to compile a Gospel from former texts, and not forbidding himself, any more than his predecessors had done, to intercalate what tradition and his own beliefs furnished him with. This man was no other than Lucanus or Luke, the disciple whom we have seen attach himself to Paul in Macedonia, follow him in his travels and in his captivity, and play an important part in his correspondence. We may readily believe that after the death of Paul he remained in Rome, and as he must have been young when Paul knew him (about the year 52), he would now be scarcely more than sixty years of age. It is impossible, in such cases, to speak with certainty; there is, however, no very strong reason for supposing that Luke was not the author of the Gospel which bears his name. Luke was not yet sufficiently famous for anyone to make use of his name to give authority to a book, as had been done in the case of the Apostles Matthew and John, later, for James and Peter.

Nor does the date appear involved in much uncertainty. All the world admits that the book is of later date than the year 70; but, on the other hand, it cannot be very much later. If it were, the predictions of the immediate appearance of Christ in the clouds, which the author copies without flinching from the oldest documents, would be sheer nonsense. The author throws back the year of the return of Jesus to an indeterminate future; "the end" is postponed as far as possible, but the connection between the catastrophe of Judea and the destruction of the world is maintained. The author preserves also the assertion of Jesus, according to which the generation which listened to him should not pass away until his predictions as to the end of the world were accomplished. Notwithstanding the extreme latitude which the apostolic exegesis claims in the interpretation of the discourses of our Lord, it cannot be allowed that an editor so intelligent as that of the third Gospel, an editor who knows so well how to make the words of Jesus pass through the changes required by the necessities of the time, should have copied a phrase which embodies a peremptory objection to the gift of prophecy attributed to the Master.

It is certainly only by conjecture that we connect Luke and his Gospel with the Christian society in Rome in the time of the Flavii. Yet it is certain that the general character of the work of Luke answers well to what such an hypothesis requires. Luke, we have already remarked, has a sort of Roman spirit; he loves order--the hierarchy; he has a profound respect for the centurions, and for the Roman functionaries, and likes to show them as favourable to Christianity. By an able turn, he succeeds in not saying that Jesus was crucified and insulted by the Romans. Between Luke and Clemens Romanus there are considerable analogies. Clemens often cites the words of Jesus from Luke, or a tradition analogous to that of Luke. The style of Luke, on the other hand, by its Latinisms, its general form, and its Hebraisms, recalls the Shepherd of Hermas. The very name of Luke is Roman, and may belong, by a bond of patron and client, or of emancipation, to some M. Annæus Lucanus, of the family of the celebrated poet, which would make a connection the more with that family of Annæa which is to be found everywhere under the dust of Christian Rome. Chapters xxv. and xxvi. of the Acts lead to the belief that the author, like Josephus, had relations with Agrippa II., Berenice, and the little Jewish coterie at Rome. Even down to Herod Antipas, whose misdeeds he almost attempts to extenuate, he represents its intervention in the Gospel history as benevolent in some aspects. May we not also find a Roman custom in that dedication to Theophilus, which recalls that of Josephus to Epaphroditus, and appears altogether foreign to the customs of Syria and Palestine in the first century of our era? We can see, besides, how such a situation recalls that of Josephus, writing almost at the same time, the one telling of the rise of Christianity, the other the Jewish revolution, with a very similar sentiment-- moderation, antipathy to extreme parties,--an official tone implying more care for defending positions than for truth,--respect, mingled with fear, for the Roman authority, whose very severities he strives to present as excusable necessities, and by whom he affects to have been sometimes protected. It is this which makes us believe that the world in which Luke lived and that of Josephus were very near to each other, and must have had more than one point of contact.

This Theophilus is otherwise unknown; his name may be only a fiction or a pseudonym to distinguish some one of the powerful adepts of the Church of Rome--one of the Clemens, for instance. A little preface clearly explains the intention and the situation of the author:--

Forasmuch as many have taken in hand to set forth in order a declaration of those things which are most surely believed among us, even as they delivered them unto us which from the beginning were eye-witnesses of the word, it seemed good to me, also having had perfect understanding of all things from the very first, to write unto thee, in order, most excellent Theophilus, that thou mightest know the certainty of those things wherein thou hast been instructed.

It does not necessarily follow from this preface that Luke must have had under his eyes, in working, these numerous writings to whose existence he bears witness; but the reading of the book leaves no doubt on that point. The verbal coincidences of the text of Luke with that of Mark, and, by consequence, with Matthew, are very frequent. No doubt Luke may have had under his eyes a text of Mark which differed very little from our own. We might say that he has assimilated it bodily, except the part of Mark vi. 45 to viii. 26, and the story of the Passion, for which he has preferred an ancient tradition. In the rest, the coincidence is literal, and when there are variants, it is easy to see the motive which has induced Luke to correct, in view of those whom he addressed, the original which he had under his hands. In the parallel passages of the three texts, the details which Matthew adds to Mark, Luke has not; what Luke appears to add, Matthew always has. In the passages which are wanting in Mark, Luke always has another recension than Matthew. In other words, in the parts common to the three Evangelists, Luke offers a sensible agreement in terms with Matthew only when the last presents a similar agreement with Mark. Luke has not certain passages of Matthew without any visible reason why he should have neglected them. The discourses of Jesus are fragmentary in Luke as in Mark; it would be incomprehensible that Luke, if he had known Matthew, should have broken up the grand discourses which the last gives. Luke, it is true, recalls a host of Logia which are not to be read in Mark, but these Logia did not come to his knowledge in the arrangement which we find in Matthew. Let us add that the legends of childhood and the genealogies have in the two evangelists in question nothing in common. Why should Luke cheerfully expose himself to evident objections? We can only conclude that Luke did not know one Matthew; and in effect, the essays of which he speaks in his prologue might bear the names of disciples or of apostles, but none of them could have borne a name like that of Matthew, since Luke distinguishes clearly between apostles, witnesses, and actors in the Gospel history, and traditionary authors and editors who have only reduced to writing the traditions without any special title to do so.

By the side of the book of Mark, Luke had surely on his table other narratives of the same kind, from which also he borrowed largely. The long passage from ix. 51 to xviii. 14, for example, has been copied from an earlier source, for it is all in confusion: Luke composed better than that when he followed oral tradition only. It has been calculated that a third of the text of Luke is to be found in neither Mark nor Matthew. Some of the Evangelists lost to us from whom Luke thus borrowed, contained very precise details; "those upon whom the tower of Siloam fell," those "whose blood Pilate had mingled with their sacrifice." Many of these documents were simply resettings of the Gospel of the Hebrews, strongly impressed with Ebionism, and thus approached Matthew. Hence may be explained in Luke certain passages analogous to Matthew which do not appear in Mark. The majority of the primitive Logia are to be found in Luke, not disposed in the form of great discourses as in our Matthew, but backed about and applied to particular circumstances. Not only has Luke not had St Matthew's Gospel under his hands, but it does not seem that he can have made use of any collection of the discourses of Jesus where already the great series of maxims of which we have verified the insertion in our Matthew were gathered. If he possessed such collections, he neglected them. On the other hand, Luke sometimes connects himself with the Gospel of the Hebrews, above all, where it is better than Matthew. It is possible that he had a Greek translation of the Hebrew Gospel.

From this it appears that Luke held with regard to Mark a position analogous to that which Matthew held to the same Evangelist. By both Mark has been enlarged by additions borrowed from documents drawn more or less from the Hebrew Gospel. To explain the numerous additions which Luke made to the common basis of Mark, and which are not in Matthew, a large part must be attributed to oral tradition. Luke plunged deeply into that tradition; he drew from it; he looked upon it as on the same footing as the numerous authors of essays on Gospel History who had existed before him. Did he scruple to insert in his text stories of his own invention, in order to stamp upon the work of Jesus the impression which he believed to be the true one? Certainly not. Tradition itself did no otherwise. Tradition is a collective work, since it expresses the mind of all; but at the same time there has always been someone who uttered for the first time the bright saying or the significant anecdote. Luke has often been that someone. The spring of the Logia had been dried up; and, to say the truth, we believe that it never produced anything more. On the contrary, the liberty of the Agada shows itself entirely in the right which Luke assumes of handling his documents according to his convenience, of culling, intercalating, transposing, and combining at his will, to obtain the arrangement which suited him the best. Not once did he say, If this history is true like this it cannot be true like that. The true material is nothing to him; the idea, the dogmatic and moral aim, are everything. I will even add the literary effect. Thus it is possible that what has caused him not to admit into his bundle of Logia collected before him or even to divide them violently, it may be a scruple of his delicate taste which has made him find these artificial groupings a little heavy. Nothing equals the ability with which he cuts down previous collections created upon the framework of Logia thus dispersed. He encases them, serves them like little gems in the delightful narratives which provoke them and lead up to them. The art of arranging has never been carried so far. Naturally, however, that method of composing brings about with Luke, as with Matthew, and generally with all the Gospels of the "second hand" artificially edited from earlier documents, repetitions, contradictions, and incoherencies, coming from the diverse documents which the last editor sought to blend together. Mark alone, by his primitive character, is exempt from this defect, and it is the best proof of his originality.

We have insisted elsewhere upon the errors which the distance of the Evangelist from Palestine has made him commit. His exegesis rests only the Septuagint, which he follows in its greatest blunders. The author was not a Jew by birth; he certainly writes for those who are not Jews; he has only a superficial acquaintance with the geography of Palestine, and the manners of the Jews. He omits everything that would be uninteresting to non-Israelites, and he adds notes which would be uninteresting to a native of Palestine. The genealogy which he attributes to Jesus leads to the belief that he was addressing people who could not easily verify a Biblical text. He extenuates all that shows the Jewish origin of Christianity, and although he may have a sort of tender compassion for Jerusalem, the Law has ceased to exist for him, save as a memory.

The spirit which inspired Luke is thus much more easy to determine than that which inspired Mark and the author of the Gospel according to Matthew. These two last Evangelists are neutral, taking no part in the quarrels which were rending the Church. The partisans of Paul, and those of James, might equally adopt them. Luke, on the contrary, is a disciple of Paul, moderate certainly, tolerant, full of respect for Peter, even for James, but a decided supporter of the adoption into the Church of Pagans, Samaritans, publicans, sinners, and heretics of all sorts. It is in him that we find the pitiful parable of the Good Samaritan, of the Prodigal Son, of the Lost Sheep, of the Lost Drachma, where the position of the penitent sinner is placed almost above that of the just man who has not failed. Certainly Luke was in that matter in agreement with the very spirit of Jesus, but there is on his part preoccupation, prejudice, fixed ideas. His boldest stroke was the conversion of one of the two thieves of Calvary. According to Mark and Matthew, the two malefactors insulted Jesus. Luke puts a fine sentiment into the mouth of one of them. "We receive the due rewards of our deeds, but this man hath done nothing amiss." In return, Jesus promises that that very day he shall be with him in Paradise. Jesus goes further. He prays for his executioners. "They know not what they do." In Matthew, Jesus appears ill-disposed towards Samaria, and recommends his disciples to avoid the cities of the Samaritans as in the way of Pagans. According to Luke, on the contrary, he is in frequent communication with the Samaritans, and speaks of them in terms of praise. It is to the journey to Samaria that Luke attaches a great amount of teaching and of narrative. Far from imprisoning Jesus in Galilee, like Mark and Matthew, Luke obeyed an anti-Galilean and anti-Judaic tendency--a tendency which will be much more visible in the fourth Gospel. In many other respects the Gospel of Luke forms a sort of intermediary between the two first Gospels and the fourth, which appears at first to offer no trace of union with them.

There is scarcely an anecdote or a parable proper to Luke which does not breathe that spirit of mercy, and of appeal to sinners. The only saying of Jesus which ever appears a little harsh becomes in his hands an apologue, full of indulgence and of long-suffering. The unfruitful tree ought not to be cut down too quickly; a good gardener opposes the anger of the proprietor, and asks leave to dig about the roots of the unhappy tree, and to dung it before condemning it altogether. The Gospel of Luke is especially the Gospel of pardon, and of pardon obtained by faith. "There is more joy in heaven over a sinner that repenteth than over ninety and nine just persons which need no repentance." "The Son of Man is come not to destroy men, but to save them." Any quantity of straining is lawful to him, if only he can make each incident of the Gospel history a history of pardoned sinners. Samaritans, publicans, centurions, guilty women, benevolent Pagans, all those whom Pharisaism despises, are his clients. The idea that Christianity has pardons for all the world is his alone. The door is open; conversion is possible to all. It is no longer a question of the Law; a new devotion, the worship of Jesus, has replaced it. Here it is the Samaritan who does the good deed, whilst the priest and the Levite pass indifferent by. There a publican comes out of the Temple justified by his humility, whilst the irreproachable but haughty Pharisee goes out more guilty than before. Elsewhere the sinful woman is raised by her love for Jesus, and is permitted to bestow on him particular marks of tenderness. Elsewhere, again, the publican Zacchaeus becomes at the first onset a son of Abraham, by the simple fact of his having shown eagerness to see Jesus. The offer of an easy pardon has always been the principal means of success in all religions. "Even the most guilty of men," says Bhagavat, "if he comes to adore me, and to turn himself to me in his worship, must be accepted as good." Luke adds the taste for humility. "That which is highly esteemed amongst men is abomination in the sight of God." The powerful shall be cast down from his throne, the humble shall be exalted; there, in brief, is the revolution wrought by Jesus. Now, the haughty is the Jew, proud of his descent from Abraham; the humble is the gentle man who draws no glory from his ancestors, and owes everything that he is to his faith in Jesus.

The perfect conformity of these views with those of Paul may readily be seen. Paul had no Gospel in the sense in which we understand the word. Paul had never heard Jesus, and intentionally speaks with much reserve of his relations with his immediate disciples. He had seen very little of them, and had passed only a few days in the centre of their traditions, at Jerusalem. He had scarcely heard tell of the Logia; of the tradition of the Gospel he knew only fragments. It must be added, however, that these fragments agree well with what we read in Luke. The account of the Last Supper, as Paul gives it, is identical, save for a few details of small importance, with that of the third Gospel. Luke, without doubt, carefully avoids all that might offend the Judeo-Christian party, and awaken controversies which he desires to put to rest; he is as respectful to the Apostles as he can be; he fears, however, that they will assume a too exclusive position. His policy, in this respect, has inspired him with the boldest of ideas. By the side of the Twelve he creates, of his own authority, seventy disciples, to whom Jesus gives a mission which in the other Gospels is reserved for the Twelve alone.

In this was an imitation of that chapter of Numbers in which God, in order to console Moses under a burden which had become too heavy, pours out upon seventy elders a part of the spirit of government which, until then, had been the gift of Moses alone. As though with the intention of rendering more conspicuous this division, and this likeness of powers, Luke divides between the Twelve and the Seventy the apostolic instructions which in the collections of Logia form only a single discourse addressed to the Twelve. This number of seventy or seventy-two had, moreover, the advantage of corresponding with the number of the nations of the earth, as the number twelve answered to the tribes of Israel. There was, indeed, an opinion that God had divided the earth amongst seventy-two nations, over each of which an angel presided. The figure was mystical; besides the seventy elders of Moses, there were seventy-one members of the Sanhedrim, seventy or seventy-two Greek translators of the Bible. The secret thought which dictated to Luke this so grave addition to the Gospel text is thus evident. It was necessary, to save the legitimacy of the apostolate of Paul, to present that apostolate as parallel to the powers of the Twelve,--to show that one might be an Apostle without being one of the Twelve --which was precisely Paul's case. The Twelve, in a word, did not exhaust the apostolate; the plenitude of their powers did not make the existence of others impossible, "and besides," the sage disciple of Paul hastens to add, "these powers, in themselves, are nothing; what is important to them, as to every other faithful man, is to have their names written in heaven." Faith is everything; faith is the gift of God, which he bestows on whom he will.

From such a point of view the privileges of the sons of Abraham are reduced to a very small thing. Jesus, rejected by his own, finds his true family only amongst the Gentiles. Men of distant countries, the Gentiles of Paul, have accepted him as king, whilst his companions, whose natural sovereign he was, have shown him that they will none of him. Woe to them! When the lawful king shall return, he will put them to death in his presence. The Jews imagine that because Jesus has eaten and drunk with them, and taught in their streets, they will always enjoy their privileges. They are in error. Many shall come from the north, and from the south, and shall sit down with Abraham, with Isaac, and with Jacob, and they shall lament at the door. The lively impression of the misfortunes which have befallen the Jewish people may be read upon every page, and these misfortunes, the author finds, the nation has merited through not having understood Jesus and the mission with which he was charged for Jerusalem. In the genealogy Luke avoids tracing the descent of Jesus from the kings of Judah. From David to Salathiel the descent is through collaterals.

Other and less open signs discover a favourable intention towards Paul. It is not unquestionably merely by chance that, after having described how Peter was the first to recognise Jesus as the Messiah, the author does not give the famous words, "Thou art Peter, and upon this rock I will build my Church;" words which were already taking their place in the tradition. The story of the Canaanitish woman, which the author had undoubtedly read in Mark, is omitted because of the harsh words which it contains, and for which the pitiful ending is no sufficient compensation. The parable of the tares, which appears to have been imagined against Paul, that untoward sower who came after the authorised sowers and made a mingled harvest out of a pure one, is also neglected. Another passage, where we think we may see an insult to the Christians who shake off the bondage of the Law, is retorted, and becomes an attack on the Judeo-Christians. The rigour of the principles of Paul upon the apostolic spirit, is pushed even further than in Matthew, and what is equally important, is that precepts addressed elsewhere to the little group of missionaries are here applied to the whole body of the faithful. "If any man come to me and hate not his father and mother, and wife and children, and brethren and sisters, yea and his own life also, he cannot be my disciple." "Whoever he be of you that forsaketh not all that he hath, he cannot be my disciple." And after these sacrifices he says yet again, "We are unprofitable servants; we have done that which it was our duty to do." Between the Apostle and Jesus there is no difference. He who hears the Apostle hears Jesus; he who despises the Apostle despises Jesus and despises also him that hath sent him.

The same exaltation may be remarked in all that relates to poverty. Luke hates riches, regards the simple attachment to property as an evil. When Jesus came into the world there was no room for him in the inn; he was born in the midst of the simplest of beings, sheep and oxen. His first worshippers were shepherds. All his life he was poor. It is absurd to save, for the rich man can carry nothing away with him. The disciple of Jesus has nothing to do with the goods of this world: he must renounce all that he possesses. The happy man is the poor man; the rich man is always guilty: hell is his certain fate. So the poverty of Jesus was absolute. The Kingdom of God will be the festival of the poor; a shifting of the social strata, an accession of new classes, will take place. With the other Evangelists the persons who are substituted for the original guests are people gathered out of the highways, the first comers; with Luke they are the poor, the halt, the lame, the blind, all who have been the sport of fortune. In this new kingdom it will be better to have made friends amongst the poor, even by injustice, than to have been correctly economical. It is not the rich who should be invited to dinners, it should be the poor; and the reward shall be paid at the resurrection of the just--that is to say, in the reign of a thousand years. Alms are a supreme precept; alms are strong enough to purify impure things; they are greater than the Law itself.

The doctrine of Luke is, it will be seen, pure Ebionism--the glorification of poverty. According to the Ebionites, Satan is king of this world, and he gives its good things to his fellows. Jesus is the prince of the world to come. To participate in the good things of the diabolical world is equivalent to exclusion from the other. Satan is the sworn enemy of Christians and of Jesus; the world, its princes and its rich men, are his allies in the work of opposition to the kingdom of Jesus. The demonology of Luke is material and bizarre. His miracle-mongering has something of the crude materialism of Mark: it terrifies the spectators. Luke does not know in this way the softened tones of Matthew.

An admirable popular sentiment, a fine and touching poetry, the clear and pure sound of a silvery soul, something removed from earthliness and exquisite in tone, prevent us from dreaming of these blemishes, these many failures of logic, these singular contradictions. The judge and the importunate widow, the friend with the three loaves, the unfaithful steward, the prodigal son, the pardoned woman that was a sinner, many of the combinations proper to Luke at first appear to positive minds little conformable to scholastic reason and to a strict morality; but these apparent weaknesses, which are like the amiable imperfections of a woman's thought, are a feature of truth the more, and may well recall the tone of emotion, soon expiring, soon breathless, the altogether womanly movement of the words of Jesus, ruled by image and by sentiment much more than by reason. It is, above all, in the stories of the childhood and of the Passion that we find a divine art. These delicious episodes of the cradle, of the shepherds, of the angel who announces great joy to the lowly, of heaven descending upon earth amongst the poor to sing the song of peace on earth to men of good will; then the old man, worthy personification of ancient Israel, whose part is finished, but who considers himself happy in that he has lived his life, since his eyes have seen the glory of his people and the light revealed to all nations; and that widow of eighty who dies consoled; and the Canticles, so pure, so gentle--Magnificat, Gloria in Excelsis, Nunc Dimittis, Benedictus--which will soon serve as the basis of a new liturgy; all that exquisite pastoral traced with a delicate outline on the forefront of Christianity--all that is assuredly the work of Luke. Never was sweeter cantilena invented to put to sleep the sorrows of poor humanity.

The taste which carried Luke towards pious narratives naturally inclined him to create for John the Baptist a childhood like that of Jesus. Elizabeth and Zecharias long barren, the vision of the priest at the hour of incense, the visit of the two mothers, the Canticle of the father of John the Baptist, were as the propylæa before the porch, imitated from the porch itself, and reproducing its principal lines. There is no necessity for denying that Luke may have found in the documents of which he made use the germs of these exquisite narratives which have been one of the principal sources of Christian art. In fact, the style of the childhoods of Luke, truncated, full of Hebraisms, is scarcely that of a prologue. Moreover, this part of the work is more Jewish than the rest: John the Baptist is of sacerdotal origin; the rites of the purification, and of circumcision, are carefully accomplished; the family of Jesus go on a pilgrimage every year; many anecdotes are altogether in the Jewish taste. A remarkable fact is that the part of Mary--nothing in Mark--grows little by little in proportion as we get further from Judea, and as Joseph loses his paternal character. The legend wants her, and allows itself to be led away to speak of her at length. It can only be imagined that the woman whom God has chosen to impregnate by the Spirit must be no ordinary woman; she it is who serves as the guarantee for whole chapters of the Gospel history; who has created for herself in the Church a position which has become more important from day to day.

Very beautiful, and also very unhistoric, are the narratives proper to the third Gospel of the Passion, death, and resurrection of Jesus. In this part of his book, Luke almost abandons his original Mark, and follows other texts. Hence we have a narrative even more legendary in character than that of

Matthew. Everything is exaggerated. At Gethsemane, Luke adds the angel, the sweating of blood, the curing of the amputated ear of Malchus. The appearance before Herod Antipas is entirely of his invention. The beautiful episode of the daughters of Jerusalem, intended to present the crowd as innocent of the death of Jesus, and to throw all the odium of it upon the great men and their chiefs, the conversion of one of the malefactors, the prayer of Jesus for his executioners, drawn from Isaiah liii. 12, are deliberate additions. For the sublime cry of despair, Eli, eli, lama sabachthani, which was no longer in harmony with the ideas of the Divinity of Jesus which were growing up, he substitutes a calmer text, "Father, into thy hands I commend my spirit." Finally the life of Jesus after his resurrection is related on an altogether artificial plan, conformable in part to that of the Gospel of the Hebrews, according to which that life beyond the tomb lasted but for one day, and was brought to a close by an ascension which Matthew and Mark altogether ignore.

The Gospel of Luke is then an amended Gospel, completed and strongly impressed with legend. Like the pseudo-Matthew, Luke corrects Mark, foreseeing objections, effacing real or apparent contradictions, suppressing more or less difficult features, and vulgar exaggerated or insignificant details. What he does not understand, he suppresses or turns with infinite skill. He adds touching and delicate details. He invents little, but he modifies much. The aesthetic transformations which he creates are surprising. The picture which he has drawn of Mary and her sister Martha, is a marvellous thing: no pen has ever traced ten more charming lines. His arrangement of the woman with the alabaster box of ointment is not less exquisite. The episode of the disciples at Emmaus, is one of the finest and most delicately-shaded in any language.

The Gospel of Luke is the most literary of the Gospels. Everything in it reveals a large and gentle mind, wise, moderate, sober, and rational, even in the midst of unreason. His exaggerations, his improbabilities, his inconsequences, are somewhat of the nature of parables, and give its charm to it. Matthew rounds off the somewhat harsh outlines of Mark; Luke does more--he writes and shows a true understanding of the art of composition. His book is a beautiful narrative well followed up, at once Hebraic and Hellenistic, uniting the emotion of the drama with the serenity of the idyll. Everyone there smiles, weeps, sings; everywhere there are tears and canticles; it is the hymn of the new people, the hosannah of the little ones and the humble introduced into the kingdom of God. A spirit of the holy childhood, of joy, of fervour, the evangelic sentiment in its originality, spreads over the whole legend a colouring of an incomparable sweetness. Never was writer less sectarian. Never a reproach, never a harsh word for the old excluded people; is not their exclusion punishment enough? It is the most beautiful book there is. The pleasure that the author must have had in writing it will never be sufficiently understood.

The historical value of the third Gospel is certainly less than that of the two first. Nevertheless, one remarkable fact which proves that the so-called synoptical Gospels really contain an echo of the words of Jesus, results from the comparison of the Gospel of Luke with the Acts of the Apostles. On both sides the author is the same. Yet when we compare the discourses of Jesus in the Gospels with the discourses of the Apostles in the Acts, the difference is absolute; here the charm of the most utter simplicity, there (I should say in the discourses of the Acts, especially towards the last chapters) a certain rhetoric, at times cold enough. Whence can this difference arise? Evidently because in the second case Luke makes the discourses himself, while in the first he follows a tradition. The words of Jesus were written before Luke; those of the Apostles were not. A considerable inference may be drawn from the account of the Last Supper in the First Epistle of St Paul to the Corinthians. The most anciently written Gospel text that there is may be found here (the First Epistle to the Corinthians is of the year 57.) Now this text coincides absolutely with that of Luke. Luke then has his own value, even when he is separated from Mark and Matthew.

Luke marks the last degree of deliberate revision at which the Gospel tradition may arrive. After him we have no more than the apocryphal Gospel based upon pure amplification and a priori supposition, without the use of any new documents. We shall see later how the texts of the kind of Mark, of Luke, and of the pseudo-Matthew were still insufficient for Christian piety, and how a new Gospel came into existence which had the pretension of surpassing them. We shall have, above all things, to explain why none of the Gospel texts succeeded in suppressing the others, and how the Christian Church exposed itself by its very good faith to the formidable objections which sprang out of their diversities.

CHAPTER XIV

THE DOMITIAN PERSECUTION

The monstrosities of the "bald Nero" made frightful progress. He reached madness, but a sombre, determined madness. Until now there had been intervals in his paroxysms; now it was a continuous frenzy. Wickedness mingled with a feverish rage, which appears to be one of the fruits of the Roman climate, the sensation of becoming ridiculous through his military failures, and by the lying triumphs which he had ordered, filled him with an implacable hatred for every honest and sensible man. He might have been called a vampire feeding greedily upon the carcase of expiring humanity; an open war was declared against all virtue. To write the biography of a great man was a crime; it seemed as though there was a wish to abolish the human intellect, and to take away the voice from conscience. Everything that was illustrious trembled; the world was full of murders and exiles. It must be said, to the honour of our poor humanity, that it went through this trial without bending. Philosophy recognised her position, and strengthened herself more than ever in this struggle against torment; there were heroic wives, devoted husbands, constant sons-in-law, faithful slaves. The family of Thrasea and Barea Soranus, was always in the front rank of the virtuous opposition. Helvidius Priscus (the son), Arulenus Rusticus, Junius Mauricus, Senecio, Pomponia Gratilla, Fannia, a whole family of great and strong souls, resisted without hope. Epictetus repeated every day in his grave voice, "Stand up and abstain. Suffering, thou wilt never make me agree that thou art an ill. Anytus and Melitus may kill me; they cannot injure me."

It was a very honourable thing for philosophy and for Christianity that under Domitian, as under Nero, they should have been persecuted in company. As Tertullian says, what such monsters condemned must have had something of good in it. It is the topstone of wickedness in a government when it does not permit the good to live even under its most resigned form. The name of philosopher implied thenceforward a profession of ascetic practices, a special kind of life, a cloak. This race of secular monks, protesting by their renunciation against the vanities of the world, were during the first century the greatest enemies of Cæsarism. Philosophy, let us say it to its glory, does not readily lend its support to the basenesses of humanity, and to the sad consequences which that baseness entails in politics. Heirs of the liberal spirit of Greece, the Stoics of the Roman epoch dreamed of virtuous democracies in a time which suited only with tyranny. The politicians whose principle it is to shut themselves up within limitations as far as possible, had naturally a strong antipathy to such a way of looking at things. Tiberius had been wont to hold the philosophers in aversion. Nero (in 66) drove away these importunates, whose presence was a perpetual reproach to his life. Vespasian (in 74) had better reasons for doing the same thing. His young dynasty was sapped every day by the republican spirit which Stoicism fostered; he did but defend himself by taking precautions against his most mortal enemies.

Nothing more than his own personal wickedness was necessary to induce Domitian to persecute the sages. He had early entertained a hatred for men of letters: every thought was a condemnation of his crimes and of his mediocrity. In his later days he could not suffer them. A decree of the senate drove the philosophers from Rome and from Italy. Epictetus, Dionysius Chrysostom, Artemidorus, departed. The courageous Sulpicia dared to raise his voice on behalf of the banished, and to address prophetic menaces to Domitian. Pliny, the younger, escaped almost by a miracle from the punishment which his distinction and his virtue merited. The treatise Octavius composed about this time contains cruel outbursts of indignation and despair:

Urbe eat nostra mitior Aulis
Et Taurorum barbara tellus;
Hospitis illic cæde litatur
Numen superum; civis gaudet
Roma cruore.

It is not surprising that the Jews and the Christians should have suffered from the recoil of these redoubtable terrors. One circumstance rendered war inevitable: Domitian, imitating the madness of Caligula, wished to receive divine honours. The road to the Capitol was crowded with herds which were taken to his statue to be sacrificed there: the form of the letters from his Chancery commenced with Dominus et Deus noster. We must read the monstrous preface which Quintilian, one of the master spirits of the age, puts at the head of one of his volumes, on the day following that on which Domitian had charged him with the education of his adopted heirs, the sons of Flavius Clemens:--"And now it would be not to understand the honour of the celestial appreciations, to remain below my task. What care the morals require if they are to obtain the approval of the most holy of censors! What attention I shall have to give to the studies not to disappoint the expectations of a prince so eminent for eloquence as for everything else! One is not astonished that the poets, after having invoked the Muses at the outset, renew their vows when they arrive at difficult passages of their tasks . . . So also I shall be pardoned for calling all the gods to my help, and in the first place he who more than any other divinity shows himself propitious to our studies. May he inspire me with the genius which the functions to which he has called me require; may he always assist me; may he make me what he has believed me."

Such is the tone adopted by a man who was "pious" in the fashion of his times. Domitian, like all hypocritical sovereigns, showed himself a severe upholder of the old worship. The word impietas especially during his reign had generally a political signification, and was synonymous with lèse majesté. Religious indifference and tyranny had reached such a point that the Emperor was the only god whose majesty was dreaded. To love the Emperor was piety; to be suspected of opposition or even of coldness was impiety. The word was not from that suspected of having lost its religious sense. The love of the Emperor, in fact, implied the respectful adoption of a whole sacred rhetoric which no sensible man could any longer accept as serious. That man was a revolutionary who did not bow before these absurdities, which had become part of the routine of the state; now the revolutionary was the impious man. The Empire thus came from it to a sort of orthodoxy, to an official pedagogy as in China. To admit what the Emperor wished with a sort of loyalism like that which the English affect towards their sovereign and their Established Church, this was what was called religio, and gained for a man the title of pius.

In such a condition of the language and of minds, Jewish and Christian monotheism must have appeared a supreme impiety. The religion of the Jew and of the Christian attached itself to a supreme God, the worship of whom was a robbery of the profane god. To worship God was to give a rival to the Emperor; to worship other gods than those of whom the Emperor was the legal patron, constituted a yet worse insult. The Christians, or rather the pious Jews, believed themselves obliged to make a more or less evident sign of protest when passing before the temples; at least they refrained absolutely from the kiss which it was the custom of pious Pagans to wave to the sacred edifice in passing before it. Christianity, by its cosmopolitan and revolutionary principle, was certainly "the enemy of the gods, of the emperors, of the laws, of morals, of all nature." The best of the emperors will not always know how to disentangle this sophism, and, without knowing it, almost without wishing it, will be persecutors. A narrow and wicked spirit, like that of Domitian, became such with pedantry and even with a sort of voluptuousness.

The Roman policy had always made in religious legislation a fundamental difference. Roman statesmen saw no harm in a provincial practising his religion in his own country without any spirit of proselytism. When this same provincial wished to worship in his own way in Italy, and, above all, in Rome, the matter became more delicate; the eyes of the true Roman were offended by the spectacle of fantastic ceremonies, and from time to time the police come to sweep out what these aristocrats regarded as ignominies. The foreign religions were besides extremely attractive to the lower classes, and it was regarded as a necessity of state to keep them within due limits. But what was held to be altogether grave was that Roman citizens, persons of importance, should abandon the religion of Rome for Oriental superstitions. That was a crime against the state. The Roman was yet the basis of the Empire. Now the Roman was not complete without the Roman religion; for him to go over to a foreign religion was to be guilty of treason to his country. Thus a Roman citizen could never be initiated into Druidism. Domitian, who aspired to the character of a restorer of the worship of the Latin gods, would not lose so fine an opportunity of delivering himself to his supreme joy, which was to punish.

We know with certainty in effect, that a great number of persons having embraced Jewish customs (the Christians were frequently placed in this category) were brought to judgment under the accusation of impiety or atheism. As under Nero, calumnies uttered by false brethren were perhaps the cause of the evil. Some were condemned to death; others were exiled or deprived of their goods. There were some apostacies. In the year 95 Flavius Clemens was Consul. In the last days of his Consulate Domitian put him to death on the slightest suspicion, coming from the basest informers. These suspicions were assuredly political, but the pretext was religion. Clemens had, without doubt, manifested little zeal for the Pagan forms with which every civil act in Rome was accompanied; possibly he had abstained from some ceremony regarded as of capital importance. Nothing more was required to justify the issue of a charge of impiety against him and against Flavia Domitilla. Clemens was put to death. As to Flavia Domitilla, she was exiled to the island of Pandataria, which had already been the scene of the exile of Julia, the daughter of Augustus, of Agrippina, the wife of Germanicus, of Octavia, the wife of Nero.

This was the crime for which Domitian paid most dearly. Domitilla, whatever was the decree of her initiation into Christianity, was a Roman woman. To avenge her husband, to save her children, compromised by the caprices of a fantastic monster, appeared to be a duty. From Pandataria she continued to maintain relations with the numerous body of slaves and freedmen whom she had at Rome, and who appear to have been strongly attached to her.

Of all the victims of the persecution of Domitian, we know one only by name--that of Flavius Clemens. The ill-will of the Government appears to have been directed far more against the Romans who were attracted to Judaism or to Christianity than against the Jews and Oriental Christians established in Rome. It does not appear that any of the presbyters or episcopi of the Church suffered martyrdom. Among the Christians who suffered, none appear to have been delivered to the beasts in the amphitheatre, for almost all belonged to what were relatively the upper classes of society. As under Nero, Rome was the principal scene of these violences; there were, however, troubles in the provinces. Some Christians faltered and left the Church, where for the moment they had found consolation for their souls, but where it was too hard to remain. Others, however, were heroic in charity, spent their goods to feed the saints, and took upon themselves the chains of those whom they judged to be more valuable to the Church than themselves.

The year 95 was not, it may be owned, as solemn a time for the Church as the year 64, but it had its importance. It was like a second consecration of Rome. After an interval of thirty-one years the maddest and wickedest of men appeared to lay himself out for the destruction of the Church of Jesus, and in reality strengthened it so that the apologists could put forth this specious argument, "All monsters have hated us; therefore we are the true."

It was probably the information which Domitian had of this remark upon Judeo-Christianity which told him of the rumours which circulated concerning the continued existence of descendants of the ancient dynasty of Judah. The imagination of the Agadists gave itself the rein on this subject, and attention, which for centuries had been diverted from the family of David, was now strongly attracted to it. Domitian took umbrage at this, and commanded all who bore that name to be put to death; but soon it was pointed out to him that amongst these supposed descendants of the antique royal race of Jerusalem there were people whose inoffensive character ought assuredly to place them beyond suspicion. There were the grandsons of Jude, the brother of Jesus, peaceably retired in Batanea. The defiant Emperor had besides heard tell of the coming triumph of Christ; all that disquieted him. An evocatus came to seek out the holy people in Syria; they were two; they were taken to the Emperor. Domitian asked them first if they were the descendants of David. They answered that they were. The Emperor then questioned them as to their means of living. "Between us," they said, "we possess only 9000 denarii, of which each of us takes half. And that property we possess not in money but in the form of a piece of land of some thirty acres upon which we pay the taxes, and we live by the labour of our hands." Then they showed their hands covered with callosities, and hardened, and red with toil. Domitian questioned them concerning Christ and his kingdom; his future appearance, and the times and places of his appearance. They answered that his kingdom was not of this world; that it was celestial, angelic; that it would be revealed at the end of time, when Christ should come in his glory to judge the quick and the dead, and render to each man according to his works. Domitian could feel only contempt for such simplicity; he set at liberty the two grand-nephews of Jesus. It appears that that simple idealism completely reassured him as to the political dangers of Christianity, and that he gave orders to cease the persecution of these dreamers.

Certain indications in effect lead to the belief that Domitian towards the end of his life relaxed his severities. It is, however, impossible to be certain in this matter; for other witnesses lead us to think that the situation of the Church was improved only after the advent of Nerva. At the moment when Clemens wrote his letter, the fire appears to have diminished. It was like the morrow of a battle; they count those who have fallen, those who are still in chains are pitied; but they are far from believing that all is over. God is entreated to defeat the perverse designs of the Gentiles, and to deliver his people from those who hate them without a cause.

The persecution of Domitian struck at Jews and Christians alike. The Flavian house thus put the topstone to its crimes, and became for the two branches of the house of Israel the most flagrant representation of impiety. It is not impossible that Josephus may have fallen a victim to the last fury of the dynasty which he had flattered. After the year 93 or 94 we hear no more of him. The works which he contemplated in 93 were not written. In that year, his life had been in danger through the curse of the times--the informers. Twice he escaped the danger, and his accusers were even punished; but it was the abominable habit of Domitian in such a case to revoke the acquittal which he had pronounced, and, after having chastised the informer, to slay the accused. The frightful rage for murder which Domitian showed in 95 and 96 against everyone connected with the Jewish world and family, scarcely permits it to be believed that he would have allowed a man to go unharmed who had spoken of Titus in a tone of panegyric (a crime in his eyes the most unpardonable of all), and had praised himself only casually. The favour of Domitia whom he detested, and whom he had resolved to put to death, was, besides, a sufficient grievance. Josephus in 96 was only 59. If he had lived under the tolerant reign of Nerva, he would have continued his writings, and probably explained some of the insinuations which the fear of the tyrant had imposed.

Have we a monument of these sombre months of terror, where all the worshippers of the true God dreamed only of martyrdom, in the discourse "on the Empire of Reason," which bears in the MSS. the name of Josephus? The thoughts, at least, are very much those of the times in which we are. A strong soul is mistress of the body which she animates, and allows herself to be conquered only by the most cruel punishments. The author proves his position by the examples of Eleazer and of the mother who, during the persecution of Antiochus Epiphanius, courageously endured death with her seven sons-- histories which may also be found in the sixth and seventh chapters of the Second Book of Maccabees.

Notwithstanding the declamatory tone, and certain ornaments which recall a little too strongly the lesson of philosophy, the book contains noble doctrines. God embodies in himself the eternal order which is made manifest to man by reason; reason is the law of life; duty consists in preferring it to the passions. As in the Second Book of Maccabees, the idea of future rewards and punishments is altogether spiritual. The righteous dead live to God for God in the sight of God, Ζῶσι τῷθεῷ. God as the author is at the same time the absolute God of philosophy, and the national God of Israel. The Jew ought to die for his Law, first, because it is the Law of his fathers, then because it is divine and true. The meats forbidden by the Law have been forbidden because they are injurious to man; in any case, to break the Law in small things is as culpable as to do so in great, since in the two cases the authority of reason is equally misunderstood. It is easy to see how such a way of looking at things connects that of Josephus and of the Jewish philosophers. From the wrath which breaks forth in every page against tyrants, and from the images of tortures which haunt the mind of the author, the book evidently dates from the time of the last outbreak of Domitian's fury. It is by no means impossible that the composition of this noble writing may have been the consolation of the last days of Josephus, when, almost certain of dying under punishment, he sought to gather together all the reasons that a wise man might find for not fearing death.

The book succeeded amongst the Christians; under the title of Fourth Book of Maccabees it was almost received into the canon; many Greek manuscripts of the Old Testament contain it. Less fortunate, however, than the Book of Judith, it was not able to keep its place; the Second Book of Maccabees afforded no sufficient reason for placing it at its side. The interesting point for us is that we may there see the first type of a species of literature which was later much cultivated,--exhortations to martyrdom, in which the author exalts to encourage the sufferers the example of feeble beings who have shown themselves heroic, or still better of these Acta martyrum, now pieces of rhetoric having edification as their aid, proceeding by oratorical amplification, without any care for historical truth, and finding in the hideous details of the antique the ferments of a sombre voluptuousness and the means of emotion.

An indistinct echo of all these events may be found in the Jewish traditions. In the month of September or October four elders of Judea, Rabbi Gamaliel, patriarch of the tribunal of Jabneh; Rabbi Eleazar ben Azariah; Rabbi Joshua; Rabbi Aquiba, later so celebrated, appeared at Rome. The journey is described in detail: every evening, because of the season, they anchored in some port; on the day of the Feast of Tabernacles the Rabbins found the means to erect on the bridge of the boat a hut of foliage, which the wind carried away the next day; the time of the navigation was occupied in discussing the manner of paying title, and of supplying the place of the loulab (palm-branch with myrtle, used at this feast) in a country where there were no palm trees. At a hundred and twenty miles from the city the travellers heard a hollow murmur; it was the sound of the Capitol. All then shed tears. Aquiba alone burst into laughter. "Why do you not weep," said the Rabbins, "at seeing how happy and tranquil are the idolators who sacrifice to false gods, while the sanctuary of our God has been consumed by fire, and serves as a den for the beasts of the field?" "Well," said Aquiba, "it is that which makes me laugh. If God grants so many good things to those who offend him, what destiny awaits those who do his will, and to whom the kingdom belongs?"

Whilst these four elders were at Rome the senate of the Emperor decreed the extermination of the Jews throughout the world. A senator, a pious man (Clemenes?) reveals this redoubtable secret to Gamaliel. The wife of the senator, even more pious than he (Domitilla??) advises him to kill himself by sucking a poison which he keeps in his ring, which will save the Jews (how one does not see). Later on, the conviction spread that this senator was circumcised, or, according to the figurative expression, "that the vessel had not quitted the port without paying the impost" According to another account, the Cæsar, enemy of the Jews, said to the great of his empire: "If one has an ulcer on the foot, should he cut off his foot or keep it at the risk of suffering?" All were for amputation, except Katia hen Shalom. This last was put to death by order of the Emperor and died whilst saying, "I am a ship which has paid its taxes; I may set sail."

There are plenty of vague images here and memories of half sane people. Some of the controversies of the four doctors at Rome are reported. "If God disapproves idolatry," they were asked, "why does he not destroy it?" "But God must then destroy the sun, moon, and stars." "No; he might destroy useless idols and leave the useful ones." "But that would at once make those things divine which he has not destroyed. The world goes its own way. The stolen seed grows like any other; the unchaste woman is not sterile because the child which shall be born of her is a bastard." In preaching, one of the four travellers utters this thought: "God is not like earthly kings, who make laws, and do not themselves observe them." A Min (a Judeo-Christian?) heard these words, and on coming out of the hall said to the doctor, "Why does not God observe the Sabbath; the world goes on just as usual on Saturday?" "Is it not lawful on the Sabbath day to move whatever is in one's house?" "Yes," said the Min. "Well, then, the whole world is the house of God."

CHAPTER XV

CLEMENS ROMANUS--PROGRESS OF THE PRESBYTERIATE

The most correct lists of the Bishops of Rome, forcing a little the signification of the word bishop, for times so remote place after Anenclet a certain Clement, who from the similarity of his name and the nearness of his time has frequently been confounded with Flavius Clemens. The name is not rare in the Judeo-Christian world. We may in strictness suppose a relationship of patron and client between our Clement and Flavius Clemens. But we must absolutely set aside both the theory of certain modern critics who insist on seeing in Bishop Clement only a fictitious personage, a double of Flavius Clemens, and the error which at various times comes to light in the ecclesiastical tradition, according to which Bishop Clement was a member of the Flavian family. Clemens Romanus was not merely a real personage, he was a personage of the first rank, a true chief of the Church, a bishop before the Episcopate was definitely constituted; I would almost dare to say a pope, if the word were not too great an anachronism in this place. His authority was recognised as the greatest in all Italy, in Greece, in Macedonia, during the last decade of the first century. At the expiration of the apostolic age he was like an apostle, an epigon in the great generation of the disciples of Jesus, one of the pillars of that Church of Rome, which, after the destruction of the Church of Jerusalem, became more and more the centre of Christianity.

Everything leads to the belief that Clement was of Jewish origin. His familiarity with the Bible, the turn of style in certain passages of his Epistle, the use which he makes of the Book of Judith and of apocryphal writings such as the assumption of Moses, do not agree with the idea of a converted Pagan. On the other hand, he appears to be little of a Hebraiser. It appears then that he was born in Rome of one of those Jewish families which had inhabited the capital of the world for many generations. His knowledge of cosmography and of profane history presuppose a careful education. It is admitted that he had been in relation with the Apostles, especially with Peter, though on this point the proof is perhaps hardly decisive. What is indubitable is the high rank which he held in the spiritual hierarchy of the Church of his time, and the unequalled credit which he enjoyed. His approval made law. All parties claimed him, and wished to shelter themselves under his authority. A thick veil hides his private opinions from us; his Epistle is a fine neutral fragment with which the disciples of Paul and the disciples of Peter might equally content themselves. It is probable that he was one of the most energetic agents in the great work which was about to be accomplished, I mean the posthumous reconciliation of Peter and Paul, and the fusion of the two parties, without the union of which the work of Christ must have perished.

The extreme importance at which Clement had arrived results, above all things, from the vast apocryphal literature which is attributed to him. When, towards the year 140, an attempt was made to gather together into one body of writing, clothed with an ecclesiastical character, the Judeo-Christian traditions concerning Peter and his apostolate, Clement was chosen as the supposed author of the work. When it was desired to codify the ancient ecclesiastical customs, and to make the collection thus formed a Corpus of "Apostolic Constitutions," it was Clement who guaranteed that apocryphal work. Other writings, all having more or less connection with the establishment of a canon law, were equally attributed to him. The fabricator of apocryphas endeavours to give weight to his forgeries. The name which he puts at the head of his compositions is always that of a celebrity. The sanction of Clement thus appears to us as the highest which can be imagined in the second century to recommend a book. Thus in the Pastor of the psuedo-Hermas, Clement's special function is assigned as being that of sending the books newly issued in Rome to the other Churches, and of causing them to be accepted. His supposed literature, whether he must be taken as assuming personal responsibility for it or not, is a literature of authority, inculcating on every page the hierarchy, obedience to the priests, to the bishops. Every phrase which is attributed to him is a law, a decretal. The right of speaking to the Universal Church is freely accorded to him. He is the first typical "Pope" whom ecclesiastical history presents. His lofty personality, increased yet more by legend, was, after that of Peter, the holiest image of Christian Rome. His venerable face was for succeeding ages that of a grave and gentle legislator, a perpetual preacher of submission and respect.

Clement passed through the persecution of Domitian without suffering from it. When the severities abated, the Church of Rome renewed its relations with the outer world. Already the idea of a certain primacy of that Church began to make itself felt. The right of advising the Churches and of adjusting their differences was accorded to it. Such privileges; it may at least be believed, were accorded to Peter and to his immediate disciples. Now, a closer and closer bond was established between St Peter and Rome. Grave dissensions had torn the Church of Corinth. That Church had scarcely changed since the days of St Paul. There was the same spirit of pride, of disputatiousness, of frivolity. We feel that the principal opposition to the hierarchy dwelt in this Greek spirit, always mobile, frivolous, undisciplined, not knowing how to reduce a crowd to the condition of a flock. The women, the children, were in full rebellion. The transcendental doctors imagined that they possessed concerning everything deep significations, mystical secrets, analogous to the gift of tongues and the discerning of spirits. Those who were honoured with these supernatural gifts despised the elders and aspired to replace them. Corinth had a respectable presbyteriate, but one which never aimed at an exalted mysticism. The illuminati pretended to throw it into the shade, and to put themselves into its place; some of the elders were even deprived. The struggle of the established hierarchy and of personal relations began, and the conflict filled all the history of the Church, the privileged soul finding it wrong that, in spite of the favours with which he had been honoured, a homely clergy, strangers to the spiritual life, should govern it officially. Not without a certain likeness to Protestantism, the rebels of Corinth formed themselves into a separate Church, or at least distributed the Eucharist in other than consecrated places. The Eucharist had always been a stumbling block to the Church of Corinth. That Church had its rich and its poor; it accommodated itself with especial difficulty to the mystery of equality. At last the innovators, proud to excess of their exalted virtue, raised chastity to the point of depreciating marriage. This was, as will be seen, the heresy of individual mysticism maintaining the rights of the spirit against authority, pretending to raise itself above the level of the faithful, and of the ordinary clergy, in the name of its direct relations with the Divinity.

The Roman Church, consulted on these internal troubles, answered with admirable good sense. The Roman Church was then above all things the Church of order, of subordination, of rule. Its fundamental principle was that humility and submission were of more value than the most sublime of gifts. The Epistle addressed to the Church of Corinth was anonymous, but one of the most ancient traditions has it that Clement's was the pen which wrote it. Three of the most considerable of the elders--Claudius Ephebus, Valerius Biton, and Fortunatus--were charged to carry the letter, and received full powers from the Church at Rome to bring about a reconciliation.

The Church of God Abiding in Rome to the Church of God in Corinth, to the Elect sanctified by the will of God and of our Lord Jesus Christ, grace and peace be upon you in abundance from God Almighty by Jesus Christ.

The misfortunes, the unforeseen catastrophes which have fallen upon us, blow upon blow, have, brethren, been the reason that we occupied ourselves but slowly with the questions which you have addressed to us, dear brethren, touching the impious and detestable revolt, cursed of the elect of God, which a small number of insolent and daring persons have raised up and carried to such a point of extravagance, that your name so famous, so venerable, and so beloved of all, has suffered great injury. Who was he who having lived among you did not esteem your virtue and the firmness of your faith? Who did not admire the wisdom and the Christian moderation of your piety? Who did not publish the largeness of your hospitality? Who did not esteem you happy in the perfection and soundness of your knowledge? You did all things without acceptation of persons, and you walked according to the laws of God, obedient to your leaders. You rendered due honour to the elders, you warned the young men to be grave and sober, and the women to act in all things with a pure and chaste conscience, loving their husbands as they ought to do, dwelling in the rule of submission, applying themselves to the government of their houses with great modesty.

You were all humble-minded, free from boastings, disposed rather to submit yourselves than to cause others to submit to you, to give than to receive. Content with the sacraments of Christ, and applying yourselves carefully to his word, you kept it in your hearts, and had always his sufferings before your eyes. Thus you rejoiced in the sweetness of a profound peace; you had an insatiable desire to do good, and the Holy Ghost was fully poured out upon you. Fitted with good-will, with zeal, and with an holy confidence, you stretched forth your hands towards Almighty God, praying for pardon for your involuntary sins. You strove day and night for all the community, so that the number of the elect of God was saved by the force of piety and of conscience. You were sincere and innocent, without resentment of injuries. All rebellion, all divisions you held in horror. You wept over the fall of your neighbours; you esteemed their faults as your own. A virtuous and respectable life was your adornment, and you did all things in the fear of God; his commandments were written upon the tables of your hearts, you were in glory and abundance, and in you was accomplished that which was written:--"The well-beloved hath eaten and drunk; he has been in abundance; he has waxed fat and kicked." (Deut. xxxii. 15.) Hence have come jealousies and hatred disputes and sedition, persecution and disorder, war and captivity. Thus the vilest persons have been raised above the most worthy; the foolish against the wise; the young against the old. Thus justice and peace have been driven away; since the fear of God has fallen off, since the faith is darkened, since all will not follow the laws, nor govern themselves according to the maxims of Jesus Christ, but follow their own evil desires, abandoning themselves to unjust and impious jealousies, by which death first came into the world.

After having quoted many sad examples of jealousy, taken from the Old Testament, he adds:--

But let us leave here these ancient examples and come to the strong men who have lately fought. Let us take the illustrious examples of our own generation. It was through jealousies and discord that the great men who were the pillars of the Church have been persecuted, and have fought to the death. Let us place before our eyes the holy Apostles, Peter, for example, who, through an unjust jealousy suffered not once or twice but many times, and who, having thus accomplished his martyrdom, has gone to the place of glory which was due to him. It was through jealousy and discord that Paul has shown how far patience can be carried; seven times in chains, banished, stoned, and after having been the herald of the Truth in the east and in the west, he has received the noble reward of his faith, after having taught justice to the whole world and being come to the very extremity of west. Having thus accomplished his martyrdom before the earthly power, he was delivered from this world, and has gone to that holy place, giving to all of us a great example of patience. To those men whose life has been holy has been joined a great company of the elect, who, always through jealousy, have endured many insults and torments, leaving amongst us an illustrious example. It was finally pursued by jealousy that the poor women, the Danaides and the Dirces, after having suffered terrible and monstrous indignities, have reached the goal in the sacred course of faith, and have received a noble recompense, feeble in body though they were.

Order and obedience are the supreme law of the Church.

It is better to displease imprudent and senseless men who raise themselves up and who glorify themselves through pride in their discourses, than to displease God. Let us respect our superiors, honour the elders, instruct the young in the fear of God, chasten our wives for their good. Let the amiable habit of chastity display itself in their conduct let them show a simple and true gentleness; let them show by their silence that they know how to rule their tongues,--that, instead of allowing their hearts to be carried away by their inclinations, they testify with holiness to an equal friendship for all who fear God. . . . Let us consider the soldiers who serve under our sovereigns; with what order, what punctuality, what submission do they obey. All are not prefects, nor tribunes, nor centurions, but each in his rank obeys the orders of the Emperor and of the chiefs. The great cannot exist without the small, nor the small without the great. In everything there is a mixture of diverse elements, and it is because of that mixture that things go on. Let us take our bodies for an example. The head without the feet is nothing; the feet are nothing without the head. The smallest of our organs are necessary, and serve the whole body; all work together and obey one same principle of subordination for the preservation of all. Let each then submit to his neighbour according to the order in which he has been placed by the grace of Christ Jesus. Let not the strong neglect the weak, let the weak respect the strong; let the rich be generous to the poor, and the poor thank God for having given him one to supply his needs. Let the wise man show his wisdom not by discourses, but by good works; let not the humble bear witness to himself, let him leave that care to others. Let him who preserves the purity of the flesh not exalt himself therefore, seeing that he has from another the gift of continence.

The Divine Service ought to be celebrated in the places and at the hours fixed by the ordained ministers, as in the Temple of Jerusalem. All power, all ecclesiastical rule, comes from God.

The Apostles have evangelised us on the part of our Lord Jesus Christ, and Jesus Christ had received his mission from God. Christ has been sent by God, and the Apostles have been sent by Christ. The two things have then been regularly done by the will of God. Provided with instruction from the Master, persuaded by the resurrection of our Lord Jesus Christ, strengthened in the faith in the Word of God by the confirmation of the Holy Ghost, the Apostles went out preaching the approach of the Kingdom of God. Preaching thus alike in the country and in the cities, they chose those who had been the first-fruits of their apostolate, and after having proved them by the Spirit, established them Episcopi and Diaconi of those who believe. And this was no novelty, for the Scripture had long spoken of Episcopi and Diaconi, since it saith in one place, "I will establish their Episcopi on the foundations of justice and their Diaconi on the bases of faith" (Isa. lx. 17). Our Apostles, enlightened by our Lord Jesus Christ, knew perfectly that there would be competition for the title of Episcopos. This is why they conferred that title in their perfect prescience on those whom we have named and prescribed, that after their death other approved men should assume their functions. These then who have been established by the Apostles or afterwards by other excellent men with the consent of all the Church, and who have served the flock of Jesus Christ without reproach, humbly, peaceably, honourably, to whom all have borne good testimony during a long time, we do not think it just to cast out of the ministry, for we could not without grave fault eject from the Episcopate those who worthily present the sacred offerings. Happy are the elders who have finished their career before us and are dead in holiness, and with fruit ! They at least have no fear lest any should come and drive them from the place to which they have been called. We see, in a word, that you have deprived some who lived well in the ministry, of which office they acquitted themselves without reproach and with honour.

Have we not the same God, the same Christ, the same Spirit of Grace poured out upon us? Why shall we tear away, why shall we cut off, the members of Christ? Why should we make war upon our own body, and come to such a point of madness as to forget that we are all members one of another? Your schism has driven away many persons, it has discouraged others, it has cast certain into doubt, and afflicted all of us; nevertheless, your rebellion continues. Take the Epistle of the blessed Paul the Apostle. What is the first thing of which he writes to you at the beginning of his Gospel? Certainly the Spirit of Truth dictated to him what he commanded you touching Cephas, Apollos, and himself. Then there were divisions amongst you, but those divisions were less guilty than the divisions of to-day. Your choice was divided amongst authorised Apostles and a man whom they had approved. Now consider who are those who have led you astray, and have injured that reputation for fraternal love for which you were venerated. It is shameful, my beloved, it is very shameful and unworthy of Christian piety to hear it said that that Church of Corinth, so firm, so ancient, is in revolt against its elders because of one or two persons. And this report has come not only to us, but to those who hold us in but little goodwill, so that the name of the Lord is blasphemed through your imprudence, and you create perils for yourselves. . . Such a faithful one is specially gifted to explain the secrets of the gnose (tongues); he has the wisdom to discern the discourse; he is pure in his actions, let him humiliate himself so that he may be greater, let him seek the common good before his own.

The best thing the authors of these troubles can do is to go away.

Is there amongst you anyone who is generous, tender, and charitable, let him say, "If I am the cause of the rebellion, the quarrel, the schisms, I will retire, I will go where you will, I will do what the majority order, I ask only one thing, which is, that the flock of Christ may be at peace with the elders who have been established." He who will thus use himself will acquire a great glory in the Lord, and will be made welcome wherever he may go. "The earth is the Lord's and all that therein is." See what they have done, and what they yet will do, who do the will of God, which never leads to repentance.

Kings and pagan chiefs have braved death in time of pestilence, to save their fellow-citizens; others have exiled themselves to put an end to civil war. "We know that many amongst us have delivered themselves to chains, that they might deliver others." If those who have caused the revolt recognise their errors, it is not to us, it is to God, to whom they will yield. All ought to receive with joy the correction of the Church.

You then who have begun the rebellion, submit yourselves to the elders, and receive the correction in the spirit of penitence, bending the knees of your hearth. Learn to submit yourselves, renouncing the vain and insolent boldness of your tongues; for it is better that you should be small but esteemed in the flock of Christ, than that you should keep up the appearance of superiority, and be deprived of your hopes in Christ.

The submission which is due to the bishops and elders, the Christian owes to the powers of the earth. At the moment of the most diabolical atrocities of Nero, we heard Paul and Peter declare that the power of this monster came from God. Clement, in the very days when Domitian was guilty of the greatest cruelties against the Church, and against the human race, held him equally as being the lieutenant of God. In a prayer which he addresses to God, he thus expresses himself:--

It is thou, supreme Master, who by thy great and unspeakable power hast given to our sovereigns and to those who govern us upon earth the power of royalty. Knowing the glory and the honour which thou hast distributed to them, we submit ourselves to them, thus avoiding placing ourselves in contradiction with thy will. Give to them, O Lord, health, peace, concord, stability, that they may exercise without hindrance the sovereignty which thou has confided to them. For it is thou, Heavenly Master, King of the Worlds, who hast given to the children of men the glory, and the honour, and the power over all that there is on the surface of the earth. Direct, O Lord! their wills for good, and according to that which is pleasing to thee, so that exercising in peace, with gentleness and piety, the power which thou has given, they may find thee propitious.

Such is this document, a remarkable monument of the practical wisdom of the Church of Rome, of its profound policy, of its spirit of government. Peter and Paul are there more and more reconciled; both are right; the dispute about Law and works is pacified; the vague expressions "our apostles," "our pillars," mask the memory of past struggles. Although a warm admirer of Paul, the author is profoundly a Jew. Jesus for him is simply "the child beloved of God;" "the great High Priest," "the chief of Christians." Far from breaking with Judaism, he preserves in its integrity the privilege of Israel; only a new chosen people amongst the Gentiles is joined with Israel. All the antique prescriptions preserve their force, even though they have ceased to bear their original meaning. Whilst Paul abrogates, Clement preserves and transforms. What he desires above all things is concord, uniformity, rule, order in the Church as in nature, and in the Roman Empire. Let everyone obey in his rank: this is the order of the world. The small cannot exist without the great, nor the great without the small; the life of the body is the result of the common action of all the members. Obedience is then the summing-up, the synonym of the word duty. The inequality of men, the subordination of one to the other, is the law of God.

The history of the ecclesiastical hierarchy is the history of a triple abdication, the community of the faithful remitting first all its powers to the hands of the elders or presbyteri; the presbyteral body joining in a single personage, who is the episcopos; then the episcopi effacing themselves in the presence of one of them, who is pope. This last process, if we may so describe it, was effected only in our own days. The creation of the Episcopate is the work of the second century. The absorption of the Church by the presbyteri was accomplished before the end of the first. In the Epistle of Clement of Rome it is not yet the episcopate, it is the presbytery, which is in question. Not a trace of a presbyteros superior to his fellows is to be found. But the author proclaims aloud that the presbyteriate, the clergy, are before the people. The Apostles, in establishing Churches, have chosen, by the inspiration of the Spirit, "the bishops and deacons of future believers." The powers emanating from the Apostles have been transmitted by a regular succession. No Church has a right to deprive its elders. The privilege of riches counts for nothing in the Church. In the same way, those who are favoured with mystical gifts ought to be the most submissive.

The great problem is approached: who form the Church? Is it the people? or the clergy? or the inspired? The question had already been asked in the time of St Paul, who solved it in the right way by mutual charity. Our Epistle defines the question in a purely Catholic sense. The apostolic title is everything; the right of the people is reduced to nothing. It may then be said that Catholicism had its origin in Rome, since the Church of Rome traced out its first rule. Precedence does not belong to spiritual gifts, to science, to distinction; it belongs to the hierarchy, to the powers transmitted by the channel of canonical ordination, which stretches back to the apostolate in an unbroken chain. We feel that a free Church such as Jesus had conceived, and as St Paul still admitted, was an anarchical utopia, which could not be looked for in the future. With gospel liberty there would have been disorder: it was not seen that with the hierarchy would come uniformity and death.

From the literary point of view the Epistle of Clement is somewhat weak and soft. It is the first monument of that prolix style, charged with superlatives, smelling of the preacher, which to this day remains that of the Papal Bulls. The imitation of St Paul is palpable; the author is governed by his memories of the sacred Scriptures. Almost every line contains an allusion to the writings of the Old Testament. Clement shows himself singularly pre-occupied with the new Bible, which is in course of formation. The Epistle to the Hebrews, which was a sort of inheritance of the Church of Rome, evidently formed his habitual reading; we may say the same of the other great Epistles of St Paul. His allusions to the Gospel texts appear to be divided between Matthew, Mark, and Luke; we might almost say that he had the same Gospel matter as we, but distributed without doubt otherwise than as we have it. The allusions to the Epistles of James and Peter are doubtful. But the allusions to the Jewish apocryphas, to which Clement accords the same authority as to the writings of the Old Testament, are striking: Judith an apocrypha of Ezekiel, the assumption of Moses, perhaps also the prayer of Manasseh. Like the Apostle Jude, Clement admitted into the Bible all those recent products of Jewish imagination or passion, inferior though they are to the old Hebrew literature, but more fitted than this last of pleasing at the time, by their tone of pathetic eloquence and of lively piety.

The Epistle of Clement attained besides the object for which it had been written. Order was re-established in the Church of Corinth. The lofty pretensions of the spiritual doctors were abated. Such was the ardent faith of these little conventicles, that they submitted to the greatest humiliations rather than quit the Church. But the work had a success which extended far beyond the limits of the Church of Corinth. There has been no writing more imitated, more quoted. Polycarpus, or the author of the Epistle attributed to him, the author of the apocryphal Epistles of Ignatius, the author of the fragment falsely called the Second Epistle of Clement, borrow from it as from a document known almost by heart. The treatise was read in the Churches like inspired Scripture. It took its place amongst the additions to the Canon of the New Testament. In one of the most ancient manuscripts of the Bible (the Codex Alexandrinus), it is found at the end of the books of the new alliance, and as one of them.

The trace left at Rome by Bishop Clement was profound from the most ancient times; a Church consecrated his memory in the valley between the Coelius and the Esquiline, in the district where, according to tradition, the paternal house was placed, and where others, through a feeling of secular hesitation, wished to recall the memory of Flavius Clemens. We shall see him later become the hero of a surprising romance, very popular in Rome, and entitled "the Recognitions," because his father, his mother, and his brothers, bewailed as dead, are found again, and recognise each other. With him was associated a certain Grapte, charged together with him with the government and teaching of widows and orphans. In the half light in which he remains enveloped, and, as it were, lost in the luminous haze of a fine historic distance, Clement is one of the great figures of nascent Christianity. Some vague rays come only out of the mystery which surrounds him; one might call him a saint's head in an old half-effaced fresco of Giotto, still recognisable by its golden aureole and by some vague tints of a pure and gentle light.

CHAPTER XVI

END OF THE FLAVII--NERVA--RECRUDESCENCE OF THE APOCALYPSES

The death of Domitian followed closely upon that of Flavius and the persecution of the Christians. There were between these events relations which are hardly to be explained. "He had been able," says Juvenal, "to deprive Rome with impunity of her most illustrious souls, without anyone arming himself to avenge them, but he perished when he became terrible to the cobblers. Behold what lost a man stained with the blood of the Lamia!" It seems probable that Domitilla and Flavius Clemens entered into the plot. Domitilla may have been recalled from Pandataria in the last months of Domitian. There was, however, a general conspiracy around the monster. Domitian felt it, and, like all egotists, he was very exigent as to the fidelity of others. He caused Epaphroditus to be put to death for having helped Nero to kill himself, in order to show what crime the freedman commits who raises his hand against his master, even with a good intention. Domitia his wife, all the people of his household, trembled, and resolved to anticipate the blow which threatened them. With them was associated Stephanus, a freedman of Domitilla, and steward of her household. As he was very robust, he offered himself for the attack, body to body. On the 18th September, towards eleven o'clock in the morning, Stephanus, with his arm in a sling, presented himself to hand to the Emperor a memorial on a conspiracy which he pretended to have discovered. The chamberlain Parthenius, who was in the plot, admitted him, and closed the door. Whilst Domitian read with attention, Stephanus drew a dagger from his bandage and stabbed him in the groin. Domitian had time to cry to the little page who attended to the altar of the Lares to give him the sword which was under his pillow and to call for help. The boy ran to the bed's head, but found only the hilt. Parthenius had foreseen all, and had closed up the ways of escape. The struggle was sufficiently long. Domitian sought to draw the dagger from the wound, and then with his fingers half cut off he tore at the eyes of the murderer, and succeeded in throwing him to the ground and placing himself upon him. Parthenius then caused the other conspirators to enter, who finished off the wretch. It was time; the guards arrived an instant later, and slew Stephanus.

The soldiers, whom Domitian had covered with shame but whose pay he had increased, wished to avenge him, and proclaimed him Divus. The senate was sufficiently strong to prevent this last ignominy. It caused all his statues to be broken or melted, his name to be effaced from the inscriptions, and his triumphal arches to be thrown down. It was ordered that he should be buried like a gladiator; but his nurse succeeded in carrying away his corpse, and in secretly uniting his ashes to those of the other members of his family in the temple of the gens Flavia.

This house, raised up by the chance of the revolutions to such strange destinies, fell thenceforward into great discredit. The persons of merit and virtue whom it yet contained were forgotten. The proud aristocracy, honest and of high nobility, who were about to reign could only feel the profoundest aversion for the relics of a middle-class family whose last chief had been the object of their just execration. During the whole of the second century nothing is heard of any Flavius. Flavia Domitilla ended her life in obscurity. It is not known what became of her two sons, whom Domitian had intended for the Empire. One indication leads to the belief that the posterity of Domitilla continued until the end of the third century. That house always preserved, it would appear, an attachment to Christianity. Its family sepulchre, situated on the Via Ardeatina, became one of the most ancient Christian catacombs. It is distinguished from all the others by its spacious approaches; its vestibule in the classical style, fully open to the public road; the size of its principal hall, destined for the reception of the sarcophagi; the elegance and the altogether profane character of the decorative paintings on the vault of this hall. if one holds to the frontispiece, everything recalls Pompeii, or, still better, the Villa of Livy, ad gallinas albas, in the Flaminian Way. In proportion as one descends the underground temple (hypogea) the aspect grows more and more Christian. It is then quite conceivable that this beautiful sepulchre may have received its first consecration from Domitilla, whose family must have been in a great part Christian. In the third century the approaches were enlarged and a collegiate schola was constructed, designed probably for agapes or sacred feasts.

The circumstances which brought the old Nerva to the Empire are obscure. The conspirators who killed the tyrant had, without doubt, a preponderating share in the choice. A reaction against the abominations of the preceding reign was inevitable; the conspirators, however, having taken part in the principal events of the reign, did not want too strong a reaction. Nerva was an excellent man, but reserved, timid, and carrying the taste for half measures almost to excess. The army desired the punishment of the murderers of Domitian; the honest party in the Senate wished for the punishment of those who had been the ministers of the crimes of the last government. Dragged about between these opposing requirements, Nerva often appeared weak. One day at his table were found united the illustrious Junius Mauricius, who had risked his life for liberty, and the ignoble Veientus, one of the men who had done the greatest evil under Domitian. The conversation fell upon Catullus Messalinus, the most abhorred of the informers:--"What would this Catullus do if he were alive?" said Nerva. "Faith," cried Mauricius, at the end of his patience, "he would dine with us."

All the good that could be done without breaking with the evil, Nerva did. Progress was never loved more sincerely; a remarkable spirit of humanity, of gentleness, entered into the government and even into the legislation. The Senate regained its authority. Men of sense thought the problem of the times, the alliance of the aristocracy with liberty, definitely resolved. The mania for religious persecution, which had been one of the saddest features of the reign of Domitian, absolutely disappeared. Nerva caused those who were under the weight of accusations of this kind to be absolved, and recalled the banished. It was forbidden to prosecute anyone for the mere practice of Jewish customs; prosecutions for impiety were suppressed; the informers were punished. The fiscus judaicus, as we have seen, afforded scope for much injustice. People who did not owe it were made to pay; in order to ascertain the quality of persons liable to it, they were subjected to disgusting inquiries. Measures were taken to prevent the revival of similar abuses, and a special coinage (FISCI IVDAICI CALVMNIA SVBLATA) recalled the memory of that measure.

All the families of Israel thus enjoyed a relative calm after a cruel storm. They breathed. For some years the Church of Rome was more happy and more flourishing than she had ever been. The apocalyptic ideas resumed their course; it was believed that God had fixed the time of his coming upon earth for the moment when the number of the elect reached a certain figure; every day they rejoiced to see that number increase. The belief in the return of Nero had not disappeared. Nero, if he had lived, would have been sixty, which was a great age for the part which was destined for him; but the imagination reasons little; besides Nero, the Antichrist became day by day a more ideal personage, placed altogether without the conditions of the natural life. For a long time people continued to speak of his return, even when it was obvious that he could no longer be alive.

The Jews were more ardent and more sombre than ever. It appears that it was a law of religious conscience with this people to pour forth in each of the great crises which tore the Roman Empire one of those allegorical compositions in which the rein was given to prognostications of the future. The situation of the year 97 in many ways resembled that of the year 68. Natural prodigies appeared to multiply. The fall of the Flavii made almost as much impression as the disappearance of the house of Julius. The Jews believed that the existence of the Empire was again in question. The two catastrophes had been preceded by sanguinary madnesses, and were followed by civil troubles, which caused doubts as to the vital powers of a state so agitated. During this eclipse of the Roman power, the imagination of the Messianists again took the field; the eccentric speculations as to the end of the Empire and the end of time resumed their course.

The Apocalypse of the reign of Nerva appeared, according to the custom of compositions of this kind, under a fictitious name, that of Esdras. This writer began by becoming very celebrated. An exaggerated part was attributed to him in the reconstitution of the sacred books. The forger for his purpose wanted besides a personage who had been contemporary with a situation of the Jewish people analogous to that through which they were passing. The work appears to have been originally written in that Greek full of Hebraisms which had already been the language of the Apocalypse of John. The original is lost, but from the Greek text translations were made into Latin, Syriac, Armenian, Ethopian, and Arabic which have preserved to us this precious document, and have allowed us to restore its first state. It is a sufficiently fine piece of writing, of a truly Hebrew taste, composed by a Pharisee probably at Rome. Christians read it with avidity, and it was unnecessary to do more than retouch one or two passages to turn it into a very edifying Christian book.

The author may in many ways be considered the last prophet of Israel. The work is divided into seven sections, for the most part affecting the form of a dialogue between Esdras, a supposed exile to Babylon, and the angel Uriel; but it is easy to see behind the biblical personage the ardent Jew of the Flavian epoch, full of rage because of the destruction of the Temple by Titus. The memory of these dark days of the year 70 rises in his soul like the smoke of the pit, and fills it with holy wrath. How far are we, with this fiery zealot, from a Josephus who treats the defenders of Jerusalem as scoundrels? Here is a veritable Jew who is sorry not to have been with those who perished in the fire of the Temple. The Revolution of Judea, according to him, was not an insanity. Those who defended Jerusalem to the uttermost, those assassins whom the moderates sacrificed and regarded as alone responsible for the misfortunes of the nations--those assassins were saints. Their fate was enviable; they will be the great men of the future.

Never did Israelite, more pious, more penetrated with the sufferings of Zion, pour out his prayers and tears before Jehovah. A profound doubt, the great doubt of the Jews, rent him,--the same which devoured the Psalmist when he "saw the ungodly in prosperity." Israel are the chosen people. God has promised happiness to them if they observe the Law. Without having fulfilled that condition in all its rigour, what would be beyond human strength, Israel is better than other nations. In any case, he has never observed the Law more scrupulously than in these last times. Why, then, is Israel the most unfortunate of peoples; and more just he is the more unfortunate? The author sees clearly that the old materialistic solutions of this problem cannot be accepted. Thus is his soul troubled even to death.

Lord, Master Universal, he cries, of all the forests of the earth, and of all the trees that are found therein, thou hast chosen a vine; of all the countries of the world, thou hast chosen a province; of all the flowers of the world, thou hast chosen a lily; of all the wilderness of water, thou host chosen a brook; amongst all the cities, thou hast sanctified Sion; of all the birds, thou hast dedicated a dove to thyself; and of all created beasts, thou wouldest take only a lamb for thyself. thus out of all the people on the face of the earth thou hast adopted one only, and to that beloved people thou hast given a Law which all admire. And now, Lord, what has he done that thou shouldest deliver thine only One to profanation, that upon the root of thy choice thou hast grafted other plants, that thou hast dispersed thy dear ones in the midst of the nations. those who deny thee crowd upon the feet of the faithful. If thou hast come to hate thy people, it must be so! But at least punish them with thine own hands, and lay not this task upon the unfaithful.

Thou hast said that it is for us that thou hast created the world; that the other nations born of Adam are in thine eyes but vile spittle (sic). . . . And now, Lord, behold these nations, thus treated as nothing, rule over us and trample us under foot. And we thy people, we whom thou hast called thy first-born, thy only Son, we the objects of thy jealousy, we are delivered unto their hands. If the world has been created for us, why do we not at least possess an heritage? How long, O Lord, how long! . . .

Sion is a desert, Babylon is happy. Is this just? Sion has sinned much. She may have, but is Babylon more innocent? I believed so until I came here, but since I came, what do I see? Such impieties that I marvel that thou bearest them, after having destroyed Sion for so much less iniquity. What nation has known thee save only Israel? What tribe has believed in thee save only that of Jacob? And who has been less rewarded? Amongst the nations I have seen them flourishing and unmindful of thy commandments. Weigh in the balance what we have done, and what they do. Amongst us I confess there are few faithful ones, but amongst them there are none at all. Now they enjoy a profound peace, and we, our life is the life of a fugitive grasshopper; we pass our days in fear and anguish. It had been better for us never to have been born than to be tormented thus without knowing in what our guilt consists. . . . Oh, that we had been burned in the fires of Sion! We are not better than those who perished there!

The angel Uriel, the interlocutor of Esdras, eludes as best he can the inflexible logic of this protestation. The mysteries of God are so profound! The mind of man is so limited! Pressed with questions, Uriel escapes by a Messianic theory like that of the Christians. The Messiah, son of God, but simple man, is on the eve of appearing in Zion in glory, in company with those who have not tasted death, that is to say, with Moses, Enoch, Elias, and Esdras himself. He will recall the ten tribes from the "land of Arzareth" (foreign country). He will fight a great fight against the wicked; after having conquered them, he will reign four hundred years upon the earth with his elect. At the end of that time, the Messiah will die, and all the living will die with him. The world will return to its primitive silence for seven days. Then a new world will appear, and the general resurrection will take place. The Most High will appear upon his throne, and will proceed to a definitive judgment.

The particular turn which Jewish Messianism tended to take, clearly appears here. Instead of an eternal reign, of which the old prophets dreamed, for the posterity of David, and which the Messianists after the pseudo-Daniel transferred to their ideal king, we arrive at the notion of a Messianic kingdom as having a limited duration. We have seen the author of the Christian Apocalypse fix that date at a thousand years. Pseudo-Esdras contents himself with four hundred years. The most diverse opinions were current on that subject amongst the Jews. Pseudo-Baruch, without specifying the limit, says distinctly that the Messianic reign will last only as long as the perishable earth. The judgment of the world from that point of view is distinguished from the advent of the Messianic kingdom, and the presidency is given to the Most High alone and not to the Messiah. Then the conception of the Eternal Messiah inaugurating an endless reign, and judging the world, carries him away altogether, and becomes the essential and distinctive feature of Christianity.

Such a theory raises a question with which we have already seen St Paul and his faithful greatly concerned. In such a conception there is an enormous difference between the fate of those who are alive at the appearance of the Messiah, and those who have died beforehand. Our seer even asks himself a question which is odd enough, but certainly logical:--Why did not God make all men alive at the same time? He gets out of the difficulty by the hypothesis of provisional "depôts" (pronaptuaria) where the souls of departed saints are held in reserve until the judgment. At the great day the depôts will be opened, so that the contemporaries of the appearance of the Messiah shall have only one advantage over the others--that of having enjoyed the reign of four hundred years. In comparison with eternity, that is a very small matter, and the author thinks himself justified in maintaining that there will be no point or privilege,--the first and the last will be all equals in the Day of Judgment. Naturally, the souls of the just, confined in a sort of prison, feel some impatience, and often say: "Until what time is this to continue? When will be the day of the harvest?" The angel Jeromiel answers them, "When the number of those like unto you is complete?" The time is coming. As the bowels of a woman nine months pregnant cannot contain the fruit which they bear, so the depôts of Sheol, too full in some sense, hasten to render up the souls which they contain. The total duration of the universe is divided into twelve parts; ten parts and a half of that period have gone by; The world is approaching its end with an incredible rapidity. The human race is decaying fast; the stature of man dwindles; like the children born of old parents, our races have no longer the vigour of the earlier ages. "The age has lost its youth, and time begins to grow old."

The signs of the last days are those which we have enumerated twenty times. The trumpet shall sound. The order of Nature will be reversed; blood shall flow from wood, and the stones shall speak. Enoch and Elias will appear to convert man. Men must hasten to die, and are as nothing compared with those that are to come. The more the world is weakened by old age, the more wicked it will become. Truth will withdraw day by day from the earth; good shall seem to be exiled.

The small number of the elect is the dominant thought of our sombre dreamer. The entrance to eternal life is like a narrow strait between two seas, like a narrow and slippery passage which gives access to a city; on the right there is a precipice of fire, on the left a sea without bottom; a single man can scarcely hold himself there. But the sea into which one enters is also immense, and the city is full of every good thing. There is in this world more silver than gold, more copper than silver, more iron than copper. The elect are the gold; the rarer things are, the more precious they are. The elect are the adornments of God; those adornments would be valueless if they were common. God is not grieved by the multitude of those who perish. Unhappy ones! they exist no longer than a puff of smoke or a flame; they are burned, they are dead. We may see how deeply rooted in Judaism the atrocious doctrines of election and of predestination had already become--doctrines which a little later were to cause such cruel tortures to so many devout souls. These frightful severities to which all the schools of thought which deal in damnation are accustomed, at times revolts the pious sentiment of the author. He allows himself to exclaim:--

Oh Earth! what hast thou done in giving birth to so many beings destined to perdition? It had been better had we no existence, rather than that we should exist only to be tortured Let humanity weep! let the beasts of the field rejoice! The condition of these last is better than ours; they do not expect the Judgment; they have no punishment to fear; after death, there is nothing for them. Of what use is life to us, since we owe to it an eternity of torments? Better annihilation than the prospect of judgment.

The Eternal God answers that intelligence has been given to man that he may be without excuse in the Day of Judgment and that he has nothing to reply.

The author plunges more and more deeply into strange questions, which raise formidable dogmas. Can it be that from the moment that one draws his last breath that he is damned and tortured, or will an interval pass, during which the soul is in repose until the Judgment? According to the author, the fate of each man is fixed at death. The wicked, excluded from the place of departed spirits, are in the condition of wandering souls, tormented provisionally with seven punishments, of which the two principal are seeing the happiness enjoyed by those in the asylum of just souls, and to assist in the preparations for the punishment reserved for themselves. The just, guarded in their limbo by angels, enjoy seven joys, of which the most agreeable is that of seeing the sufferings of the wicked, and the tortures which await them. The soul of the author, pitiful at bottom, protests against the monstrosities of his theology. "The just at least," asks Esdras, "may not they pray for the damned,--the son for his father, the brother for his brother, the friend for his friend?" The answer is terrible. "Just as in the present life the father cannot be the substitute for the son, nor the son for the father, the master for his slave, nor the friend for his friend, to be sick, to sleep, to eat, to be cured in his place; so in that day no one can interfere for another, each shall bear his own justice or his own injustice." Esdras adduces in vain the examples of Abraham, and of other holy persons who have prayed for their brethren. The Day of Judgment will be the first of a definite state, where the triumph of justice will be such that the righteous himself cannot pity the damned. Assuredly we agree with the author when he exclaims after these responses, supposed to be divine,

I have already said, and I say again,--"Better were it for us that Adam had not been created upon the earth. At least after having placed him there God should have prevented him from doing evil. What advantage is it for man to pass his life in sadness and in misery, when after his death he can expect nothing else than punishments and torments? Oh, Adam! how enormous was thy crime! By sinning thou didst lose thyself and hast dragged down in thy fall all the men of whom thou went the father. And of what value is immortality to us if we have done only deeds worthy of death?"

Pseudo-Esdras admits liberty; but liberty has but a small right of existence in a system which makes so cardinal a point of predestination. It is for Israel that the world was created; the rest of the human race are damned.

And now, Lord, I pray not for all men (thou knowest better than I what concerns them), but I will entreat thee on behalf of thy people; of thy heritage; of the perpetual source of my tears. . . .

Inquire of the earth and she will tell thee that it is to her that the right of weeping belongs. All those who are born or who will be born come out of the earth; yet almost all of them hasten to destruction, and the greater part of them are destined to perish! . . .

Disquiet not thyself because of the great number of those who must perish, for they also having received liberty have scoffed at the Most High, have rejected his holy law, have trampled his just ones under foot, and have said in their hearts "There is no God." So whilst ye enjoy the rewards that have been promised, they will partake of the thirst and the torments which have been prepared for them. It is not that God hath desired the destruction of men; but the men who are the work of his hands have defiled the name of their Maker, and have been ungrateful to him who has given them life. . . .

I have reserved to myself a grape of the bunch, a plant from the forest. Let the multitude then perish who have been born in vain, if only I may keep my single grape, my plant that I have tended with so much care! . . .

A special vision is designed, as in almost all apocalypses, to give in an enigmatic fashion the philosophy of contemporary history, and as usual also the date of the book may be precisely arrived at from it. An immense eagle (the eagle is the symbol of the Roman Empire in Daniel) extends its wings over all the earth and holds it in its grip. It has six pairs of great wings, four pairs of pinions or opposing wings, and three heads. The six pairs of great wings are six Emperors. The second amongst them reigns for so long that none of those who succeed him reach half the number of his years. This is obviously Augustus; and the six Emperors referred to are the six Emperors of the house of Julius--Cæsar, Augustus, Tiberius, Caligula, Claudius, Nero, masters of the East and of the West. The four pinions or opposing wings are the four usurpers or Anti-Cæsars--Galba, Otho, Vitellius, Nerva, who, according to the author, must not be considered as true Emperors. The reigns of the three first Anti-Cæsars are periods of trouble, during which we may believe that the Empire is at an end; but the Empire rises again, though not as she was at the first. The three heads (the Flavii) represent this new resuscitated Empire. The three heads always act together, make many innovations, surpass the Julii in tyranny, put the topstone to the impieties of the Empire of the Eagle (by the destruction of Jerusalem), and mark the end. The middle head (Vespasian) is the greatest; all the three devour the pinions (Galba, Otho, Vitellius), who aspire to reign. The middle head dies; the two others (Titus and Domitian) reign; but the head on the right devours that on the left (an evident allusion to the popular belief as to the fratricide of Domitian); the head on the right, after having killed the other, is killed in its turn; only the great head dies in its bed; but not without cruel torments (an allusion to the Rabbinical fables as to the maladies by which Vespasian expiated his crimes towards the Jewish nation).

Then comes the turn of the last pair of pinions, that is to say, of Nerva, the usurper, who succeeded, the right hand head (Domitian) and is with regard to Flavius in the same relation as Galba, Otho, and Vitellius were with Julius. The last reign is short and full of trouble; it is less a reign than an arrangement made by God to bring about the end of the world. In fact, after some moments, according to our visionary, the last Anti-Cæsar (Nerva) disappears; the body of the eagle takes fire, and all the earth is stricken with astonishment. The end of the profane world arrives, and the Messiah comes to overwhelm the Roman Empire with the bitterest reproaches.

Thou hast reigned over the world by terror and not by truth; thou hast crushed the poor; thou hast persecuted peaceable people; than hast hated the just; thou hast loved the liars; thou hast broken down the walls of those who have done thee no wrong. Thy violences have gone up before the throne of the Eternal God, and thy pride has reached even unto the Almighty. The Most High hath regarded his table of the times and hast seen that the measure is full and that the moment has arrived. Wherefore thou shall disappear, O Eagle! thou and thy horrible wings and thy accursed pinions, thy perverse heads and thy detestable claws and all thy wicked body, so that the earth may breathe again, may live again, delivered from tyranny, and may begin to hope once more in the justice and mercy of him who has done it.

The Romans will then be judged; judged living, and exterminated on the spot. Then the Jewish people will breathe. God will preserve them in joy until the Day of Judgment.

It will scarcely be doubted after this that the author wrote during the reign of Nerva, a reign which appeared without solidity or future, because of the age and of the weakness of the sovereign, until the adoption of Trajan (end of 97). The author of the Apocalypse of Esdras, like the author of the Apocalypse of John, ignorant of real politics, believes that the Empire which he hates, and the infinite resources of which he does not see, is approaching the end of its career. The authors of the two Revelations, passionately Jewish, clap their hands in advance over the ruin of their enemy. We shall see the same hopes renewed after the reverses of Trajan in Mesopotamia. Always on the look out for the moments of weakness on the part of the Empire, the Jewish party, at the appearance of any black spot on the horizon, break out in advance into shouts of triumph, and applaud, by anticipation. The hope of a Jewish Empire succeeding to the Roman Empire, still filled these burning souls whom the frightful massacres of the year 70 had not crushed. The author of the Apocalypse of Esdras had perhaps in his youth fought in Judea; sometimes he appears to regret that he did not find his death. We see that the fire is not extinct, that it still lives in the ashes, and that before abandoning all hope, Israel will tempt her fortune more than once. The Jewish revolts under Trajan and Adrian will answer to this enthusiastic cry. The extermination of Bether will be required to bring to reason the new generation of revolutionaries who have risen from the ashes of 70.

The fate of the Apocalypse of Esdras was as strange as the work itself. Like the Book of Judith and the discourse upon the Empire of Reason, it was neglected by the Jews, in whose eyes every book written in Greek became at once a foreign book; but immediately upon its appearance it was eagerly adopted by the Christians, and accepted as a book of the Canon of the Old Testament, really written by Esdras. The author of the Epistle attributed to St Barnabas, the author of the apocryphal epistle which is called the Second of Peter, certainly read it. The false Herman appears to imitate its plan, order, use of visions, and turn of dialogue. Clement of Alexandria makes a great show of it. The Greek Church, departing further and further from Judeo-Christianity, abandons it, and allows the original to be lost. The Latin Church is divided. The learned doctors, such as St Jerome, see the apocryphal character of the whole composition, and reject it with disdain, whilst St Ambrose makes more use of it than of no matter what other holy book, and distinguishes it in no way from the revealed Scriptures. Vigilance detects there the germ of its heresy as to the uselessness of prayers for the dead. The Liturgy borrows from it. Roger Bacon quotes it with respect. Christopher Columbus finds in it arguments for the existence of another world. The enthusiasts of the sixteenth century nourish themselves upon it. Antoinette Bourignon, the illuminée, sees in it the most beautiful of the holy books.

In reality, few books have furnished so many elements of Christian theology as this anti-Christian work. Limbo, original sin, the small number of the elect, the eternity of the pains of hell, the punishment by fire, the free choice of God, have there found their crudest expression. If the terrors of death have been greatly aggravated by Christianity, it is upon books like this that the responsibility must rest. The sombre office, so full of grandiose dreams, which the Church recites over the coffins, appears to have been inspired by the visions, or, if you choose, by the nightmares of Esdras. Christian iconography itself, borrowed much from these bizarre pages, in all that relates to the representation of the state of the dead. The Byzantine mosaics, and the miniatures which offer representations of the Last Judgment, seem to be based upon the description which our author gives of the place of departed spirits. From its assertions principally is derived the idea that Esdras recomposed the lost Scriptures. The angel Uriel owes to him his place in Christian art. The addition of this new celestial personage to Michael, Gabriel, and Raphael gives to the four corners of the Throne of God, and consequently to the four cardinal points, their respective guardians. The Council of Trent, whilst excluding from the Latin Canon the book so much admired by the Early Fathers, did not forbid it to be reprinted at the end of the editions of the Vulgate, in a different character.

If anything proves the promptitude with which the false prophecy of Esdras was received by the Christians, it is the use which was made of it in the little treatise of Alexandrian exegesis, imitated from the Epistle to the Hebrews, to which the name of Barnabas was attached from a very early date. The author of this treatise cites the false Esdras as he quotes Daniel, Enoch, and the old prophets. One feature of Esdras is especially striking--the wood from which the blood flows--in which is naturally seen the image of the Cross. Now everything leads us to believe that the treatise attributed to Barnabas was composed, like the Apocalypse of Esdras, in the reign of Nerva. The writer applies, or rather alters to make applicable to his time, a prophecy of Daniel concerning ten reigns (Cæsar, Augustus, Tiberius, Caligula, Claudius, Nero, Galba, Otho, Vespasian, Titus), and a little king (Nerva), who shall humiliate the three (Flavius), reduced to one (Domitian), who have preceded him.

The facility with which the author has been able to adopt the prophecy of the false Esdras, is so much the more singular, since few Christian doctors express as energetically as he the necessity for an absolute separation from Judaism. The Gnostics in this respect have said nothing stronger. The author presents himself to us as an ex-Jew, well versed in the Ritual, the agada, and the rabbinical disquisitions, but strongly opposed to the religion which he has left. Circumcision appears to him to have always been a mistake of the Jews--a misunderstanding into which they have been betrayed by some perverse genius. The Temple itself was a mistake; the worship which was practised in it was almost idolatrous; it rested wholly upon the Pagan idea that God could be shut up in a house. The Temple destroyed through the fault of the Jews, would never be re-erected; the true Temple is that spiritual house which is raised in the hearts of Christians. Judaism, in general, has been only an aberration, the work of a bad angel, who has led the Jews in opposition to the commands of God. What the author fears most is lest the Christian should have only the air of a Jewish proselyte. All has been changed by Jesus, even the Sabbath. The Sabbath formerly represented the end of the world; transplanted to the first day of the week, it represents, by the joy with which it is celebrated, the opening of a new world inaugurated by the resurrection and ascension of Jesus Christ. Sacrifices and the Law are alike at an end. The whole of the Old Testament was but a symbol. The cross of Jesus solves all problems; the author finds it everywhere, by means of bizarre ghematrioth. The Passion of Jesus is the propitiatory sacrifice of which others were merely the image. The taste which Egypt, ancient Egypt and Jewish Egypt, had for allegories, appears to revive in these explanations, wherein it is impossible to see anything besides arbitrary turns. Like all the readers of the apocalypses, the author believed that he was on the eve of the Judgment. The times are evil; Satan has all power over earthly matters; but the day is not far distant when he and his will alike perish. "The Lord is at hand with his recompense."

The scenes of disorder which followed each other from day to day in the Empire gave, moreover, only too much reason for the sombre predictions of the pseudo-Esdras and the pretended Barnabas. The reign of the feeble old man whom all parties had agreed to put into power, in the hours of surprise which followed the death of Domitian, was an agony. The timidity with which he was reproached was really sagacity. Nerva felt that the army always regretted Domitian, and bore only with impatience the domination of the civil element. Honest men were in power, but the reign of honest men, when it is not supported by an army, is always weak. A terrible incident showed the depth of the evil. About the 27th October 97 the Prætorians, having found a leader in Casperius Ælianus, besieged the palace, demanding with loud cries the punishment of those who had slain Domitian. Nerva's somewhat soft temperament was not suited to such scenes. He virtuously offered his own life, but he could not prevent the massacre of Parthenius and of those who had made him Emperor. The day was decisive, and saved the Republic. Nerva, like a wise man, understood that he ought to associate with himself a young captain whose energy should supply what he was deficient in. He had relations, but, attentive only to the good of the state, he sought the worthiest. The Liberal party counted amongst its members an admirable soldier, Trajan, who then commanded upon the Rhine at Cologne. Nerva chose him. This great act of political virtue assured the victory of the Liberals, which had remained always doubtful since the death of Domitian. The true law of Cæsarism, adoption, was found. The military were bridled. Logic required that a Septimus Severus, with his detestable maxim, "Please the soldier; mock at the rest," should succeed Domitian. Thanks to Trajan, the catastrophe of history was adjourned and retarded for a century. The evil was conquered, not for a thousand years, as John believed, nor even for four hundred years, as the pseudo-Esdras dreamed, but for a hundred years--which is much.

CHAPTER XVII

TRAJAN--THE GOOD AND GREAT EMPERORS

The adoption of Trajan assured to civilised humanity after cruel trials a century of happiness. The Empire was saved. The malignant predictions of the apocalypse makers were completely contradicted. The world still desired to live: the Empire, in spite of the fall of the Julii and the Flavii, found in its strong military organisation resources which the superficial provincials never suspected. Trajan, whom the choice of Nerva was to carry to the Imperial throne, was a very great man, a true Roman, master of himself, cool in command, of a grave and dignified bearing. He had certainly less political genius than a Cæsar, an Augustus, a Tiberius, but he was their superior in justice and in goodness, while in military talent, he was the equal of Cæsar. He made no profession of philosophy like Marcus Aurelius, but he equalled him in practical wisdom and benevolence. His firm faith in Liberalism never faltered; he showed, by an illustrious example, that the heroically optimist party which makes us admit that men are good when they are not proved to be bad, may be reconciled with the firmness of a sovereign. Surprising thing! this world of idealogues and of men of opposition, whom the death of Domitian carried into power, knew how to govern. He frankly reconciled himself to the necessity, and it was then seen how excellent a thing is a monarchy made by converted Republicans. The old Virginius Rufus, the great citizen who had dreamed all his life of a Republic, and who did all that he could to get it proclaimed at the death of Nero as it had been at the death of Caligula, Virginius illustrious for having many times refused the Empire, was completely won over, and served as a centre for that distinguished society. The Radical party renounced its dream, and admitted that if the principate and liberty had until then been irreconcilable, the happiness of the times had made such a miracle easy.

Galba had been the first to recognise that combination of apparently contradictory elements. Nerva and Trajan realised it. The Empire with them became Republican, or rather the Emperor was the first and only Republican in the Empire. The great men who are praised in the world which surrounds the sovereign are Thrasea, Helvidius, Senecion, Cato, Brutus, the Greek heroes who expelled the tyrants from their country. Therein lies the explanation of the fact that after the year 98 nothing more is heard of protests against the principate. The philosophers who had been until then in some sort the soul of the Radical opposition, and whose attitude had been so hostile under the Flavii, suddenly held their peace: they were satisfied. Between the new régime and philosophy there was an intimate alliance. It must be said that never in the government of human affairs was to be seen a group of men so worthy to preside. There were Pliny, Tacitus, Virginius Rufus, Junius Mauricus, Gratilla, Fannia, noble men, chaste women, all having been persecuted by Domitian, all lamenting some relation, some friend, victim of the abhorred reign.

The age of monsters had gone by. That haughty race of the Julii, and the families which were allied to them, had unfolded before the world the strangest spectacle of folly, grandeur, and perversity. Henceforward the bitterness of the Roman blood appears exhausted. Rome has sweated away all her malice. It is the peculiarity of an aristocracy which has lived its life without restraint, to become in its old age rigid, orthodox, puritan. The Roman nobility, the most terrible that ever existed, is now distinguished chiefly by refinements, extremes of virtue, delicacy, modesty.

This transformation was in a great measure the work of Greece. The Greek schoolmaster had succeeded in making himself accepted by the Roman noblesse, by dint of submitting to its pride, its coarseness, its contempt for matters of mind. In the time of Julius Cæsar, Sextius, the father, brought from Athens to Rome the proud moral discipline of Stoicism, the examination of conscience, asceticism, abstinence, love of poverty. After him, Sextius, the son, Sohon of Alexandria, Attala, Demetrius the cynic, Metronax, Claranus, Fabianus, Seneca, gave the model of an active and practical philosophy, employing all means--preaching, direction of conscience--for the propagation of virtue. The noble struggle of the philosophers against Nero and Domitian, their banishments, their punishments, had all ended in making them dear to the best Roman society. Their credit continues increasing until the time of Marcus Aurelius, under whom they reigned. The strength of a party is always in proportion to the number of its martyrs. Philosophy had had its own. It, like everything else that was noble, had suffered from the abominable governments under which it had existed; it profited by the moral reaction provoked by the excess of evil. Then arose an idea dear to rhetoricians; the tyrant, born enemy of philosophy; philosophy, the born enemy of tyrants. All the masters of the Antonines are full of this idea; the good Marcus Aurelius passed his youth in declaiming against the tyrants; the horror for Nero and for those Emperors whom Pliny the Elder called "the firebrands of the human race," fills the literature of the time. Trajan had always for philosophers the greatest regard and the most delicate attentions. Between Greek discipline and Roman pride the alliance is henceforward intimate. "To live as beseems a Roman and a man," is the dream of everyone who respects himself; Marcus Aurelius is not yet born, but he is here morally; the spiritual matrix from which he will issue, is completely constructed.

Ancient philosophy assuredly had days of greater originality, but it had never penetrated life and society more deeply. The differences of the schools were almost effaced; general systems were abandoned; a superficial eclecticism, such as men of the world like when they are anxious to do well, was the fashion. The philosophy became oratorical, literary preaching tending more towards moral amelioration than to the satisfaction of curiosity. A host of persons made it their rule and even the law of their exterior life. Musonius Rufus and Artemidorus were true confessors of their faith, heroes of stoical virtue. Euphrates of Tyre offered the ideal of the gentleman philosopher, his person had a great charm, his manners were of the rarest distinction. Dion Chrysostom created a series of lectures akin to sermons, and obtained immense successes, without ever falling short of the most elevated tone. The good Plutarch wrote for the future, Morality in Action, of good sense, of honesty, and imagined that Greek antiquity, gentle and paternal, little resembling the true (which was resplendent with beauty, liberty, and genius), but better suited than the true to the necessities of education. Epictetus himself had the words of eternity, and took his place by the side of Jesus, not upon the golden mountains of Galilee, enlightened by the sun of the kingdom of God, but in the ideal world of perfect virtue. Without a resurrection, without a chimerical Tabor, without a kingdom of God, he preached self-sacrifice, renunciation, abnegation. He was the sublime snow point which humanity contemplates with a sort of terror on its horizon; Jesus had the more lovable part of God amongst men--a smile, gaiety, forgiveness of sins were permitted to him.

Literature, on its side, having become all at once grave and worthy, exhibits an immense progress in the manners of good society. Quintilian already, in the worst days of the reign of Domitian, had laid out the code of oratorical probity which ought to be in such perfect accord with our greatest minds of the seventeenth and eighteenth centuries, Rollin, M.M. de Port Royal. Now literary honesty never goes alone; it is only serious ages that can have a serious literature. Tacitus wrote history with a high aristocratic sense, which did not save him from errors of detail, but which inspired him with those outbursts of virtuous passion which have made of him for all eternity the spectre of tyrants. Suetonius prepared himself, by labours of solid erudition, for his part of exact and impartial biographer. Pliny, a man of good birth, liberal, humane, charitable, refined, founds schools and public libraries; he might be a Frenchman of the most amiable society of the eighteenth century. Juvenal, sincere in declamation, and moral in his painting of vice, has fine accents of humanity, and preserves, notwithstanding the stains on his life, a sentiment of Roman pride. It was like a tardy flowering of the beautiful intellectual culture, created by the collaboration of the Greek and the Italian genius. That culture was already stricken with death at the root; but before dying, it produced a last crop of leaves and flowers.

The world is then at last to be governed by reason. Philosophy will enjoy for a hundred years the right which it is credited with of rendering people happy. A great number of excellent laws, forming the best part of the Roman law, are of this date. Public assistance begins; children are, above all, the object of the solicitude of the State. A real moral sentiment animates the government; never before the eighteenth century was so much done for the amelioration of the condition of the human race. The Emperor is a god accomplishing his journey upon earth, and signalising his passage by benefits.

Such a system must, of course, differ greatly from what we consider as essentially a Liberal government. We should seek vainly for any trace of parliamentary or representative institutions: the state of the world was Incompatible with such things. The opinion of the politicians of the time is that power belongs, by a sort of natural delegation, to honest, sensible, moderate men. That designation was made by the Tatum; when it was once accepted, the Emperor governs the Empire as the ram conducts his troop, and the bull his herd. By the side of this a language altogether Republican. With the best faith in the world these excellent sovereigns thought that they would be able to realise a State founded upon the natural equality of all citizens, a royalty having as its basis respect for liberty. Liberty, justice, respect for opponents, were their fundamental maxims. But these words, borrowed from the history of the Greek Republics, where letters were cultivated, had but little meaning in the real society of the time. Civil equality did not exist. The difference between rich and poor was written in the law, the Roman or Italiote aristocracy preserved all its privileges; the Senate, re-established in its rights and dignity by Nerva, remained as much walled in as it had ever been; the cursus honorum was the exclusive privilege of the nobility. The good Roman families have reconquered their exclusive predominance in politics: outside of them, it does not happen.

The victory of these families was assuredly a just victory, for under the odious reigns of Nero and Domitian they had given an asylum to virtue, to self-respect, to the instinct of reasonable command, to good literary and philosophical education; but these same families, as usually happens, formed a very closely-enclosed world. The advent of Nerva and Trajan, which was the work of an aristocratic, Liberal-Conservative party, put an end to two things--barrack troubles, and the importance of the Orientals, the domestics, and favourites of the Emperors. The freedmen, people of Egypt and Syria, will no longer be able to trouble all that is best in Rome. These wretches, who made themselves masters by their guilty complaisances in the reigns of Caligula, Claudius, and Nero, who had even been the counsellors and the confidants of the debaucheries of Titus before his accession, fell into contempt. The irritation which the Romans felt at the honours decreed to a Herod Agrippa, to a Tiberius Alexander, was not again felt after the fall of Flavius. The Senate increased as much in power; but the action of the provinces was lessened; the attempts to break the ice of the official world were almost reduced to impotence.

Hellenism did not suffer; for it knew by its suppleness or by its high distinction how to make itself acceptable to the best of the Roman world. But Judaism and Christianity suffered for it. We have seen on two occasions in the first century, under Nero and under the Flavii, Jews and Christians approach the house of the Emperor, and exercise considerable influence there. From Nerva to Commodus they were a thousand leagues apart. For one thing, the Jews had no nobility; the worldly Jews, like the Herodians, the Tiberius Alexanders, were dead; every Jew is henceforward a fanatic separated from the rest of the world by an abyss of contempt. A mass of impurities, ineptitudes, absurdities--that is what Mosaism was for the most enlightened men of the time. The Jews appeared to be at the same time superstitious and irreligious; atheists devoted to the most vulgar beliefs. Their religion appeared like a world turned upside down, a defiance of reason, a pledge to contradict in everything the customs of other people. Travestied in a grotesque fashion, their history served a theme for endless pleasantries; it was generally thought to be a form of the worship of Bacchus. "Antiochus," it was said, "tried in vain to improve this detestable race." One accusation especially--that of hating all who were not of them, was murderous, for it was based upon specious motives of a kind to mislead public opinion. Still more dangerous was the idea according to which the proselyte who attached himself to Mosaism learned as his first lesson to despise the gods, to cast off every patriotic sentiment, to forget parents, children, and friends. Their benevolence, it was said, was but egotism; their morality only apparent; amongst them everything is permitted.

Trajan, Adrian, Antonine, Marcus Aurelius, held themselves in this way with regard to Judaism and to Christianity in a sort of haughty isolation. They did not know it; they did not care to study it. Tacitus, who wrote for the great world, speaks of the Jews as an exotic curiosity, totally ignored by those to whom he addresses himself, and his errors are surprising. The exclusive confidence of these noble minds in the Roman discipline rendered them careless of a doctrine which presented itself to them as foreign and absurd. History ought to speak only with respect of honest and courageous politicians who lifted the world out of the mire into which it had been cast by the last Julius and the last Flavius; but they had imperfections which were really the result of their qualities. They were aristocrats, men of traditions, of the race of English Tories, drawing their strength from their very prejudices. They were profoundly Roman. Persuaded that no man who is not rich or well-born can possibly be an honest man, they did not feel for the foreign doctrines that weakness which the Flavii, men of lower birth, could not avoid. Their surroundings, the society which rose into power along with them--Tacitus, Pliny--have the same contempt for the barbarous doctrines. A ditch seems to have been dug during the whole of the second century between Christianity and the special world. The four great and good Emperors are clearly hostile to it, and it is under the monster Commodus that we find once more, as under Claudius, under Nero, and under the Flavii, "Christians of the House of Cæsar." The defects of these virtuous Emperors are those of the Romans themselves,--too much confidence in the Latin tradition, a disagreeable obstinacy in not admitting honour out of Rome, much pride and harshness towards the humble, the poor, foreigners, Syrians, and for all the people whom Augustus disdainfully called "the Greeks," and to whom he permitted adulations forbidden to the Italiots. These outcasts took their revenge, showing that they also have their nobility and are capable of virtue.

The question of liberty is thus raised as it has never been raised before in any of the republics of antiquity. The ancient city, which was only an enlarged family, could have only one religion, that of the city itself; that religion was almost always the worship of mythical founders, of the very idea of the city. When it was not practised, the idea of the city was excluded. Such a religion was logical even when it was intolerant; but Alexander had been unreasonable. Antiochus Epiphanes was so in the highest degree, in wishing to persecute to the profit of a particular religion, since their States resulting from conquest formed various cities whose political existence had been suppressed. Cæsar, with his marvellous lucidity of mind, understood that. Then the narrow idea of the Roman city regained the ascendency, feebly and by short intermissions in the first century, in a manner much followed in the second. Already under Tiberius, a Valerius Maximus, maker of indifferent books, and a dishonest man, preached the religion with an astonishing air of convection. We have seen even Domitian extend a powerful protection to the Latin religion, attempt a sort of union of "the throne and the altar." All that sprang out of a sentiment analogous to that which attaches to the Catholicism of our own days, a host of people who believe very little, but who are convinced that this worship is the religion of France. Martial and Statius, gazetteers of the scandalous chronicle of the times, who at heart regret the fine times of Nero, become grave and religious, applaud the censorship of manners, preach respect for authority. Social and political crises usually have the effect of provoking political reactions of this kind. Society in peril attaches itself where it can. A threatened world ranges itself in order of battle; convinced that every thought turns to evil, becomes timid, holds its breath as it were, since it fears that every movement may overthrow the frail edifice which serves it as shelter.

Trajan and his successors scarcely cared to renew the sad excess of sneaking hypocrisy which characterised the reign of Domitian. Yet these princes and their surroundings showed themselves very Conservative in religion. They saw salvation only in the old Roman spirit. Marcus Aurelius, philosopher though he was, is in no way exempt from superstition. He is a rigid observer of the official religion. The brotherhood of the Salii had no more devout member. He affected to imitate Numa, from whom he claimed to be descended, and maintained with severity the laws which forbade foreign religions. Devotions on the eve of death! The day when one holds most to these memories is the day that in which they go astray. How much injury has accrued to the House of Bourbon through thinking too much of St Louis, and claiming to be descended from Cloris and Charlemagne!

To that strong preference for the national worship was joined, with the great emperors of the second century, the fear of the heteria, coetus illiciti, or associations which might become factions in the cities. A simple body of firemen were suspected. Too many people at a family festivity disquieted the authorities. Trajan required that the invitations should be limited and given by name. Even the associations ad sustinendam tenuiorum inopiam were permitted only in the cities which had special charters for the purpose. In that matter Trajan followed the tradition of all the great Emperors after Cæsar. It is impossible that such measures could have appeared necessary to such great men if they had not been justified in some respects. But the administrative spirit of the second century was carried to excess. Instead of practising public benevolence, as the State had begun to do, how much better it would have been to leave the associations free to exercise it! These associations aspired to spring up in all parts; the State was full of injustice and harshness for them. It wanted peace at any price, but peace, when it is based by authority on the suppression of private effort, is more prejudicial to society than the very troubles of which it is desired to get rid by the sacrifice of all liberty.

In that lies the cause of that phenomenon, in itself so singular, of Christianity being found worse under the wise administration of the great emperors of the second century than under the furious rage with which the scoundrels of the first attacked it. The violences of Nero, of Domitian, lasted only a few weeks or months; they were either passing acts of brutality or else the results of annoyances springing out of a fantastic and shady policy. In the interval which passed between the appearance of Christianity and the accession of Trajan, never once do we find the criminal law put in force against Christians. Legislation on the subject of the illicit colleges already existed in part, but it was never applied with so much rigour as was done later. On the contrary, the very legal but very governmental rule (as we should say nowadays) of the Trajans and the Antonines, will be more oppressive to Christianity than the ferocity and the wickedness of the tyrants. These great Conservatives of things Roman will perceive, not without reason, a serious danger to the Empire in that too firm faith in a kingdom of God which is the inversion of existing society. The theocratic element which underlies Judaism and Christianity alike terrifies them. They see indistinctly but certainly what the Decii, the Aurelians, the Diocletians will see more clearly after them, all the restorers of the Empire failing in the third century,--that a choice must be made between the Empire and the Church,--that full liberty of the Church means the end of the Empire. They struggle as a matter of duty; they allow a harsh law to be applied, since it is the condition of the existence of society in their time. Thus a fair understanding with Christianity was much more remote than under Nero or under Flavius. Public men had felt the danger, and stood on guard. Stoicism had grown more rigid; the world was no longer for tender souls full of feminine sentiments like Virgil. The disciples of Jesus have now to deal with stern men, inflexible doctrinaires, men sure of being right, capable of being systematically harsh, since they can give proof of acting only for the good of the State, and of saying, with an imperturbable gentleness, "What is not useful to the swarm is no more useful to the bee."

Assuredly, according to our ideas, Trajan and Marcus Aurelius would have done better had they been Liberals altogether, had they fully conceded the right of association, of recognising corporations as being capable of holding property; free, in case of schism, to divide the property of the corporation amongst the members, in proportion to the number of adherents to each party. This last point would have been sufficient to get rid of all danger. Already in the third century it is the Empire which maintains the unity of the Church in making it a rule that he shall be regarded as the true bishop of a church in any city who corresponds with the Bishop of Rome, and is recognised by him. What would have happened in the fourth, in the midst of those embittered struggles with Arianism? Numberless and irremediable schisms. The emperors, and then the barbarian kings, alone could put an end to the matter by limiting the question of orthodoxy to "who was the canonical bishop?" Corporations not connected with the State are never very formidable to the State, when the State remains really neutral, does not assume the office of judge of the denominations, and in the legal proceedings before it for the possession of goods, observes the rule of dividing the capital in strict proportion to numbers. Thus all associations which might become dangerous to the peace of the State may readily be dissolved; division will reduce them to dust. The authority of the State alone can cause schisms in bodies of this kind to cease; the neutrality of the State renders them incurable. The Liberal system is the surest solvent of too powerful associations, as has been proved on many occasions. But Trajan and Marcus Aurelius did not know this. Their error in this as in so many other points where we find their legislative work defective, was one which centuries alone could correct.

Permanent persecution by the State. Such, then, is in brief the story of the era which is now opening for Christianity. It has been thought sometimes that there was a special edict in these terms:-- Non licet esse Christianos, which served as basis for all the proceedings against the Christians. It is possible, but it is not necessary, to suppose that there was. Christians were, by the very fact of their existence, in conflict with the laws concerning association. They were guilty of sacrilege, of lèse majesté, of nightly meetings. They could not render to the Emperor the honours which a loyal subject should. Now the crime of lèse majesté was punished with the most cruel tortures: no one accused of the crime was exempt from the torture. And there was that sombre category of flagitia nomini cohærentia, crimes which it was not necessary to prove, which the name of Christian alone was supposed to be sufficient to prove à priori, and which entailed the character of hostis publicus. Such crimes were officially prosecuted. Such, in particular, was the crime of arson, constantly kept in mind by the remembrance of 64, and also by the persistence with which the apocalypses returned to the idea of a final conflagration. To this was joined the constant suspicion of secret infamies, of nightly meetings, of guilty commerce with women, young girls, and children. From thence to judge the Christians capable of every crime and to attribute to them all misdeeds, was but one step, and that step the crowd rather than the magistracy took every day.

When to all this is added the terrible discretion which was left to the judges, especially in the choice of punishment, and it will be understood how, without exceptional laws, without special legislation, it was possible to produce the desolating spectacle which the history of the Roman Empire presents at its best periods. The law may be applied with greater or less rigour, but it is still the law. This condition of things will last like a low and slow fever throughout the second century, with intervals of exasperation and remission in the third. It will end only with the terrible outburst of the first years of the fourth century, and will be definitely closed by the edict of Milan of 313. Every revival of the Roman spirit will be a redoubling of persecution. The emperors who, on divers occasions in the fourth century, undertook to restore the Empire, are the persecutors. The tolerant emperors--Alexander, Severus, Philip--are those who have no Roman blood in their veins, and who sacrifice Latin traditions to the cosmopolitanism of the East.

Venerate the Divine in all things and everywhere, according to the usages of the nation, and force others to honour him. Hate and punish the partisans of foreign ceremonies, not merely out of respect for the gods, but especially because those who introduce new divinities thereby spread the taste for foreign customs, which leads to conjurations, to coalitions to associations, things which agree in no way with the Monarchy. Neither permit any man to profess at atheism or magic. Divination is necessary; let augurs and auspices be officially named, therefore, to whom those who wish to consult them may address themselves, but let there be no free magicians, for such persona, mixing some truths with many lies, may urge the citizens to rebellion. The same thing may be said of many of those who call themselves philosophers; beware of them; they only do mischief to private persons and to the peoples.

It was in such terms that a statesman of the generation which followed the Antonines summed up their religious policy. As in a time nearer to our own, the State thought itself to be displaying immense ability when it made use of superstition as a means of government. The municipalities enjoyed the same right by delegation. Religion was only a simple affair of the police,--a system of absolute isolation, where every movement is repressed, where every individual act is accounted dangerous, where the isolated individual, without a religious bond with other men, is no more than a purely official being, placed between a family reduced to the paltriest proportions and a state too great to be a country, to form the mind, to make the heart beat; such was the ideal which was dreamed of. Everything that was thought capable of affecting men, of producing emotion, was a crime which was to be prevented by death or exile. It was in this way that the Roman Empire killed the antique life, killed the soul, killed science, formed that school of heavy and restricted minds, of narrow politics, which, under the pretence of abolishing superstition, brought about in reality the triumph of theocracy.

A great intellectual decline was the result of these efforts to restore a faith which no one held. A sort of commonplaceness spread itself over beliefs, and took away from them everything that was serious. Free-thinkers, innumerable in the century before and the century after Jesus Christ, diminished in numbers and disappeared. The easy tone of the great Latin literature was lost, and gave place to a heavy credulity. Science extinguished itself from day to day. After the death of Seneca it could hardly be said that there was a single savant who was altogether a rationalist. Pliny the elder is curious, but is no critic. Tacitus, Pliny the younger, Suetonius, avoid all expression of opinion on the inanity of the most ridiculous imagination. Pliny the younger believes in childish ghost stories. Epictetus desires to practise the established religion. Even a writer as frivolous as Apuleius believes himself, when the gods are in question, obliged to take the tone of a rigid Conservative. A single man about the middle of this century appears altogether free from supernatural beliefs--Lucan. The scientific spirit which is the negation of the supernatural, exists no longer save amongst an extremely small number; superstition invades everything, enervates all reason.

Whilst religion was corrupting philosophy, philosophy sought for apparent reconciliations with the supernatural. A foolish and hollow theology, mixed with imposture, came into fashion Apuleius will soon call the philosophers "the priests of all the gods." Alexander of Abonotica will found a religion upon conjuring tricks. Religious quackery, miracle-mongering, relieved by a false varnish of philosophy, became the fashion. Apollonius of Tyana afforded the first example of it, although it would be difficult to say who this singular personage was in reality, It was at a later date that he was imagined to be a religious revealer, a sort of philosophical demi-god. Such was the promptitude of the decadence of the human mind that a wretched theurgist who, in the time of Trajan, would hardly have been accepted by the Gapers of Asia Minor, became a hundred years afterwards, thanks to shameless writers, who used him to amuse a public fallen altogether into credulity, a personage of the first order, a divine incarnation whom they dared to compare with Jesus.

Public instruction obtained from the emperors much more attention than under the Cæsars and even under the Flavii; but there was no question of literature; the grand discipline of the mind which comes especially from science will obtain from these professors but little profit. Philosophy was specially favoured by Antoninus and Marcus Aurelius; but philosophy, which is the supreme object of life, which includes everything else, can scarcely be taught by the State. In any case, that instruction affected the people very little. It was something abstract and elevated, something which passed over their heads, and as, on the other hand, the Temple gave nothing of that moral teaching which the Church has more recently dispensed, the lower classes stagnated in a deplorable condition of abandonment. All this implies no reproach upon the great emperors who did not succeed in the impossible task of saving the ancient civilisation. Time failed them. One evening, after having endured during the day the assault of declaimers who promised him an infinite glory if he converted the world to philosophy, Marcus Aurelius wrote upon his tablets the following reflection, for his own use only:--"The universal cause is a torrent which draws all things with it. How simple are these pretended politicians who imagine that they can manage affairs by the maxims of philosophy. They are children who are babbling still. Do not hope that there will ever be a Republic of Plato; content thyself with small improvements, and if thou succeedest, do not imagine that that will be a small thing. Who can in effect change the inward dispositions of men? And without the change of hearts and of opinions, of what avail is all the rest? Thou wilt never do more than make slaves and hypocrites. The work of philosophy is a simple and a modest thing: far from us be all this pretentious gibberish?" Ah! honest man!

To sum up! Notwithstanding all its defects, society in the second century was making progress. There was intellectual decadence but moral improvement, as appears to be the case in our own days in the upper ranks of French society. The ideas of charity, of assistance to the poor, of disgust at the (gladiatorial) spectacles, increased everywhere. So much did this excellent spirit preside over the destinies of the Empire, that at the death of Marcus Aurelius Christianity seemed to be brought to a standstill It pressed forward, on the contrary, with an irresistible movement when in the third century the noble maxims of the Antonines were forgotten. As we have already said, Nerva, Trajan, Adrian, Antoninus, Marcus Aurelius, prolonged the life of the emperors for a hundred years; we may almost say that they retarded the advance of Christianity for the same time. The progress which Christianity made in the first and in the third centuries was gigantic as compared with that of the second. In the second century, Christianity was confronted by a great force, that of practical philosophy labouring rationally for the amelioration of human society. From the time of Commodus, individual egotism, and what may be called the egotism of the State, left no place for ideal aspirations except in the Church. The Church thus became the asylum of all the heart and soul; shortly after, civil and political life concentrated themselves equally within it.

CHAPTER XVIII

EPHESUS--THE OLD AGE OF JOHN--CERINTHUS--DOCETISM

Doubt, which is never absent from this history, becomes always an opaque cloud when it is a question of Ephesus and of the dark passions which agitated it. We have admitted as probable the traditional opinion, according to which the Apostle John, surviving the majority of the disciples of Jesus, having escaped from the storms of Rome and Judea successively, took refuge in Ephesus, and there lived to an advanced age, surrounded with the respect of all the Churches of Asia. Irenæus, without doubt, on the authority of Polycarp, affirming that the old Apostle lived until the reign of Trajan, appears to us to have even heard him. If these facts are true, they must have had grave consequences. The memory of the punishment which John had escaped at Rome, caused him to be classed amongst the martyrs even during his lifetime, in the same way as his brother James. In connecting the words in which Jesus had announced that the generation which listened to him should not pass away before his appearance in the clouds, with the great age which the only surviving Apostle of Jesus had attained, the logical idea that that disciple should never die was arrived at--that is to say, that he would see the inauguration of the Kingdom of God without first tasting death. John related, or allowed it to be believed, that Jesus after his resurrection had had on that subject an enigmatical conversation with Peter. Hence resulted for John, in his very lifetime, a sort of marvellous halo. Legend began to deal with him even before the grave received him.

The old Apostle, in these last years veiled in mystery, appears to have been much beset. Miracles and even resurrections from the dead were ascribed to him. A circle of disciples gathered around him. What passed in that private coenaculum? What traditions were elaborated there? What stories did the old man tell? Did he not soften in his last days the strong antipathy which he had always shown to the disciples of Paul? In his narratives did he not seek, as happened more than once in the lifetime of Jesus, to ascribe to himself the first place by the side of his Master, to put himself nearest to His heart? Did some of the doctrines which were described later as Johannian begin already to be discussed between the aged and weary master and the young and bright spirits in search of novelties, seeking perhaps to persuade the old man that he had always had on his own account the ideas which they suggested? We do not know; and here is one of the gravest difficulties which encompass the origin of Christianity This time, in effect, it is not only the exaggeration and the uncertainty of the legends of which we have to complain. There was probably in the bosom of that delusive Church of Ephesus a disposition towards dissimulation and pious frauds which has made the task of the critic who is called upon to disentangle such confusion, singularly difficult.

Philo, at about the time when Jesus lived, had developed a philosophy of Judaism, which, although prepared by previous speculations of Israelitish thinkers, took under his pen only a definite form. The basis of that philosophy was a sort of abstract metaphysic, introducing into the one God various hypostases, and snaking of the Divine Reason (in Greek Logos, in Syro-Chaldaic Memera) a sort of distinct principle from the Eternal Father. Egypt and Phoenicia already knew of similar doublings of one same God. The Hermetic Books were later to erect the theology of the hypostases into a philosophy parallel to that of Christianity. Jesus appears to have been left out of these speculations, which, had he known of them, would have had few charms for his poetic imagination and his loving heart. His school, on the contrary, was, so to speak, besieged by it; Apollos was perhaps no stranger to it. St Paul, in the latter part of his life, appears to have allowed himself to be greatly preoccupied with it. The apocalypse gives us the mysterious name of its triumphant Λόγος τοῦ Θεοῦ. Judeo-Christianity, faithful to the spirit of orthodox Judaism, did not allow such ideas to enter their midst, save in the most limited fashion. But when the Churches out of Syria were more and more detached from Judaism, the invasion of the new spirit was accomplished with an irresistible force. Jesus, who at first had been for his hearers only as a prophet, a Son of God, in whom the most exalted had seen the Messiah or that Son of Man whom the pseudo-Daniel had shown as the brilliant centre of future apparitions, became now the Logos, the Reason, the Word of God. Ephesus appears to have been the place where this fashion of regarding the part of Jesus took the deepest root, and from which it spread over the Christian world.

It is not in effect with the Apostle John alone that tradition connects the solemn promulgation of this novel dogma. Around John tradition shows us his doctrine raising storms, troubling consciences, provoking schisms and anathemas. About the time at which we have arrived, there appeared at Ephesus, coming from Alexandria like another Apollos, a man who appears, after a generation, to have had many points of likeness with this last. The man in question was Cerinthus, which others call Merinthas, without its being possible to know what mystery is hidden under that assonance. Like Apollus, Cerinthus was born a Jew, and before becoming acquainted with Christianity had been imbued with the Judeo-Alexandrine philosophy. He embraced the faith of Jesus in a manner altogether different from that of the good Israelites who believed the kingdom of God realised in the Idyll of Nazareth, and of the pious Pagans, whom a secret attraction drew towards that mitigated form of Judaism. His mind, besides, appears to have had little fixity, and to have been willingly carried from one extreme to the other. Sometimes his conceptions approached those of the Ebionites; sometimes they inclined to millenarianism; sometimes they floated in pure gnosticism, or presented an analogy with those of Philo. The creator of the world and the author of the Jewish law--the God of Israel, in short--was not the Eternal Father; he was an angel, a sort of demigod, subordinated to the great and Almighty God. The spirit of this great God, long unknown to the world, has been revealed only in Jesus. The Gospel of Cerinthus was the Gospel of the Hebrews, without doubt translated into Greek. One of the characteristic features of the Gospel was the account of the baptism of Jesus, after which a divine spirit, the spirit of prophecy, at that solemn moment descended upon Jesus, and raised him to a dignity which he had not previously had. Cerinthus thought that even until his baptism Jesus was simply a man, the most just and the most wise of men it is true; by his baptism, the spirit of the omnipotent God came to dwell in him. The mission of Jesus thus become the Christ, was to reveal the Supreme God by his preaching and his miracles; but it was not true in that way of seeing him that the Christ had suffered upon the Cross; before the Passion, the Christ, impassible by nature, separated himself from the man Jesus; he alone was crucified, died and rose again. At other times Cerinthus denied even the Resurrection, and pretended that Jesus would rise again with all the world at the Day of Judgment.

That doctrine, which we have already found at least in germ amongst many of the families of the Ebionim, whose propaganda was carried on beyond the Jordan in Asia, and which in fifty years Narcion and the Gnostics would take up with greater vigour, appeared a frightful scandal to the Christian conscience. In separating from Jesus the fantastic being called Christos, it did nothing less than divide the person of Jesus, carrying off all personality from the most beautiful part of his active life, since the Christ found himself to have been in him only as something foreign and impersonal to him. It was thought indeed that the friends of Jesus, those who had seen and loved him, child, young man, martyr, corpse, would be indignant. The memories presented Jesus to them as amiable as God, from one moment to mother; they wished that he should be adopted and revered altogether. John, it would seem, rejected the doctrines of Cerinthus with wrath. His fidelity to a childish affection might alone excuse certain fanatical traits which are attributed to him, and which, besides, appear to have been not out of keeping with his habitual character. One day on entering the bath at Ephesus, and perceiving Cerinthus, he exclaimed:--"Let us fly; the building will fall in, since Cerinthus, the enemy of the truth, is there!" These violent hatreds produce sectaries. He who loves much, hates much.

On all sides the difficulty of reconciling the two parts of Jesus, of causing to co-exist in the same being the wise man and the Christ, produced imaginations like those which excited the wrath of John. Docetism was, if we may so express it, the heresy of the time. Many could not admit that the Christ had been crucified and laid in the tomb. Some like Cerinthus admitted a sort of intermittance in the divine work of Jesus; others supposed that the body of Jesus had been fantastic, that all his material life, above all, his life of suffering, had been but apparitional. These imaginations came from the opinion, very wide spread at that period, that matter is a fall, a degradation of the spirit; that the material manifestation is the degradation of the idea. The Gospel history is thus volatilised as it were into something impalpable. It is curious that Islamism, which is only a sort of Arab prolongation of Judeo-Christianity, should have adopted this idea about Jesus. At Jerusalem, in particular, the Mussulmans have always denied absolutely that Isa died upon Golgotha; they pretend that someone like him was crucified in his stead. The supposed place of the Ascension upon the Mount of Olives is for the Shaykhs the true Holy Place of Jerusalem connected with Isa, for it is there that the impassible Messiah, born of the sacred breath and not of the flesh, appeared for the last time united to the appearance which he had chosen.

Whatever he may have been, Cerinthus became in the Christian tradition a sort of Simon Magus, a personage almost fabulous, the typical representative of Docetic Christianity, brother of Ebionite and Judeo-Christian Christianity. As Simon Magus was the sworn enemy of Peter, Cerinthus was considered to be the bitter opponent of Paul. He was put on the same footing as Ebion; there was soon a habit of not separating them, and as Ebion was the abstract personification of the Judeo-Christian-speaking Hebrew, Cerinthus became a sort of generic word to designate Judeo-Christianity-speaking Greek. Phrases like the following were coined:--"Who dares to reproach Peter with having admitted Pagans into the Church? Who showered insults upon Paul? Who provoked a sedition against Titus the uncircumcised? It was Ebion: it was Cerinthus"--phrases which, taken literally, cause it to be supposed that Cerinthus had had a part in Jerusalem in the earliest ages of the Church. As Cerinthus has left no writings, the ecclesiastical tradition went on in all that concerned him from one inexactitude to another. In this tissue of contradictions there is not one word of truth. Cerinthus was really the first heretic, the author of a doctrine destined to remain a dead branch in the great tree of the Christian doctrine. In opposing itself to him, in denying his claims, the Christian Church made the greatest step towards the constitution of an orthodox faith.

By these struggles, and these contradictions in effect, Christian theology developed itself. The person of Jesus, and the singular combination of man, and the Divinity that were believed to exist in him, formed the basis of these speculations. We shall see gnosticism come to light in a current of like ideas, and seek in its turn to decompose the unity of the Christ; but the orthodox Church will be steady in repelling such conceptions; the existence of Christianity, founded upon the reality of the personal action of Jesus, was at this price.

John, without doubt, consoled himself for these aberrations, the fruits of a mind strange to the Galilean tradition, by the fidelity and affection with which his disciples surrounded him. In the first rank was a young Asiatic, named Polycarp, who must have been about thirty years of age during the extreme old age of John, and who appears to have been converted to the faith in Christ in his infancy. The extreme respect which he had for the Apostle made him look upon him with the curious eye of youth, in which everything enlarges and transforms itself. The living image of this old man had fixed itself in his mind, and throughout his life he spoke of it as of a glimpse of the Divine world. It was at Smyrna that he was chiefly active, and it is not impossible that he had been selected by John to preside over the already ancient Church in that city, as Irenæus has it.

Thanks to Polycarp, the memory of John remained in Asia, and consequently at Lyons, and amongst the Gauls, a living tradition. Everything that Polycarp said of the Lord, of his doctrine, and of his miracles, connected him as having received it from the eye-witnesses of the Life of Jesus. He was accustomed to express himself thus:--"This I have from the Apostles." . . . "I who have been taught by the Apostles, and who have lived with many of those who have seen the Christ." This way of speaking caused it to be supposed that Polycarp had known other Apostles besides John--Philip, for example. It is, however, more probable that there was some hyperbole here. The expression "the Apostles," without doubt means John, who might besides be accompanied by many unknown Galilean disciples. We may also understand thereby, if we choose, Presbyteros Joannes and Aristion, who, according to certain texts, would have been the immediate disciples of the Lord. As to Caius, Diotrephes, Demetrius, and the pious Cyria whom the Epistles of the Presbyteros present as making part of the Ephesian circle, it would be to risk by dwelling too strongly on these names, discussing beings who, as the Talmud says, "have never been created," and who owe their existence only to the artifices of forgers, or even, like Cyria, to misunderstandings.

Nothing, in short, is more doubtful than everything which relates to this homonym of the Apostle, this Presbyteros Joannes, who only appears near to John in his later years, and who, according to some traditions, succeeded him in the presidency of the Church of Ephesus. His existence, however, seems probable. The title of Presbyteros may be the appellation by which he was distinguished from Apostolos. After the death of the Apostle, he may have long continued to describe himself as Presbyteros, omitting his name. Aristion, whom very ancient information places by the side of the Presbyteros as a traditionist of the highest authority, and who appears to have been claimed by the Church of Smyrna, is also an enigma. All that can be said is that there was at Ephesus a group of men who, towards the end of the first century, gave themselves out as the last eye-witnesses of the Life of Jesus. Papias knew them, or at least came very near to them, and collected their traditions.

We shall see later the publication of a Gospel, of an altogether special character, produced by this little circle, which appears to have obtained the entire confidence of the old Apostle, and which perhaps believed itself authorised to speak in his name. At the period at which we are, and before the death of John, some of his disciples, who appear to have surrounded him, and, as it were, to have monopolised the old age of the last survivor of the Apostles, did they not seek to make use of the rich treasure which he had at their disposal? We may suppose so; we ourselves were formerly inclined that way. We think now that it is more probable that some part of the Gospel which bears the name of John may have been written by himself, or by one of his disciples during his lifetime. But we persist in believing that John had a manner of his own of telling the life of Jesus, a manner very different from the narratives of Batanea, superior in some respects, and in particular the parts of the life of Jesus which were passed in Jerusalem afforded him more room for development. We believe that the Apostle John, whose character appears to have been sufficiently personal, and who, during the life-time of Jesus, aspired with his brother to the first place in the Kingdom of God, gave himself with much simplicity that place in his narrative. If he had read the Gospels of Mark or of Luke, which is quite possible, he must have found that there was not sufficient mention of him, that the importance attributed to him was not so great as he had had. He claimed as is known to have been, the disciple whom Jesus especially loved; he wished that it should be believed that he had played the first part in the Gospel drama. With the vanity of an old man he assumed all the importance, and his long stories have frequently no other object than that of showing that he had been the favourite disciple of Jesus,--that at solemn moments he had rested upon his heart,--that Jesus had confided to him his mother, that in a host of circumstances where the first place had been given to Peter, it really belonged to him--John. His great age gave rise to all kinds of reflections, his longevity passed for a sign from Heaven. As, furthermore, his surroundings were not distinguished by absolute good faith, and as even a little charlatanism may have been mixed up with them, we can imagine what strange productions might spring up in this nest of pious intrigues around an old man whose head might be weak, and who found himself powerless in the hands of those who took care of him.

John continued a strict Jew to the end, observing the Law in all its rigour; it is doubtful whether the transcendental theories which began to be disseminated as to the identity of Jesus with the Logos can ever have been comprehended by him; but, as happens in schools of thought in which the master attains a great age, his school went on without him and outside of him, even whilst pretending to base itself upon him. John appeared fated to be made use of by the authors of fictitious pieces. We have seen how much there was that was suspicious in the origin of the Apocalypse; objections almost equally grave may be made to theories which maintain the authenticity of this singular book, and which declare it apocryphal. What shall be said of that other eccentricity, that a whole branch of the ecclesiastical tradition, the school of Alexandria, has determined not merely that the Apocalypse shall not be John's, but that it belongs to his opponent Cerinthus. We shall find the same equivocations surrounding the second class of Johannian writings which will soon be produced, and one thing only remaining clear--that John cannot have been the author of the two series of works which bear his name. One of the two series, at all events, may possibly be his; but both are certainly not.

There was great emotion on the day which witnessed the death of the Apostle in whom for many years had been summed up the whole Christian tradition, and by whom it was believed that there was still connection with Jesus, and with the beginning of the new word. All the pillars of the Church had disappeared. He whom Jesus, according to the common belief, had promised not to allow to taste of death until he came again, had in turn gone down into the grave. It was a cruel deception, and in order to justify the prophecy of Jesus, it was necessary to have recourse to subtleties. It was not true, said the friends of John, that Jesus had announced that his beloved Apostle should remain alive until his reappearance. He had simply said to Peter, "If I will that he tarry till I come, what is that to thee?" a vague formula which left the field open to all sorts of explanations, and allowed it to be believed that John, like Enoch, Elias, Esdras, were held in reserve until the coming of the Christ. It was now in any case a solemn moment. No one now could say, "I have seen him." Jesus and the first years of the Church of Jerusalem were lost in an obscure past. The importance then passed to those who had known the Apostles, to Mark and to Luke, disciples of Peter and Paul, to the daughters of Philip, who continued his marvellous gifts. Polycarp all his life quoted the connection which he had had with John. Aristion and Presbyteros Johannes lived upon the same memories. To have seen Peter, Andrew, Thomas, Philip became the leading qualification in the eyes of those who wished to know the truth as to the appearances of the Christ. Books, as we have said twenty times, counted for very little; oral tradition was everything. The transmission of the doctrine, and the transmission of apostolic powers, were regarded as part of a kind of delegation, of ordination, of consecration, the primary source of which was the apostolic college. Soon every Church wishes to show the succession of the men who made the chain going back in a right line to the Apostles. Ecclesiastical precedence was regarded as a sort of inoculation with spiritual powers, suffering no interruption. The ideas of the social hierarchy thus made rapid progress; the episcopate consolidated itself from day to day.

The tomb of John was shown at Ephesus ninety years later; it is probable that upon this venerable monument was raised the basilica which afterwards became celebrated, and the site of which appears to have been in the neighbourhood of the present citadel of Aïa Solouk. By the side of the tomb of the Apostle was to be seen in the third century a second tomb, which was also attributed to a person named John, whence resulted great confusion. We shall have to speak of it again.

CHAPTER XIX

LUKE, THE FIRST HISTORIAN OF CHRISTIANITY

With John disappeared the last man of the strange generation which had believed itself to have seen God upon the earth, and had hoped not to die. It was about the same time that that charming book appeared which has preserved to us across the mists of legends the image of the age of gold. Luke, or whoever the author of the third Gospel may have been, undertook that task, which was congenial to his refined soul, to his pure and gentle talents. The prefaces which stand at the head of the third Gospel and at the head of the Acts appear at the first glance to indicate that Luke conceived his work as consisting of two books, one of which contained the Life of Jesus, the other the history of the Apostles as he had known them. There are, however, strong reasons for believing that the compilation of the two works was separated by some interval. The preface to the Gospel does not necessarily imply the intention of composing the Acts. It may be that Luke added this second book to his work only at the end of several years, and at the request of persons with whom the first book had had so much success.

This hypothesis is supported by the part which the author has taken in the first lines of the Acts relative to the ascension of Jesus. In the other Gospels the period of the apparitions of Jesus fades away little by little, without any definite end. The imagination comes to desire a final catastrophe; a definite way of escaping from a state of things which could not continue indefinitely. This myth, the completion of the legend of Jesus, was slowly and painfully evolved. The author of the apocalypse in 69 certainly believed in the Ascension. Jesus, according to him, is carried up into heaven and placed by the throne of God. In the same book the two prophets copied from Jesus, killed like him, rise after three and a half days; after their resurrection, they ascend to heaven in a cloud in the sight of their enemies. Luke, in his Gospel, leaves the matter in suspense, but at the beginning of the Acts he relates, with all desirable accompaniments, the crowning event of the life of Jesus. He knows even how long the life of Jesus lasted beyond the tomb. It was forty days, a remarkable coincidence with the apocalypse of Esdras. Luke at Rome may have been one of the earliest readers of this document, which must have made a profound impression upon him. The spirit of the Acts is the same as that of the third Gospel: gentleness, tolerance, conciliation, sympathy with the humble, aversion from the proud. The author is certainly he who wrote, "Peace to men of good will." We have explained elsewhere the singular distortions which these excellent intentions have made him give to historic accuracy, and how his book is the first document of the mind of the Roman Church, indifferent to facts and dominated in all things by the official tendencies. Luke is the founder of that eternal fiction which is called ecclesiastical history, with its insipidity, its habit of smoothing off all angles, its foolishly sanctified turns. The à priori of a Church always wise, always moderate, is the basis of his narrative. The principal point for him is to show that the disciples of Paul are the disciples not of an intruder but of an apostle like the others who has been in perfect communion with the others. The rest is of small consequence to him. Everything passes as in an idyll. Peter was at heart of Paul's opinion; Paul was of the opinion of Peter. An inspired assembly has seen all the members of the apostolic college united in the same thought. The first Pagan baptism was performed by Peter; Paul, on the other hand, submitted to the legal prescriptions, and observed them publicly at Jerusalem. All frank expression of a decided opinion is repugnant to this prudent narrator. The Jews are treated as false witnesses because they quote an authentic statement of Jesus, and attribute to the Founder of Christianity an intention of bringing about changes in Mosaism. According to the occasion, Christianity is nothing else than Judaism, or else it is quite a different thing. When the Jew bows before Jesus, his privilege is loudly recognised. Luke then has the most unctuous words for these elders of the family who must be reconciled with the younger brothers. But that does not prevent him from insisting complacently on the Pagans who have been converted, or from opposing them to the hardened Jew, uncircumcised of heart. He may see that at bottom his sympathies are with the former. He greatly prefers the Pagans who are Christians in spirit, the centurions who love the Jews, the plebeians who avow their humility. Return to God, faith in Jesus,--these are matters which equalise all differences, extinguish all rivalries. It is the doctrine of Paul set free from those rudenesses which fill the life of the Apostle with bitterness and disgust.

From the point of view of historical value, two parts, absolutely distinct, ought to be made in the Acts, according to which Luke relates the facts of the life of Paul, of which he had personal knowledge, or as he presents to us the accepted theory of his times as to the first years of the Church at Jerusalem. The first years were like a distant mirage, full of illusions. Luke was as ill-placed as possible to understand that world which has disappeared. All that had happened during the years which followed the death of Jesus, was regarded as symbolical and mysterious. Across that deceiving vapour, everything became sacramental. Thus were formed, besides the myth of the Ascension of Jesus, the narrative of the descent of the Holy Ghost, which was connected with the day of the Feast of Pentecost, the exaggerated ideas of the community of goods in the Primitive Church, the terrible legend of Ananias and Sapphira, the fancies which were indulged in as to the altogether hierarchical character of the College of the Twelve, the contradictions as to the gift of tongues, the effect of which was to transform into a public miracle a spiritual phenomenon of the interior of the Churches. All that relates to the institution of the Seven, the conversion of Cornelius, the Council of Jerusalem, and the decrees which are supposed to have been issued from thence by a common consent, arise out of the same tendency. It is now very difficult to discover in these curious pages the truth of the legend or even of the myth. As the desire of finding a Gospel basis for all the dogmas and the institutions which were hatched out every day had encumbered the life of Jesus with fabulous anecdotes, so the desire of finding for these same institutions, for these same dogmas, an apostolic basis, charged the history of the first years of the Church at Jerusalem, with a host of narratives conceived à priori. To write history ad narrandum, non ad probandum, is a feat of disinterested curiosity of which there is no example in the creative periods of the faith.

We have had too many occasions to show in detail the principles which govern the narrative of Luke, to be compelled to revert to them here. The reunion of the two parties into which the Church of Jesus was divided, is its principal object. Rome was the point where that supreme work was accomplished. Clemens Romanus had already preluded it. He had probably never seen either Peter or Paul. His great practical sense showed him that the safety of the Christian Church required the reconciliation of its two founders. Did he inspire St Luke, who appears to have been in communication with him, or did these two pious souls fall spontaneously into agreement as to the direction which it was desirable to give to Christian opinion? We do not know, for want of documents. What we do know is that it was a Roman work. Rome possessed two Churches, one coming from Peter, and one from Paul. To those numerous converts who came to Jesus, some by way of the school of Peter, and others by way of the school of Paul, and who were tempted to cry out, "What! are there then two Christs?" it was necessary to be able to say, "No. Peter and Paul are in perfect agreement. The Christianity of the one is the Christianity of the other." Perhaps a slight colouring was on this account imported into the Gospel legend of the miraculous Draught of Fishes. According to the account of Luke, the nets of Peter were not able to contain the multitude of fishes which were anxious to be captured; Peter is obliged to make signs to his collaborators to come to his aid; a second ship (Paul and his friends) is filled in the same way as the first, and the haul of the kingdom of God is superabundant.

Something analogous to this may be found in what happened about the time of the Revolution, in the party which undertook to restore the worship of the French Revolution. Amongst the heroes of the Revolution, the struggles had been ardent and bitter; there was hatred even to the death. But twenty-five years afterwards nothing remained of all that but a great neutral result. It was forgotten that the Girondins, Danton, Robespierre, had cut off each other's heads. Save for some few and rare exceptions, there were no longer any partisans of the Girondins, of Danton, or of Robespierre; all were partisans of what was considered their common work--that is to say, the Revolution. In the same Pantheon were placed as brethren men who had proscribed each other. In great historical movements there is the moment of exaltation when men associated in view of a common work separate from each other or kill each other for a shade of difference; then comes the moment of reconciliation, when it is sought to prove that these apparent enemies understood each other and laboured for the same end. At the end of a certain time, out of all these disagreements comes forth a single doctrine, and a perfect agreement reigns between the disciples of the men who anathematised each other.

Another essentially Roman feature of Luke, is one which brings him into closer relation with Clement, is his respect for the Imperial authority, and the precautions which he takes not to wound it. We do not find amongst these two writers the bitter hatred of Rome which characterises the authors of the apocalypse and the Sibylline poems. The author of the Acts avoids everything which could present Rome as the enemy of Christianity. On the contrary, he endeavours to show that on many occasions they have defended Paul and the Christians against the Jews. There is never an insulting word for the civil magistrates. If he stops short in his narrative at the arrival of Paul at Rome, it is perhaps because he does not wish to be compelled to relate the monstrosities of Nero. Luke does not admit that the Christians may ever have been legally compromised. If Paul had not appealed to the Emperor, he might have been acquitted. A judicial afterthought in perfect agreement with the era of Trajan preoccupies him: he wishes to create precedents, to show that there is no method of prosecuting those who had been so often acquitted. Bad processes do not repel him. Never have patience and optimism been pushed farther. The taste for persecution, the joy of sufferings endured for the name of Jesus, fill the soul of

Luke, and make his book the manual par excellence of the Christian missionary.

The perfect unity of the book scarcely allows us to decide whether Luke in composing it had under his eyes previously-written documents, or if he was the first to write the history of the Apostles from oral tradition. There were many Acts of the Apostles, just as there were many Gospels; but whilst several Gospels have been retained in the Canon, only a single book of Acts has been preserved. The "Preaching of Peter," the object of which was to present Jerusalem as the source of all Christianity, and Peter as the centre of the Hierosolymitan Christianity, is perhaps as ancient at bottom as the Acts; but Luke certainly did not know it. It is gratuitous also to suppose that Luke revised and completed, in the sense of the reconciliation of the Judeo-Christian with Paul, a more ancient document composed to the greater glory of the Church of Jerusalem and the Twelve. The design of putting Paul on a level with the Twelve, and, above all, to connect Peter and Paul, is manifest in our author; but it appears that he followed in his narrative only the framework of a long-established oral tradition. The chiefs of the Church of Rome appear to have a consecrated manner of relating the apostolic history. Luke conformed to it, adding a sufficiently detailed memoir of Paul, and towards the end some personal recollections. Like all the historians of antiquity, he did not deny himself the use of a little innocent rhetoric. At Rome his Greek education had been completed, and the sentiment of oratorical composition in the Greek manner awoke in him.

The book of the Acts, like the third Gospel written for the Christian society of Rome, remained for a long time confined to it. So long as the Church developed herself by direct tradition and by internal necessities, only a secondary importance was attached to it, but when the decisive argument in the discussions relative to the ecclesiastical organisations was to remount to the primitive Church as to an ideal, the book of the Acts became of the highest authority. It told of the Ascension, the Pentecost, the Coenaculum, the miracles of the apostolic Word, the Council of Jerusalem. The foregone conclusions of Luke imposed themselves upon history; and even to the penetrating observers of the modern criticism, the thirty years which were most fertile in ecclesiastical annals, were known only by him. The material truth suffered from it, for that material truth Luke scarcely knew, while he cared still less about it; but almost as much as the Gospels, the Acts fashioned the future. The manner in which things are told is of more consequence in great secular developments than the manner in which they happened. Those who constructed the legend of Jesus have a part in the work of Christianity almost equal to his; that which made the legend of the primitive Church has weighed with an enormous weight in the creation of that spiritual society where so many centuries have found the repose of their souls. Multitudinis credentium erat cor unum et anima una. When one has written that, one has thrust into the heart of humanity the goad which never allows it to rest until what may have been discovered, and what has been seen in slumber, and what has been seen in dreams, and touched that of which we have dreamed.

CHAPTER XX

SYRIAN SECTS--ELKASAÏ

Whilst the Western Churches, yielding more or less to the influence of the Roman spirit, moved rapidly towards an orthodox Catholicism, and aspired to give to itself a central government excluding the varieties of the sects, the Churches of the Ebionim in Syria were crumbling away more and more, and wasted themselves in all sorts of aberrations. The sect is not the Church; too often, on the contrary, the sect eats away the Church and dissolves it. A veritable Proteus, Judeo-Christianity engaged itself by turns in the most opposite directions. Notwithstanding the privilege enjoyed by the Syrian Christians of possessing the members of the family of Jesus, and of attaching to itself a tradition much closer than those of the Churches of Asia, of Greece, and of Rome, it is not to be doubted that, left to themselves, these little associations would have melted away like a dream at the end of two or three hundred years. On the one hand, the exclusive use of Syriac deprived them of all fertile contact with the works of Greek genius; on the other, a host of Oriental influences, full of danger, acted upon them, and threatened them with a prompt corruption. Their imperfect reasoning powers delivered them over to the seductions of the theosophic follies--of Babylonian, Persian, or Egyptian origin; which, in about forty years, caused the nascent Christianity that grave malady of Gnosticism, which can only be compared to a terrible croup, from which the child barely escapes by a miracle.

The atmosphere in which these Ebionite Churches of Syria, and beyond the Jordan, lived, was exceedingly disturbed. Jewish sects abounded in these districts, and followed an altogether different course from that of the orthodox doctors. After the destruction of Jerusalem, Judaism, deprived of the prophetic spur, had only two poles of religious activity--the Casuistic, represented by the Talmud, and the mystical dreams of the new-born Cabbala. Lydda and Jabneh were the centres of the religious elaboration of the Talmud; the country beyond Jordan served as a cradle to the Cabbala. The Essenians were not dead; under the names of Essenes, Ossenes, or Osseens, they were scarcely to be distinguished from Nazarenes or Ebionites, and continued their special asceticisms and fastings with so much the more ardour since the destruction of the Temple had suppressed the ritualism of the Thora. The Galileans of Judah, the Gaulonite, existed, it appears, as a Church apart. It is scarcely known what the Masbotheans were, still less what were the Genisti, the Meristi, and some other obscure heretics.

The Samaritans were divided on their side into a crowd of sects, more or less connected with Simon of Gitton. Cleobius, Menander, the Gorotheans, the Sebueans, are already Gnostics: the Cabbalistic mysticism ran high amongst them. The absence of all authority still permitted the gravest confusions. The Samaritan sects which swarmed by the side of the Church sometimes entered within its limits or sought to force their way in. We may connect with these times the book of the Grand Exposition attributed to Simon of Gitton. Menander and Capharateus had succeeded to all the ambitions of Simon. He, like his master, imagined that he possessed the supreme virtue hidden from the rest of men. Between God and the creation he placed an innumerable world of angels, over whom magic had all power. Of that magic he pretended to know the profoundest secrets. It appears that he baptised in his own name. This baptism conferred the right to the resurrection and to immortality. It was at Antioch that Menander reckoned the greatest number of followers. His disciples sought, as it would seem, to usurp the name of Christians, but the Christians vigorously repulsed them and gave them the name of Menandrians. It was the same with certain Simonian sectaries named Eutychites, worshippers of Eons, against whom were brought the gravest accusations.

Another Samaritan, Dositheus or Dosthaï, played the part of a sort of Christ, of Son of God, and sought to pass himself off as the great prophet equal to Moses of whom the promise might be read in Deuteronomy (xviii. 15), and in these feverish times he was constantly expected. Essenism, with its tendency to multiply angels, was at the root of all these aberrations; the Messiah himself was no more than an angel, and Jesus, in the Churches placed under that influence, risked the loss of his beautiful title of Son of God, to become only a great angel--an Eon of the first rank.

The intimate connection which existed between Christians and the mass of Israel, the want of direction which characterised the trans-Jordanic Churches, caused each of these sects to have its counterpart in the Church of Jesus. We do not well understand what Hegesippus endeavours to say when he traces for the Church of Jerusalem a period of absolute virginity, finishing about the time at which we now are, and when he attributes all the evil of the time which followed to a certain Trebuthis, who, out of spite at not having been named bishop, infected the Church with errors borrowed from seven Jewish sects. What is true is that in the lost provinces of the East strange alliances were produced. Sometimes even the mania for incoherent mixtures did not stop at the limits of Judaism; the religions of Upper Asia furnished more than one element to the cauldron in which the most discordant elements fermented together. Baptism is a rite originally from the region of the Lower Euphrates; but baptism was the most common feature amongst the Jewish sects which sought to free themselves from the Temple and the priests at Jerusalem. John the Baptist still had disciples. The Essenians, the Ebionites, were almost all given to ablutions. After the destruction of the Temple, baptism gained greater strength. The sectaries plunged into water every day and on any excuse. We heard about the year 80 accounts which appeared to come from this sect. Under Trojan, the fashion of baptism redoubled. This growing favour was due in part to the influence of a certain Elkasaï, who we may suppose to have been in many ways the imitator of John the Baptist and of Jesus.

This Elkasaï appears to have been an Essene of the country beyond Jordan. He had, perhaps, resided in Babylonia, whence he pretended to have brought the book of his revelation. He raised his prophetic standard in the third year of the reign of Trajan, preaching repentance, and a new baptism more efficacious than all these which had preceded it, capable, in a word, of washing away the most enormous sins. He presented, as a proof of his divine mission, a bizarre apocalypse, probably written in Syriac, which he sought to surround with a charlatanesque mystery, by representing it as having come down from heaven at Sera, the capital of the fabulous country of the Serans, beyond Parthia. A gigantic angel, thirty-two leagues in height, representing the Son of God, there played the part of revealer; by his side, a female angel of the same height, the Holy Spirit, appeared like a statue in the clouds between two mountains. Elkasaï, now the depositary of the book, transmits it to a certain Sobiaï. Some fragments of this strange document are known to us. Nothing there rises above the level of a vulgar mystifier, who wishes to make his fortune with pretended formulas of expiation and ridiculous mummeries. Magic formulas composed of Syriac phrases read backwards, puerile predictions as to lucky and unlucky days, mad medicine of exorcisms and sortileges, prescriptions against devils and dogs, astrological predictions--such is the Gospel of Elkasaï. Like all the makers of apocalypses, he announced catastrophes for the Roman Empire, the date of which he fixed for the sixth year after Trajan.

Was Elkasaï really Christian? It has sometimes been doubted. He spoke often about the Messiah, but he equivocated concerning Jesus. It may be imagined that, walking in the footsteps of Simon of Gitton, Elkasaï knew and copied Christianity. Like Mahomet, at a later period, he adopted Jesus as a divine personage. The Ebionites were the only Christians with whom he had relations; for his Christology is distinctly that of Ebion. By its example, he maintained the Law, circumcision, the Sabbath, rejected the ancient prophets, hated Paul, abstained from flesh, and turned towards Jerusalem in prayer. His disciples appear to have approached Buddhism; they admitted many Christs, passing one into the others by a sort of transmigration, or rather a single Christ incarnating himself and appearing in the world at intervals. Jesus was one of these apparitions, Adam having been the first. These dreams make one think of the avatars of Vishnu and the successive lives of Krishna

We feel in all this the crude syncretism of a sectary very like Mahomet, who coolly jumbles together and confounds the ideas which he gleans from right and left according to his caprice or interest. The most recognisable influence is that of Persian naturalism and the Babylonian Cabbala. The Elkasaïtes adored water as the source of life, and detested fire. Their baptism administered, "in the name of the Most High God, and in the name of the Son, the great King," effaced all sins and cured all sickness, when to it was joined the invocation of seven mysterious witnesses, the heaven, water, the holy spirits, the angels of prayer, oil, salt, earth. From the Essenes Elkasaï borrowed fasting, the horror of bloody sacrifices. The privilege of announcing the future and of healing the sick by magical operations, was also a pretension of the Essenes. But the morals of Elkasaï resembled those of these good Cenobites as little as might be. He reproved virginity, and, to avoid persecution, he allowed the simulation of idolatry, even to denying with the mouth the faith professed.

These doctrines were more or less adopted by all the Ebionite sects. The living impress of them may be found in the pseudo-Clementine narratives, the work of the Ebionites at Rome, and vague reflections of them in the epistle falsely attributed to John. The book of Elkasaï was, however, not known by the Greek and Latin Churches until the third century, and had amongst them no success. It was, on the other hand, adopted with enthusiasm by the Osseans, the Nazarenes, and the Ebionites of the East. All the region beyond Jordan, Perea, Moab, Iturea, the country of the Nabatheans, the banks of the Dead Sea towards Arnon, were filled with these sectaries. Later they were called Samseans, an expression of obscure meaning. In the fourth century the fanaticism of the sect was such that people caused themselves to be killed for the family of Elkasaï. His family, in fact, still existed and carried on its vulgar charlatanry. Two women, Marthous and Marthana, who claimed descent from him, were almost worshipped; the dust of their feet, their spittle, were treated as relics. In Arabia, the Elkasaïtes, like the Ebionites and the Judeo-Christians in general, lived close to Islam and were confounded with it.

The theory of Mahomet as to Jesus is scarcely separable from that of Elkasaï. The idea of the Kibla, or direction for prayer, perhaps comes from the trans-Jordanic sectaries.

It is impossible to insist too strongly on the point that before the great schism of the Greek and Latin Churches, equally orthodox and Catholic, there had been another schism--an Oriental, a Syrian schism, if we may so explain it--which put out of the pale of Christianity, or, more exactly, left upon its confines a whole world of Judeo-Christian or Ebionite sects, in no way Catholic (Essenians, Osseans, Samseans, Jesseans, Elkasaïtes), in whose midst Mahomet learned Christianity, and of which Islam was the result. A proof, in some sort still a living proof, of this great fact, is the name of Nazarenes, which Mussulmans have always given to Christians. Another proof that the Christianity of Mahomet was Ebionism of Nazarism is that obstinate docetism which has caused it to be believed by the Mussulmans of all times that Jesus was not crucified in person,--that a ghost alone suffered in his place. We might fancy that we heard Cerinthus, or some of the Gnostics so energetically opposed by Irenæus.

The Syriac name of these various sects of Baptists was Sabiin, the exact equivalent of "baptisers." This is the origin of the name of Sabiens which serves even now to designate the Mendaïtes, the Nazarenes, or Christians of St John, who drag out their poor existence in the marshy district of Wasith and of Howeysa, not far from the confluence of the Tigris and of the Euphrates. In the seventh century Mahomet treated them with a special consideration. In the tenth the Arab polygraphs called them Elmogtasileh, "those who bathed." The first Europeans who knew them took them for disciples of John the Baptist, who had quitted the banks of the Jordan before receiving the preaching of Jesus. It is hardly possible to doubt the identity of these sectaries with the Elkasaïtes, when we find them calling their founder El hasih, and, above all, when we study their doctrines, which are a sort of Judeo-Babylonian Gnosticism analogous in many ways to that of Elkasaï. The use of ablutions, the taste for astrology, the habit of ascribing books to Adam as the first of revelators, the qualities attributed to angels, a sort of naturalism and of belief in the magical virtue of the elements, the horror of celibacy, are so many features common to the Elkasaïtes and to the sectaries of Bassora.

Like Elkasaï the Mendaïtes believed in water as the principle of life; fire as a principle of darkness and destruction. Although they lived far from the Jordan, that stream is always the baptismal stream. Their antipathy for Jerusalem and Judaism, the dislike which they manifested for Jesus and for Christianity, did not prevent their organisation of bishops, priests, and faithful from recalling in all respects the organisation of Christianity, or their liturgy from being copied from that of a Church, and bordering upon true Sacraments. Their books do not appear to be very ancient, but they seem to have replaced older ones. Of this number was perhaps the Apocalypse or Penitence of Adam, a singular book about the celestial liturgies for every hour of the day and night, and upon the sacramental acts which belong to each.

Does Mendaïsm come from a single source--Essenism and Jewish baptism? Certainly not. In many respects a branch of the Babylonian religion may be seen in it, that religion may have entered into close alliance with a Judeo-Christian sect, itself already impressed with Babylonish ideas. The unbridled syncretism which has always been the rule with Oriental sects, renders an exact analysis of such monstrosities impossible. The ulterior relations of the Sabiens with Manicheism remain very obscure. All that can be said is that Elkasaïsm lasts even in our own days, and represents alone in the marshes of Bassora the Judeo-Christian sects which formerly flourished beyond Jordan.

The family of Jesus which still survived in Syria was undoubtedly opposed to these unhealthy dreams. About the time we are considering, the last nephews of the Galilean founder died out, surrounded with the most profound respect by the trans-Jordanic communities, but almost forgotten by the other Churches. After their appearance before Domitian, the sons of Jude, returned to Batanea, were considered martyrs. They were placed at the head of the Churches, and they enjoyed a preponderating authority until their death, under Trajan. The sons of Cleophas during this time appear to have continued to bear the title of presidents of the Church of Jerusalem. To Simeon, son of Cleophas, had succeeded his nephew Judah, son of James, to whom appears to have succeeded another Simeon, the great-grandson of Cleophas.

An important political event occurred in the year 105, in Syria, which had grave consequences for the future of Christianity. The Nabathean kingdom, which, until then, had remained independent, bordered Palestine on the east and included the cities of Petra, of Bostra, and in fact, if not in law, the city of Damascus, was destroyed by Cornelius Palma, and became the Roman province of Arabia. About the same time the little royalties feudatory to the Empire which until then were maintained in Syria, the Herods, the Soëmi of Edessa, the little sovereign of Chalcis, of Arbila, the Solencides of the Comagena, had disappeared. The Roman domination then assumed in the East a regularity which it had never had before. Beyond its frontiers there was only the inaccessible desert. The trans-Jordanic world which until then entered into the Empire only by its most westerly parts, was there swallowed up wholly. Palmyra, which so far had given to Rome only auxiliaries, entered altogether into the Roman domination. The entire field of Christian work is henceforward submitted to Rome, and is about to enjoy the absolute repose which the end of the pre-occupations of local patriotism brings about. All the

East adopted Roman manners; the cities until then Oriental were rebuilt according to the rules of contemporary art. The prophecies of the Jewish apocalypses were not fulfilled. The Empire was at the height of its power; one single government extended from York to Assouan, from Gibraltar to the Carpathians and to the Syrian desert. The follies of Caligula and of Nero, the wickedness of Tiberius and Domitian, were forgotten. In that immense area there was only one natural protestation--that of the Jews; all bent without murmuring before the greatest force which had ever been seen in the world until then.

CHAPTER XXI

TRAJAN AS A PERSECUTOR--LETTER OF PLINY

In a multitude of ways this force was benevolent. There were many countries, and, in consequence, many wars. With the reforms which might be hoped for from the excellent statesmen who were at the head of affairs, the aims of humanity seemed to be attained. We have already shown how that species of golden age of the Liberals, that government of the wisest and most honest men was hard,--worse, in a sense, than that of Nero and Domitian. Cold, correct, moderate statesmen, knowing only the law, applying it even with indulgence, could not fail to be persecutors; for the law was a persecutor; it did not permit what the Church of Jesus regarded as of the very essence of its divine institution.

Everything proves, in fact, that Trajan was the first systematic persecutor of Christianity. The proceedings against the Christians, without being very frequent, took place many times under his reign. His political principles, his zeal for the official religion, his aversion for everything that resembled a secret society, involved him in it. He was equally urged forward by public opinion. Outbreaks against the Christians were not rare. The government, whilst satisfying its own suspicions, acquired by its severities against the calumniated sect a varnish of popularity. The riots and the persecutions which followed them, were altogether local in character. There was not under Trajan what under Decius and Diocletian was called a general persecution, but the condition of the Church was unstable and unequal. It was dependent upon caprices, and such caprices as came from the crowd were usually more to be feared than those of the agents of authority. Amongst the agents of authority themselves, the most enlightened--Tacitus, for example, and Suetonius--nourished the most deeply-rooted prejudices against "the new superstition." Tacitus regards it as the first duty of a good statesman to stifle at the same time both Judaism and Christianity, "melancholy offshoots of the same stalk."

That becomes manifest in a very sensible manner when one of the most honest, the most upright, the most educated, the most liberal men of the time found himself brought by his duties into the presence of the problem which was coming to the front, and was beginning to embarrass the best minds. Pliny was named in the year 111 Imperial Legate Extraordinary in the provinces of Bithynia and Pontus, that is to say, in all the north of Asia Minor. This country had until then been governed by annual pro-consuls, senators drawn by lot, who had administered it with the greatest negligence. In some respects liberty had gained thereby. Shut off from high political questions, these administrators of a day occupied themselves less than they might have done with the future of the Empire. The public treasury had fallen into a state of extreme dilapidation; finances and the public works of the province were in a pitiable state; but whilst they were occupied in amusing or enriching themselves, these governors bad left the country to follow its own instincts at will. Disorder, as often happens, had profited by liberty.

The official religion had to sustain it only the support which it received from the Empire: abandoned to itself by those indifferent prefects, it had fallen altogether into disrepute. In certain districts, the temples were in ruins. The professional and religious associations, the heteries, which were so strongly to the taste of Asia Minor, had been infinitely developed; Christianity, profiting by the facilities offered by the officials charged with its suppression, gained in all districts. We have seen that Asia and Galatia were the places where in all the world the new religion had found the greatest favour. Thence it had made surprising progress towards the Black Sea. Manners were altogether changed. Meats offered to idols, which were one of the sources of the provision of the markets, could not be sold. The firm knot of faithful might not be very numerous, but around it sympathetic crowds were grouped, half initiated, inconstant, capable of hiding their faith at the appearance of danger, but at bottom not detaching themselves from it. There were in those corporate conversions fashionable enthusiasms, gusts of wind which from time to time carried to the Church, and took away from it, waves of unstable populations, but the courage of the leaders was superior to all trials; their hatred of idolatry led them to brave everything to maintain the point of honour of the faith which they had embraced.

Pliny, a perfectly honest man and scrupulous executor of the Imperial orders, was soon at work to bring back to the provinces which had been entrusted to him both order and law. Experience was wanting to him; he was rather an amiable man of letters than an able administrator; in almost all matters of business he was in the habit of consulting directly with the Emperor. Trajan answered him, letter for letter, and that precious correspondence has been preserved to us. Upon the daily orders of the Emperor everything was watched over, reformed; he required authorisations for the smallest matters. A formal edict suppressed the heteries; the most inoffensive corporations were dissolved. It was the custom in Bithynia to celebrate certain family events and local festivities by great assemblies in which a thousand persons might be gathered. They were suppressed. Liberty, which in most cases slips into the world in a surreptitious fashion only, was reduced to almost nothing.

It was inevitable that the Christian Churches should be attacked by a meticulous policy which saw everywhere the spectre of the heteries, and disquieted itself over a society of five hundred workmen instituted by authority to act as firemen. Pliny often met on his path innocent sectaries, the danger of whom he did not readily see. In the different stages of his career as an advocate and magistrate he had never been concerned in any proceedings against the Christians. Denunciations now multiplied daily; arrests must follow. The Imperial Legate, following the summary procedure of the justice of the time, made some examples; he decided to send to Rome those who were Roman citizens; he put two deaconesses to the torture. All that he discovered appeared to him childish. He wished to shut his eyes, but the laws of the Empire were absolute; the informations passed all measure; he found himself in the way to put the entire country under arrest.

It was at Amisus, on the border of the Black Sea, in the autumn of the year 112, that this difficulty became a dominant care for him. It is probable that the last incidents which disturbed him had taken place at Amastris, a city which in the second century was the centre of Christianity in Pontus. Pliny, according to custom, wrote of it to the Emperor:

I consider it my duty, sire, to refer to you all matters on which I have doubts. Who can direct my hesitations or instruct my ignorance better than you? I have never taken part in any proceedings against the Christians, hence I know not whether I ought to punish or to hunt them out, nor how far I ought to go. For example, I do not know if I ought to make any distinction of age, or if in such a matter there ought to be no difference between youth and ripe age; if I must pardon upon repentance, or if he who has become altogether a Christian ought to profit by ceasing to be one; if it is the name itself apart from all crime that should be punished, or the crimes which are inseparable from the name. In the meantime, the course which I have adopted with regard to all those who have been brought before me as Christians, has been to inquire first if they are Christians; those who have avowed themselves to be such, I have interrogated a second time; a third time threatening them with punishment; those who have persisted, I have sent to death; one point in effect beyond all doubt for me being that, whether the fact admitted be criminal or not, that inflexible obstinacy and persistency deserved to be punished. There are some other unhappy persons attacked with the same madness, who, in view of their rank as Roman citizens, I have directed to be sent to Rome. Then in the course of the process the crime as generally happens, branching out widely, many species of it are presented. An anonymous libel has been deposited containing many names. Those who have denied that they either were or had been Christians, I have thought it right to release, when after me they have invoked the gods, when they have offered incense and wine to your image, with which I have supplemented the statues of the divinities, and when moreover, they have cursed Christus, all which things I am assured they could not be forced to do if they were Christians. Others named by the informer have said that they were Christians, and immediately have denied that they were, avowing that they had been, but asserting that they had ceased to be, some for three years, some for still longer, others for as many as twenty years. All these also have paid honour to your image, and to the statues of the gods, and have cursed Christ. Now these affirm that all their offence or all their error was confined to meeting habitually on fixed days before sunrise to sing together alternately (? antiphonically) a hymn to Christus as God, and to swear not to such and such certain crimes, but not to commit thefts, highway robbery, adultery, not fail to keep sworn faith, not to refuse to restore a pledge; that that done they used to retire, then to meet together again to take a meal, but an ordinary and perfectly innocent meal; that even that had ceased, since by your orders I had forbidden the heteries. That made it necessary in my eyes to proceed to discover the truth by the torture of two servants, of those whom they call deaconesses. I found nothing but an evil, unmeasured superstition. So, suspending the inquiry, I resolved to consult you. The business has appeared to me to require that I should do so, especially because of the number of those who are in peril. A great number of persons in effect, of every age, of every condition, of both sexes, are called to justice or will be; it is not only in the cities, but in the towns and in the rural districts that the contagion of this superstition has spread. I think that it may yet be stopped and remedied. Already it is reported that the temples which were almost abandoned, have begun to be frequented once more, that the solemn festivals which had long been interrupted, have recommenced, and that the flesh of victims ("meats offered to idols") is again exposed, though the buyers have been few. From which it may readily be believed how great a number of men may be reclaimed if a place of repentance be left open.

Trajan answered:

Thou hast followed the path thou should'st have taken, my dear Secundus, in examining the cases of those who have been brought before thy tribunal as Christians. In such a matter it is impossible to devise a fixed rule for all cases. They should not be sought out. If they are denounced and are convicted, they must be punished in such a way, however, that he who denies that he is a Christian, and who proves his words by his acts,--that is to say, by addressing his supplications to our gods, shall obtain pardon as a reward for his repentance, whatever may have been the suspicions which weigh upon him for the past. As for anonymous denunciations, we most not take account of the species of accusation which is brought, for this concerns a detestable example which is no longer of our time.

No more misunderstandings! To be a Christian, is to be in disagreement with the law, is to merit death From Trajan's time Christianity is a crime against the State. Some tolerant Emperors of the third century will alone consent to shut their eyes and allow men to be Christians if they chose. A good administration, according to the most benevolent ideas of the Emperors, ought not to try to find too many criminals; it does not encourage informers, but it encourages apostasy by pardoning renegades. To teach, to advise, to reward the most immoral acts, that which most lowers a man in his own eyes, appears wholly natural. Here is the error into which one of the best governments that ever existed has allowed itself to be drawn, because it has touched matters of conscience, and has preserved the old principle of the State religion, a principle which was natural enough in the small cities of antiquity, which were only an extension of the family, but dangerous in a great Empire composed of parts having neither the same history nor the same moral needs.

It is equally evident from these invaluable documents that Christians were not persecuted as Jews, as has been the case under Domitian. They are persecuted as Christians. There is no longer any confusion in the judicial world, though in the world outside it still existed. Judaism was not a crime: it had even outside its days of revolt, its guarantees, and privileges. Strange thing! Judaism, which revolted thrice against the Empire with a nameless fury, was never officially persecuted; the evil treatment which the Jews endured are, like those of the Rayahs in Mahometan countries, the consequence of a subordinate position, not a legal punishment; very rarely, in the second and third century, because he will not sacrifice to idols or to the image of the Emperor. More than once even we find the Jews protected by the administration against the Christians. On the contrary, Christianity, which was never in revolt, was in reality outside the law. Judaism had, if it may be so expressed, its Concordat with the Empire; Christianity had none. The Roman policy felt that Christianity was the white ant which was eating away the heart of antique society. Judaism did not aspire to penetrate the Empire; it dreamed of its supernatural overthrow; in its hours of insanity it took arms, killed everyone, struck blindly, then, like a raving madman, allowed itself to be chained after its paroxysm, whilst Christianity continued its work slowly, gently. Humble and modest in appearance, it had a boundless ambition; between it and the Empire the struggle was to the death.

Trajan's answer to Pliny was not a law; but it supposed laws and fixed the interpretation of them. The temperaments indicated by the wise Emperor should have been of small consequence. It was too easy to find pretexts, for the ill-will with which Christians were regarded to find itself hampered. A signed denunciation relating to an ostensible act was all that was necessary. Now the attitude of a Christian in passing before temples, his questions in the markets as to the origin of the meats he found there; his absence from public festivals, pointed him out at once. Thus local persecutions never ceased. It was less the Emperors than the Pro-Consuls who persecuted. All depended upon the good or the ill-will of the governors, and the good-will was rare. The time had gone by when the Roman aristocracy would receive these exotic novelties with a sort of benevolent curiosity. It had now but a cold disdain for the follies it declined out of pure moderation and pity for human weaknesses to suppress at a moment's notice. The people, on the other hand, showed themselves fanatical enough. He who never sacrificed, or who, in passing before a sacred edifice. did not waft it a kiss of adoration, went in danger of his life.

CHAPTER XXII

IGNATIUS OF ANTIOCH

Antioch had its part, and a very violent one, in those cruel measures which proved to be so absolutely inefficacious. The Church of Antioch, or, at least, the fraction of that Church which attached itself to St Paul, had at this moment a chief, regarded with the most profound respect, who was called Ignatius. This name is probably the Latin equivalent of the Syriac name Nourana. The reputation of Ignatius had spread through all the Churches, especially in Asia Minor. Under circumstances which are unknown to us, probably as the result of some popular movement, he was arrested, condemned to death, and, as he was not a Roman citizen, ordered to be taken to Rome to be delivered to the beasts in the amphitheatre. For that fate the noblest victims were reserved, men worthy to be shown to the Roman people. The journey of this courageous confessor from Antioch to Rome along the coasts of Asia, Macedonia, and Greece was a sort of triumphal progress. The Churches of the cities at which he touched flocked around him, asking for his counsels. He, on his part, wrote letters full of instruction, to which his position, like that of St Paul, prisoner of Jesus Christ, gave the highest authority. At Smyrna, in particular, Ignatius found himself in communication with all the Churches of Asia. Polycarp, Bishop of Smyrna, saw him, and retained a profound memory of him. Ignatius had from that place an extensive correspondence: his letters were received with almost as such respect as the apostolic writings. Surrounded by couriers of a sacred character, who came and went, he was more like a powerful personage than a prisoner. The spectacle impressed the very Pagans, and served as the foundation for a curious romance which has been handed down to us.

Almost the whole of the authentic epistles of Ignatius appear to have been lost. Those which we possess under his name addressed to the Ephesians, to the Magnesian, to the Tralliens, to the Philadelphians, to the Smyrniotes, to Polycarp, are apocryphal. The four first were written from Smyrna; the two last from Alexandria-Troas. The six works are more or less feeble reproductions of the same original. Genius and individuality are absolutely wanting. But it appears that amongst the letters which Ignatius wrote from Smyrna, there was one addressed to the faithful at Rome, after the manner of St Paul. This piece, such as we have it, impressed all ecclesiastical antiquity. Irenæus, Origen, and Eusebius cite it and admire it. Its style has a harsh and pronounced flavour, something strong and popular; pleasantry is pushed even to playing upon words; as a matter of taste, certain points are urged with a shocking exaggeration, but the liveliest faith, the most ardent thirst for death, have never inspired such passionate accents. The enthusiasm of the martyr who for six hundred years was the dominant spirit of Christendom, has received from the author of this extraordinary fragment, whoever he may be, its most exalted expressions.

After many prayers I am permitted to see your holy faces; I have even obtained more than I asked; for if God give me grace to endure to the end, I hope that I shall embrace you as the prisoner of Jesus Christ. The business has begun well, seeing that nothing prevents me from awaiting the lot which has been appointed to me. Verily it is for you that I am concerned. I fear lest your affection should be hurtful to me. You would risk nothing, but I should lose God himself if you succeed in saving me , , . Never again shall I find such an opportunity, and you, if you will have the charity to remain quiet, never will you have taken part in a better work. If you keep silence, in short, I shall belong to God; if you love my flesh, I shall again be cast into the conflict. Let me suffer whilst the altar is ready, so that, united in chorus by love, you may sing to the Father in Christ Jesus,--"Oh, great goodness of God who hath deigned to bring the Bishop of Syria from the rising to the going down of the sun!" It is good to lie down from the world with God that we may rise with him.

You have never done evil to any; why then begin to-day? You have been masters to so many others! I ask but one thing; do what you teach, what you prescribe. Ask only for me strength from within and from without, so that I may be not only called Christian but really a Christian, when I shall have passed away from this world. Nothing that is visible is good. What thou seest is temporal. What thou seest not is eternal. Our God, Jesus Christ, existing in his father, appears no more. Christianity is not only a work of silence; it becomes a work of splendour when it is hated of the world.

I write to the Churches: I inform all that I am assured of dying for God, if you do not prevent me. I beg you not to prove yourselves by your intemperate goodness my worst enemies. Let me be the food of beasts, thanks to whom it shall be given me to enjoy God; I am the wheat of God, I must be ground by the teeth of beasts that I may be found the pure bread of Christ. Rejoice therefore that they shall be my tomb, and that nothing shall be left of my body, that my funeral shall thus cost no man aught. Then shall I be truly the disciple of Christ, when the world shall see my body no more.

From Syria to Rome, upon land, upon sea, by day and by night, I fight already against the beasts, chained as I am to ten leopards (I speak of the soldiers who guard me, and who show themselves the more cruel the more good is done to them). Thanks to their ill-treatment, I am formed, "but I am not thereby justified." I shall gain, I assure you, when I find myself face to face with the beasts which await me. I hope to meet them in good temper; if needs be, I will caress them with my hands, that they may devour me alone, and that they may not, as they have done to some, show themselves afraid to touch me. If they do it unwillingly, I will force them.

Forgive me. I know which is best for me. It is now that I begin to be a true disciple. No! no power, visible or invisible, shall prevent me from rejoicing in Jesus Christ. Fire and cross; troops of beasts; broken bones; limbs lopped off; crushing of the whole body, all the punishments of the devil, may fall upon me, if only I may rejoice in Jesus Christ . . . My love has been crucified, and there is no longer in me ardour for the material part; there is within me only a living water which murmurs and says to me, "Come to the Father." I take pleasure no longer in corruptible food, nor in the joys of this life. I desire the bread of God, the bread of life, which is the flesh of Jesus Christ, the Son of God, born in the end of time, of the race of David, and of Abraham; and I desire to drink his blood, which is incorruptible love and life eternal.

Sixty years after the death of Ignatius, the characteristic phrase of this fragment, "I am the wheat of God," was traditional in the Church, and was repeated to sustain the courage of martyrs. Perhaps this was a matter of oral tradition; perhaps also the letter is authentic at bottom--I mean as to those energetic phrases by which Ignatius expressed his desire to suffer, and his love for Jesus. In the authentic narrative of the martyrdom of Polycarp (155), there are, it would appear, allusions to the very text of that Epistle to the Romans which we now possess. Ignatius becomes thus the great master of martyrdom, the exciter to enthusiasm for death for Jesus. His letters, true or superstitious, were the collection from which might be drawn striking expressions and exalted sentiments. The deacon Stephen had by his heroism sanctified the Diaconate and the ecclesiastical ministries; with still great splendour the Bishop of Antioch surrounded with an aureole, the functions of the Episcopate. It was not without reason that writings were attributed to him in which those functions were hyperbolically depicted. Ignatius was really the patron saint of the Episcopate, the creator of the privilege of the chiefs of the Church, the first victim of their redoubtable duties.

The most curious thing is that this history, told more recently by one of the most intelligent writers of the age by Lucian, inspired him with the principal features of his little picture of manners, entitled "Of the Death of Peregrinus." It is scarcely to be doubted that Lucian borrowed from the narratives of Ignatius the passages in which he represents his charlatan playing the part of Bishop and Confessor, chained in Syria, shipped for Italy, surrounded by the faithful with cares and attentions, receiving from all parts deputations of ministers sent to console him. Peregrinus, like Ignatius, addresses from his captivity to the celebrated towns which he finds upon his way, letters full of counsels and of exhortations that they should observe the laws; he institutes, in view of these messages, missions clothed with a religious character; finally he appears before the Emperor, and defies his power, with an audacity which Lucian finds impertinent, but which the admirers of the fanatic represent as a movement of holy liberty.

In the Church the memory of Ignatius was especially exalted by the partisans of St Paul. To have seen Ignatius was a favour almost as great as to have seen St Paul. The high authority of the martyr was one of the reasons which contributed to the success of this group, whose right to exist in the Church of Jesus was still so greatly contested. Towards the year 170, a disciple of St Paul, zealous for the establishment of episcopal authority, conceived the project, in imitation of the pastoral epistles attributed to the Apostle, of composing, under the name of Ignatius, a series of epistles designed to inculcate an anti-Jewish conception of Christianity, as well as ideas of strict hierarchy and Catholic orthodoxy in opposition to the errors of the Docetists and of certain Gnostic sects. These writings, which it was desired should be regarded as having been collected by Polycarp, were accepted with enthusiasm, and had in the constitution of discipline and dogma a commanding influence.

By the side of Ignatius we may see, in the oldest documents, two persons figure who appear to have been associated with him, Zozimus and Rufus. Ignatius does not appear to have had travelling companions; Zozimus and Rufus were perhaps persons well known in the ecclesiastical circles of Greece and of Asia, and recommended by their high devotion to the Church of Christ.

About the same time another martyr may have suffered, to whom his title of head of the Church of Jerusalem and his relationship with Jesus gave great notoriety. I mean Simeon, son, or rather great-grandson, of Cleophas. The opinion decided amongst the Christians, and probably accepted by those around them, according to which Jesus had been of the race of David, attributed this title to all his blood-relations. Now in the state of effervescence in which Palestine was, such a title could not be borne without risk. Already under Domitian we have seen the Roman authority entertain apprehensions apropos of the pretensions avowed by the sons of Jude. Under Trajan the same disquietude came to light. The descendants of Cleophas, who presided over the Church of Jerusalem, were too modest to boast much of a descent which non-Christians might perhaps have disputed, but they could not hide it from the affiliated of the Church of Jesus; from those heretics--Ebionites, Essenes, Elkasaïtes--some of whom were hardly Christians. A denunciation was addressed by some of those sectaries to the Roman authority, and Simeon, son of Cleophas, was brought to judgment. The Consular Legate of Judea at this moment was Tiberius Claudius Atticus, who appears to have been the father of the celebrated Herod Atticus. He was an obscure Athenian, whom the discovery of an immense treasure had suddenly enriched, and who by his fortune had succeeded in obtaining the title of surrogate consul. He showed himself, in the circumstances of this case, extremely cruel. During many days he tortured the unhappy Simeon, without doubt to force him to reveal pretended secrets. Atticus and his assessors admired his courage, but he finished by crucifying him. Hegesippus, from whom we have these details, assures us that the accusers of Simeon were themselves convinced that they were of the race of David, and perished with him. We ought not to be too much surprised by such denunciations. We have already seen that the internal rivalries of the Jewish and Christian sects had the greatest share in the persecution of the year 64, or at least in the deaths of the Apostles Peter and Paul.

Rome at that period appears to have had no martyrs. Among the Presbyteri and Episcopi who governed that capital Church are reckoned Evarestes, Alexander, and Xystus, who appear to have died in peace.

CHAPTER XXIII

END OF TRAJAN--REVOLT OF THE JEWS

Trajan, the conqueror of the Dacii, adorned with all the triumphs, arrived at the highest degree of power which man had until then attained, revolved, notwithstanding his sixty years, boundless projects with regard to the East. The limit of the Empire in Syria and in Asia Minor was as yet but ill-assured. The recent destruction of the Nabathean kingdom postponed for centuries all danger from the Arabs. But the kingdom of Armenia, although in law vassal to the Romans, constantly inclined towards the Parthian alliance. In the Dacian war, the Arsacides had had relations with Decebalus. The Parthian Empire, master of Mesopotamia, menaced Antioch, and created, for provinces incapable of defending themselves, a perpetual danger. An Eastern expedition, having for its object the annexation to the Empire of Armenia, Osrohenia and Mygdonia, countries which in effect, after the campaigns of Lucius Verus and of Septimius Severus, belonged to the Empire, would have been reasonable. But Trajan did not take sufficient account of the state of the East. He did not see that beyond Syria, Armenia, and the north of Mesapotamia, which it is easy to make the rampart of Western civilisation, extends the ancient East; traversed by nomadic tribes, containing, side by side with the cities, indocile populations, amongst which it is impossible to establish order after the European fashion. This East has never been conquered by civilisation in a durable manner; even Greece reigned there only in the most transitory way. To hew out Roman provinces in a world totally different in climate, races, manner of living, from what Rome had hitherto assimilated, was a veritable chimera. The Empire, which had need of all its strength against the German impulse on the Rhine and the Danube, was about to prepare upon the Tigris a struggle not less difficult, for supposing that the Tigris had really become in all its course a river-frontier, Rome would not have had behind the great ditch the support of the solid Gallic and Germanic populations of the West. Through not having understood that, Trajan made a mistake which can only be compared with that of Napoleon in 1812. His expedition against the Parthians was analogous to that of the Russian campaign. Admirably planned out, the expedition started with a series of victories, then degenerated into a struggle against nature, and concluded with a retreat which cast a sombre veil over the end of a most brilliant reign.

Trajan left Italy, which he was not again to see, in the month of October 113. He passed the winter months at Antioch, and in the spring of 114 began the campaign of Armenia. The result was prodigious: in September, Armenia was reduced to a Roman province; the limits of the Empire extended to the Caucasus and the Caspian Sea. Trajan rested the following winter at Antioch.

The results of the year 115 were not less extraordinary. ordinary. The Mesopotamia of the North, with its more or less independent principalities, was conquered or subjected. The Tigris was attained. The Jews were numerous in these parts. The dynasty of the Izates and Monobazes, always vassal to the Parthians, was mistress of Nisibe. As in 70, it no doubt resisted the Romans, but it was necessary to yield. Trajan passed the following winter at Antioch, where, on the 13th December, he was nearly destroyed in a frightful earthquake which destroyed the city, and from which he escaped only with the greatest difficulty.

The year 116 witnessed miracles: the times of Alexander seemed restored. Trajan conquered Adiabene, beyond the Tigris, in spite of a vigorous resistance. There he should have stopped. Pushing his fortune to its limit, Trajan penetrated to the heart of the Parthian Empire. The strategy of the Parthians, like that of the Russians in 1813, consisted in at first offering no resistance. Trajan marched without opposition as far as Babylon; took Æsiphon, the western capital of the Empire, thence descended the Tigris to the Persian Gulf, saw those distant seas which appeared to the Romans only as a vision, and regained Babylon. Then the black spots began to accumulate upon the horizon. Towards the end of 116 Trajan heard at Babylon that revolt had broken out behind him. The Jews had without doubt taken a great part in it. They were numerous in Babylonia. The relations between the Jews of Palestine and those of Babylonia were continual--the doctors passed from one country to the other with great facility. A vast secret society escaping thus from all supervision created a political vehicle of the most active kind. Trajan confided the duty of crushing this dangerous movement to Lusius Quietus, chief of the Berber cavalry, who had placed himself with his goum at the service of the Romans, and had rendered the greatest services in the Parthian wars. Quietus re?conquered Nisibe, Edessa; but Trajan began to see the impossibilities of the enterprise in which he was engaged, and meditated retreat.

Disquieting news reached him, blow upon blow. The Jews were everywhere in revolt. Nameless horrors passed in Cyrenaica. The Jewish fury attained to heights which had never yet been known. This poor people again lost their heads. Perhaps there was already, in Africa, a presentiment of the revival of fortune which was awaiting Trajan; it may be that the Jewish rebellions of Cyrene, the most fanatical of all, were anticipated on the faith of some prophet, that the day of wrath against the Pagans had arrived, and that it was time to begin the Messianic exterminations. All the Jews were agitated as under a demoniacal attack. It was less a revolt than a massacre, with details of indescribable ferocity. Having at their head a certain Lucora, who enjoyed amongst his friends the title of King, these madmen set to work to butcher Greeks and Romans, eating the flesh of those whom they had slaughtered, making belts of their bowels, rubbing themselves with their blood, skinning them and clothing themselves with the skin. Madmen were seen sawing unfortunate men in two through the midst of their bodies. At other times the insurgents delivered the Pagans to the beasts, in memory of what they themselves had suffered, and forced them to fight with each other like gladiators. Two hundred and twenty thousand Cyreneans are believed to have been slaughtered in this way. It was almost the entire population: the province became a desert. To repeople it, Hadrian was obliged to bring colonists from other places, but the country never again flourished as it had done under the Greeks.

From Cyrenaica the epidemic of massacre extended to Egypt and to Cyprus. The latter witnessed atrocities. Under the leadership of a certain Artemion the fanatics destroyed the town of Salamine and exterminated the entire population. The number of Cypriotes butchered, was estimated at 240,000. The resentment for such cruelties was such that the Cypriotes decreed the exclusion of the Jews from their island in perpetuity; even the Jew cast upon their coast by the act of God was put to death.

In Egypt the Jewish insurrection assumed the proportions of a veritable war. At first the rebels had the advantage. Lupus, Prefect of Egypt, was obliged to retreat. The alarm in Alexandria was acute. The Jews, to fortify themselves, destroyed the Temple of Nemesis raised by Cæsar to Pompey. The Greek population succeeded, however, not without a struggle, in gaining the upper hand. All the Greeks of Lower Egypt took refuge with Lupus in the city, and made there a great entrenched camp. It was time. The Cyreneans, led by Lucora, came to join their brethren of Alexandria, and to form with them a single army. Deprived of the support of their Alexandrini co-religionists, all killed or prisoners, but strengthened by bands from other parts of Egypt, they dispersed themselves, killing and plundering, over the Thebaïd. They especially sought to seize the functionaries who tried to gain the cities of the coast, Alexandria and Pelusia. Appian, the future historian, then young, who exercised municipal functions in Alexandria, his country, was nearly captured by these madmen. Lower Egypt was inundated with blood. The fugitive Pagans found themselves pursued like wild beasts; the deserts by the side of the Isthmus of Suez were filled with people who hid themselves and endeavoured to come to an understanding with the Arabs, so as to escape from death.

The position of Trajan in Babylonia became more and more critical. The wandering Arabs in the space between the two rivers caused him much difficulty. The impregnable stronghold of Hatra, inhabited by a war like tribe, stopped him altogether. The surrounding country is deserted, unhealthy, without wood or water, desolated by mosquitoes, exposed to frightful atmospheric troubles. Trajan committed, without doubt from a sense of honour, the mistake of wishing to reduce it As later Septimus Severus and Ardeschir Babek, he failed. The army was frightfully wasted with sickness. The city was a great centre of sun-worship; it was thought that the god was fighting for his temple; storms breaking out at the moment of attack, filled the soldiers with terror. Trajan, who was already suffering from the malady which carried him off a few months later, raised the siege. The retreat was difficult, and marked by more than one partial disaster.

About the month of April 117, the Emperor set out on his return to Antioch, sad, ill, and irritable. The East had conquered him without fighting. All those who had bowed before the conqueror raised their heads again The results of three years of campaigning, full of marvellous struggles against nature, were lost. Trajan had to begin over again, if he were not to lose his reputation for invincibility. All at once grave news came to prove to him what grave dangers were concealed in the situation created by the recent reverses. The Jewish revolt, until then limited to Cyrenaica and Egypt, threatened to extend itself through Palestine, Syria, and Mesopotamia. Always on the watch for signs of weakness in the Roman Empire, the enthusiasts fancied for the tenth time that they saw the preliminary signs of the end of an abhorred domination. Excited by books like Judith and the apocalypse of Esdras, they believed that the day of Edom was come. The cries of joy which they had uttered at the deaths of Nero and Domitian, they uttered once more. The generation which had made the great Revolution had almost disappeared; the new had learned nothing. These hard heads, obstinate and full of passion, were incapable of enlarging the narrow circle of iron that an inveterate psychological heredity had riveted around them. What passed in Judea is obscure, and it is not proved that any positive act of war or of massacre took place there. From Antioch, where he resided, Adrian, Governor of Syria, appears to have succeeded in maintaining order. Far from encouraging rebellion, the doctors of Jabneh had shown, in the scrupulous observation of the Law, a new way of arriving at the peace of the soul. Casuistry had in their hands become a plaything, which like all playthings ought to invite much to patience. As to Mesopotamia, it is natural that a half-subdued population which a year before were in arms, and amongst whom there were not merely dispersed Jews but Jewish armies and dynasties, should have broken out after the check of Hatra, and upon the first indications of the approaching death of Trajan. It appears, besides, that the Romans acted with vigour, often upon mere suspicion They feared that the example of Cyrenaica, of Egypt, and of Cyprus might be contagious. Before the massacres had broken out, Trajan confided to Lucius Quietus the duty of expelling all the Jews from the conquered provinces. Quietus went thither as to an expedition. This African, cruel and pitiless, supported by light Moorish cavalry, men who rode bare-backed without saddle or bridle, went like the modern Bashi-Bazouk, massacring right and left. A very large part of the Jewish population of Mesopotamia were exterminated. To reward the services of Quietus, Trajan detached Palestine from the province of Syria for him, and created him Imperial Legate, thus placing him in the same rank as Adrian.

The revolt of Cyrenaica, of Egypt, and of Cyprus, still continued. Trajan chose one of his most distinguished lieutenants, Marcius Turbo, to suppress it. He gave him a land and a sea force, and numerous cavalry. A regular war with many battles was required to put an end to these madmen. There were regular butcheries. All the Cyrenian Jews, and those from Egypt who had joined them, were massacred. Alexandria--the blockade raised at last--breathed once more, but the destruction of the city had been considerable. One of the first acts of Hadrian after becoming Emperor, was to repair the ruins and to give himself out as the restorer.

Such was this deplorable movement, in which the Jews appear to have been wrong from the first, and which finished by ruining them in the opinion of the civilised world. Poor Israel fell into furious madness. These horrible cruelties, so far removed from the Christian spirit, widened the ditch of separation between Judaism and the Church. The Christian, becoming more and more of an idealist, consoled himself more and more by his gentleness, by his resigned attitude. Israel had made himself a cannibal, rather than allow his prophets to be liars. Pseudo-Esdras, twenty years before, contented himself with the tender reproach of a pious soul which thinks itself forgotten of God: now it is a question of killing everybody, of annihilating the Pagans, that it may not be said that God has failed to keep his promise to Jacob. Every great fanaticism, pressed by the ruin of its hopes, ends in madness, and becomes a peril to the reason of all humanity.

The material diminution of Judaism, as the result of this inept campaign, was very considerable. The number of those who perished was enormous. From that moment the Jewry of Cyrene and Egypt almost disappeared. The powerful community of Alexandria, which had been an essential element of Oriental life, was no longer important. The great synagogue of Diapleuston, which passed in the eyes of the Jews for one of the wonders of the world, was destroyed. The Jewish quarter near the Lochias became a field of ruins and of tombs.

CHAPTER XXIV

DEFINITIVE SEPARATION OF THE CHURCH AND THE SYNAGOGUE

Fanaticism knows no repentance. The monstrous error of 117 scarcely left more than the recollection of a festivity in the Jewish mind. Amongst the number of days when fasting was forbidden, and mourning must be suspended, figures the 12th December, the iom Traïanos or "day of Trajan," not because the war of 116-117 gave reason for any anniversary of victory, but because of the tragic end which the agada ascribed to the enemy of Israel. The massacres of Quietus remained, on the other hand, in tradition, under the name of polémos schel Quitos. A progress of Israel in the way of mourning was attached to it:--

After the polémos schel Aspasionos, crowns and the use of tambourines are forbidden to bridegrooms.

After the polémos schel Quitos, crowns were forbidden to brides, and the teaching of the Greek language to one's son was prohibited.

After the last Polémos, the bride was forbidden to go out of the town in a litter.

Thus every folly brought about a new sequestration, a new renunciation of some part of life. Whilst Christianity became more and more Greek and Latin, and its writers conformed to a good Hellenic style, the Jew interdicted the study of Greek, and shut himself up obstinately in his unintelligible Syro-Hebraic dialect. The root of all good intellectual culture is cut off for him for a thousand years. It is especially in this period that the decisions were given which present Greek education as an impurity, or at best as a frivolity.

The man who announced himself at Jabneh, and grew from day to day as the future chief of Israel, was a certain Aquiba, pupil of the Rabbi Tarphon, of obscure origin, unconnected with the great families who held the chairs and filled the great offices of the nation. He was descended from proselytes, and had had a poverty-stricken youth. He was, it would seem, a sort of democrat, full at first of a ferocious hatred against the doctors in the midst of whom he might one day sit. His exegesis, and his casuistry, were the height of subtlety. Every letter, every syllable of the Canonical texts, became significant, and attempts were made to draw meanings from them. Aquiba was the author of the method which, according to the expression of the Talmud, "from every feature of a letter draws whole bushels of decision." We can only admit that in the revealed Code there was the least that was voluntary, the smallest liberty of style, or of orthography. Thus the particle which is the simple mark of the objective case, and which may be inserted or omitted in Hebrew, furnished puerile inductions.

This touched madness; we are only two steps from the Cabbala and the Notarikon, silly combinations, in which the texts represent no longer the language of humanity, but is taken for a divine book of magic. In detail the consultations of Aquiba are recommended by their moderation, the sentences which are attributed to him have even the marks of a certain liberal spirit. But a violent fanaticism spoiled all his qualities. The greatest contradictions spring up in those minds which are at once subtle and uncultivated, whence the superstitious study of a solitary text had banished the right sense of language and of reason. Incessantly travelling from synagogue to synagogue in all the countries of the Mediterranean, and perhaps even amongst the Parthians, Aquiba kept up amongst his co-religionaries the strange fire with which he himself was filled, and which soon became so melancholy for his country.

A monument of the mournful sadness of these times appears in the apocalypse of Baruch. The work is an imitation of the apocalypse of Esdras, and, like it, is divided into seven visions. Baruch, secretary to Jeremiah, receives from God the order to remain in Jerusalem, to assist in the punishment of the guilty city. He curses the fate which has given him birth, only that he may witness the outrages offered to his mother. He prays God to spare Israel. But for Israel, who wilt praise him? Who will explain his law? Is the world then destined to return to its primitive silence? and what joy for the Pagans if they are able to go into the countries of their idols to rejoice before them over the defeats which they have inflicted upon the true God.

The divine interlocutor answers that the Jerusalem which had been destroyed was not the Eternal Jerusalem, prepared since the times of Paradise, which was shown to Adam before his fall, and a glimpse of which was seen by Abraham and Moses. It was not the Pagans who destroyed the city; it was the wrath of God which annihilated it. An angel descends from heaven, carries all the sacred objects from the Temple, and buries them. The angels then demolish the city. Baruch sings a song of mourning. He is indignant that nature should continue her course, that the earth smiles, and is not burned up by an eternal midday sun.

Labourers, cease to sow, and thou, O Earth, cease to bring forth harvests; wherefore dost thou waste thy wine, O thou Vine, since Zion is no more? Bridegrooms, denounce your rights; virgins, deck yourselves no more with crowns; women, cease to pray that ye may become mothers. Henceforth the barren shall rejoice, and the fruitful mothers shall weep; for why bring forth children in sorrow, whom ye must bury with tears? Henceforth, speak no more of charms; neither discuss beauty. Take the keys of the sanctuary, O priests, cast them towards heaven, return them to the Lord, and say to him,--"Preserve now thine own house!" And ye, O virgins, who sew your linen and your silk with the gold of Ophir, hasten and cast all into the fire, that the flames may carry all these things to him that hath made them, and that our enemies may not rejoice in them. Earth, attend! Dust take heart, to announce in Sheol and say to the dead: "Happy are ye as compared with ourselves!"

Pseudo-Baruch, no better than pseudo-Esdras, can render account of the conduct of God towards his people. Assuredly the turn of the Gentiles will come. If God has given to his people such severe lessons, what will he do with those who have turned his benefits against him? But how explain the fate of so many of the just who have scrupulously observed the Law and have been exterminated? Why has not the Eternal had pity upon Zion for their sakes? Why has he taken account only of the wicked? "What hast thou done with thy servants?" cries the pious writer. "We can no longer understand why thou art our Creator. When the world had no inhabitants, thou didst create man as minister of thy works, to show that the world existed only for man, and not man for the world. And now, behold, the world which thou hast made for us lasts, and we, for whom thou hast made it, disappear."

God answers that man has been made free and intelligent. If he has been punished, it is only his desert. This world for the just man is a trial; the world to come will be a crown. Length of time is a relative matter. Better to have commenced by ignominy and finished with happiness than to have begun in glory and finished in shame. Time is, moreover, pressing on, and will go by much more quickly in the future than in the past.

"If man had but this life," answers the melancholy dreamer, "nothing could be more bitter than his fate. How long shall the triumph of impiety continue? How long, O Lord! wilt thou leave it to be believed that thy patience is weakness? Arise; close Sheol; forbid it henceforward to receive fresh dead men; and cause limbo to give up the souls that are enclosed therein. Behold how long Abraham, Isaac, Jacob and the others, who sleep in the earth, have been waiting, those for whom thou hast said that the world was created! Show thy glory; delay it no longer."

God contents himself with saying that the time is fixed and that the end is not far distant. The Messianic sorrows have already begun; but the signs of the catastrophe will be isolated, partial, so that men shall scarcely be able to see them. At the moment when it shall be said, "The Almighty has forgotten the earth," when the despair of the just shall be at its height, this shall be the hour of awakening. Signs shall stretch forth over the whole universe. Palestine alone shall be safe from calamity. Then the Messiah shall be revealed. Behemoth and Leviathan shall serve as food to those who shall be saved. The earth shall yield up ten thousand for one; a single stem of the vine shall have a thousand branches; every branch shall bear a thousand grapes, and every grape shall yield a hogshead of wine. Joy shall be perfect. In the morning a breath shall leave the bosom of God, bearing the perfume of the most exquisite flowers; in the evening, another breath bearing a wholesome dew. Manna shall fall from Heaven. The dead who sleep in hope of the Messiah shall rise. The receptacles of the souls of the just shall open; the multitude of happy souls shall be all of one mind; the first shall rejoice and the last shall not be sad. The impious shall be consumed with rage, seeing that the moment of their punishment is come. Jerusalem shall be renewed, and crowned for Eternity.

The Roman Empire then appears to our seer like a forest which covers the earth; the shadow of the forest veils the truth; all that there is of evil in the world hides itself there and finds a shelter. It is the harshest and the worst of all the Empires which succeed each other. The Messianic Kingdom, on the contrary, is represented by a vine under whose shadow a sweet and gentle spring arises which runs towards the forest. In approaching this last, the current changes into impetuous waves which uproot it as well as the mountains which surround it. The forest is carried away, until there remains of it nothing but a cedar. This cedar represents the last Roman sovereign remaining standing when all the legions shall have been exterminated (according to us, Trajan, after his reverses in Macedonia). He is overthrown in his turn. The vine then says to him:--

Is it not thou, O Cedar! who art the relic of the forest of malice; who seizest upon what does not belong to thee; who never hast pity upon that which is thine own; who wouldest reign over that which was far from thee; who boldest in the nets of impiety all that approacheth thee; and who art proud as though thou couldest never be uprooted? Behold thine hour is come. Go, O Cedar; share the fate of the forest which has disappeared before thee, and let thine ashes mingle with it."

The cedar is short, is cast down to the earth, and fire is kindled. The chief is enchained and brought upon Mount Sion. There the Messiah convicts him of impiety, shows him the wickedness which has been wrought by his armies, and kills him. The vine then extends itself on all sides and covers the earth; the earth reclothes itself with flowers which never fade. The Messiah will reign until the end of the corruptible world. The wicked, during this time, shall burn in a fire where none shall pity them.

Oh, blindness of man, who will not discern the approach of the Great Day! On the eve of the event they will live calm and careless. They will see miracles without understanding them; true and false prophecies shall grow in all parts. Like pseudo-Esdras, our visionary believes in the small number of the elect, and in the enormous number of the damned. "Just men rejoice in your sufferings; for a day of trial here below, ye shall have an eternity of glory." Like pseudo-Esdras again he disquiets himself with great naïveté concerning the physical difficulties of the Resurrection. In what form shall the dead arise? Will they keep the same body that they had before? Pseudo-Baruch does not hesitate. The earth will restore the dead which have been entrusted to her, as she has received them. "She shall give them back," saith God, "as I have given them to her." That will be necessary to convince the sceptical of the resurrection; they must have ocular evidence of the identity of those whom they have known.

After the judgment, a marvellous change will be wrought. The damned shall become more ugly than they were; the just shall become beautiful, brilliant, glorious; their figures shall be transformed into a luminous ideal. The rage of the wicked shall be frightful, seeing those whom they have persecuted here below glorified above them. They will be forced to assist at this spectacle, before being taken away for punishment. The just shall see marvels; the invisible world shall be unrolled before them; the hidden times shall be discovered. No more old age; equal to the angels; like the stars; they may change themselves into whatever form they will; they will go from beauty to beauty, from glory to glory; all Paradise shall be open to them; they shall contemplate the majesty of the mystical beasts which are under the throne; all the armies of angels shall await their arrival. The first who enter shall receive the last; the last shall recognise those whom they knew to have preceded them.

These dreams are pervaded by some glimpses of a sufficiently lucid good sense. More than pseudo-Esdras, pseudo-Baruch has pity on man, and protests against a theology which has no bowels. Man has not said to his father, "Beget me," nor has he said to Sheol, "Open to receive me." The individual is responsible only for himself; each of us is Adam for his own soul. But fanaticism leads him soon to the most terrible thoughts. He sees rising from the sea a cloud composed alternately of zones of black and of clear water. These are the alternations of faith and unfaith in Israel. The angel Ramiel, who explains these mysteries to him, has judgments of the most sombre rigorism. The fine epochs are those in which they have massacred the nations which sinned, and burned and stoned the heterodox, when they dug up the bones of the wicked to burn them, when every sin against legal purity was punished with death. The good King "for whom the celestial glory was created," is he who does not suffer an uncircumcised man upon the earth.

After the spectacle of the twelve zones a deluge of black water descends, mingled with stenches and with fire. It is the period of transition between the kingdom of Israel and the coming of the Messiah--a time of abominations, of wars, of plagues, of earthquakes. The earth seems to wish to devour its inhabitants. A flash of lightning (the Messiah) sweeps out all, purifies all, cures all. The miserable survivors of the plagues shall be given over to the Messiah, who will kill them. All who have not oppressed Israel shall live. Every nation which has governed Israel with violence shall be put to the sword. In the midst of these sufferings the Holy Land alone shall be at peace and shall protect its people.

Paradise shall then be realised upon earth; no more pain, no more suffering, no more sickness, no more toil. Animals shall serve man spontaneously. Men will still die, but never prematurely; women shall feel no more the pangs of travail; the harvest shall be gathered without effort; the houses shall be built without fatigue. Hatred, injustice, vengeance, calumny, shall disappear.

The people received the prophecy of Baruch with delight. But it was only right that the Jews dispersed in distant countries should not be deprived of so beautiful a revelation. Baruch wrote, therefore, to the ten tribes and a half of the dispersion, a letter which he entrusted to an eagle, and which is an abridgment of the entire book. There, even more clearly than in the book itself, may be seen the fundamental idea of the author, which is to bring about the return of the dispersed Jews to the Holy Land, that land alone during the Messianic crisis being able to offer them an assured asylum. The day is approaching when God will return to the enemies of Israel the evil which they have done to his people. The youth of the world is past; the vigour of creation is spent. The bucket is near to the well; the ship to the port; the caravan to the city; life to its end.

We see the infidel nations prosperous, although they act with impiety; but their prosperity is like a vapour. We see them rich although they act with iniquity; but their riches will last them as long as a drop of water. We see the solidity of their power, although they resist God; but it is worth no more than spittle. We contemplate their splendour whilst they do not observe the precepts of the Most High; but they shall vanish away like smoke. . . . Let nothing which belongs to the present time enter into your thoughts; have patience, for all that has been promised shall happen. We will not stop over the spectacle of the delights which foreign nations may enjoy. Let us beware lest we be excluded at once from the heritage of two worlds; captives here, tortured hereafter. Let us prepare our souls that we may rest with our fathers and may not be punished with our enemies.

Baruch receives the assurance that he will be taken to heaven like Enoch without having tasted death. We have seen that favour granted, in like manner, to Esdras, by the author of the apocalypse which is attributed to this last.

The work of the pseudo-Baruch, like that of the pseudo-Esdras, was as successful amongst the Christians as amongst the Jews--perhaps even more so. The original Greek was soon lost, but a Syriac translation was made which has come down to us. The final letter alone, however, was adapted for the use of the Church. This letter forms an integral part of the Syriac Bible, at least amongst the Jacobites, and lessons are taken from it for the Burial Office. We have seen pseudo-Esdras also furnish for our office for the dead some of its most gloomy thoughts. Death, in fact, appears to reign as mistress in these last fruits of the wandering imagination of Israel.

Pseudo-Baruch is the last writer of the apocryphal literature of the Old Testament. The Bible which he knew is the same as that which we perceive behind the Epistle of Jude and the pretended Epistle of Barnabas, that is to say, the canonical books of the Old Testament. The author adds, whilst putting them on the same footing, books recently fabricated, such as the Revelations of Moses, the Prayer of Manasseh, and other agadic compilations. These works, written in a biblical style, divided into verses, became a sort of supplement to the Bible. Often even, precisely because of their modern character, such apocryphal productions had greater popularity than the ancient Bible, and were accepted as Holy Scripture on the day of their appearance, at least by the Christians, who were more easy in that respect than the Jews. For the future there will be no more of these books. The Jews compose no more pasticcios of the Sacred Text; we feel amongst them even fears and precautions on this subject. Hebrew religious poetry of a later date seems to be expressly written in a style which is not that of the Bible.

It is possible that the troubles in Palestine, under Trajan, may have been the occasion for transporting the Beth-din of Jabneh to Ouscha. The Beth-din, as far as possible, must be fixed in Judea; but Jabneh, a mixed town, sufficiently large, not far from Jerusalem, might become uninhabitable for the Jews after the horrible excesses which they had committed in Egypt and Cyprus. Ouscha was an altogether obscure part of Galilee. The new patriarchate was of much less importance than that of Jabneh. The patriarch of Jabneh was a prince (nasi); he had a sort of court; he drew a great prestige from the pretensions of the family of Hillel to descend from David. The supreme council of the nation was now going to reside in the obscure villages of Galilee. "The institutions of Ouscha"--that is to say, the rules which were settled by the doctors of Ouscha--had none the less an authority of the first order: they occupied a considerable place in the history of the Talmud.

What was called the Church of Jerusalem continued its tranquil existence a thousand leagues removed from the seditious ideas which animated the nation. A great number of Jews were converted, and continued to observe strictly the prescriptions of the Law. The chiefs of that Church were, moreover, taken from amongst the circumcised Christians, and all the Church, not to wound the rigorists, constrained itself to follow the Mosaic rules. The list of these bishops of the circumcision is full of uncertainties. The best-known appears to have been one named Justus. The controversy between the converted and those who persisted in pure Mosaism was active but less acrimonious than after Bar Coziba. A certain Juda ben Nakouza appears to have played an especially brilliant part. The Christians endeavoured to prove that the Bible did not exclude the divinity of Jesus Christ. They insisted upon the word Elohim, upon the plural employed by God upon several occasions (for example, in Genesis i. 26), upon the repetition of the different names of God, etc. The Jews had no difficulty in showing that the tendencies of the new sect were in contradiction with the fundamental doctrines of the religion of Israel.

In Galilee, the relations of the two sects appear to have been friendly. A Judeo-Christian of Galilee, Jacob of Caphar-Shekaniah, appears about this time to have been much mixed up with the Jewish world of Sephoris, of the little towns of the neighbourhood. Not only did he converse with the doctors and quote to them pretended words of Jesus, but he practised, like James, the brother of the Lord, spiritual medicine, and pretended to cure the bite of a serpent by the name of Jesus. Rabbi Eliezer was, it is said, persecuted as inclined to Christianity. Rabbi Joshua ben Hanania died preoccupied with the new ideas. Christians repeated to him in every tone that God had turned away from the Jewish nation: "No," he answered, "His hand is still stretched out over us." There were conversions in his own family. His nephew Hananiah being come to Caphar-Nahum, "was bewitched by the minim" to such a point that he was seen on an ass on the Sabbath day. When he came to the house of his uncle Joshua, he cured him of the sorcery by means of an ointment, but insisted upon his retirement to Babylon. At another time the Talmudist narrator appears to desire that it shall be believed that amongst Christians infamies existed like those which were laid to the charge of the pretended Nicholas. Rabbi Isaiah of Cæsarea included in the same curse the Judeo-Christians who supported these polemics and the heretical population of Caphar-Nahum, the primary source of all the evil.

In general the minim, especially those of Caphar-Nahum, passed for great magicians, and their successes were attributed to spells and to ocular illusions. We have already seen that until the third century at least Jewish doctors continued to work their cures in the name of Jesus. But the Gospel was cursed: reading it was strictly forbidden; the very name of Gospel gave rise to a play upon words which made it signify "evident iniquity." A certain Eliza ben Abouyah, surnamed Aher, who professed a species of gnostic Christianity, was for his former co-religonists the type of a perfect apostate. Little by little the Judeo-Christians were placed by the Jews in the same rank as the Pagans, and much below the Samaritans. Their bread and their wine were held to be unclean; their means of cure proscribed; their books considered as repertoires of the most dangerous magic. Hence, the Churches of Paul offered to the Jews who wished to be converted a more advantageous position than the Judeo-Christian Churches, exposed as they were on the part of Judaism to all the hatred of which brothers who have quarrelled are capable.

The truth of the apocalyptic image was striking. The woman protected by God, the Church, had truly received two eagles' wings to fly into the desert far from the crises of the world and from its sanguinary dramas. There she grew in peace, and all that was done against her turned to her. The dangers of her first childhood are passed; her growth is henceforward assured.

END OF THE GOSPELS.

APPENDIX

The inaccuracy of the information furnished by the Gospels as to the material circumstances of the life of Jesus, the dubiety of the traditions of the first century, collected by Hegesippus, the frequent homonyms which occasion so much embarrassment in the history of the Jews at all epochs, render the questions relating to the family of Jesus almost insoluble. If we hold by a passage from the synoptic Gospels, Matt. xiii. 55, 56; Mark vi. 3, Jesus should have four brothers and several sisters. His four brothers were called James, Joseph or Jose, Simon, and Jude, respectively. Two of these names figure, in fact, in all the ecclesiastical and apostolic traditions as being "brothers of the Lord." The personage of "James, brother of the Lord," is, after that of St Paul, the most perfectly sketched of any of the first Christian generation. The Epistle of St Paul to the Galatians, the Acts of the Apostles, the superscriptions of the authentic epistles, or those not ascribed to James and Jude, the historian Josephus, the Ebionite legend of Peter, the old Judeo-Christian historian Hegesippus, are agreed in making him the chief of the old Judeo-Christian Church. The most authentic of these proofs, the passage in the Epistle to the Galatians, gives him distinctly the title of ἀδελφὸς τοῦ Κυρίου.

One Jude appears also to have a most indisputable right to this title. The Jude whose epistle we possess gives himself the title of ἀδελφός de Iachobou. A person of the name of James, of sufficient importance to be taken notice of, and who was given the authority to call himself His brother, can hardly be the celebrated James of the Epistle to the Galatians, the Acts, of Josephus, of Hegesippus, of the pseudo-Clementine writings. If this James was "brother of the Lord," Jude, the true or supposed author of the epistle which forms a part of the canon, was then also a brother of the Lord. Hegesippus certainly understood him so to be. This Jude, whose grandson (ὑιωνοί) was sought out and presented to Domitian as the last representative of the race of David, was, in the view of the antique historian of the Church, the brother of Jesus according to the flesh. Several reasons lead even to the supposition that this Jude was in his turn the chief of the Church of Jerusalem. Here is then a second personage who is included in the series of the four names given by the synoptic Gospels as those of the brothers of Jesus.

Simon and Jose are not known otherwise than as brothers of the Lord. But there would be nothing singular in the fact that two members of the family should remain obscure. What is much more surprising is that in reconciling other facts furnished by the Gospels, Hegesippus, and the oldest traditions of the Church of Jerusalem, a family of cousins-german of Jesus is formed, bearing almost the same names which are given by Matthew (xiii. 55) and by Mark (vi. 3), as those of the brothers of Jesus.

In fact, amongst the women whom the synoptics place at the foot of the cross of Jesus, and who testify to the resurrection, there is found one "Mary," mother of James the Less (ὁ μιχρός) and of Jose (Matt. xvii. 56; Mark xv. 40, 47; xiv. 1; Luke xxiv. 10). This Mary is certainly the same as the one whom the fourth Gospel (xix. 25) places also at the foot of the cross, who is called Μαρία ἡ τοῦ Κλωπᾶ (which signifies without doubt "Mary, the wife of Clopas"), and which makes her a sister of the mother of Jesus. The difficulty which is thus occasioned by the two sisters being called by the same name is hardly taken into account by the fourth Evangelist, who only once gives to the mother of Jesus the name of Mary. Be this as it may, we have already two cousins-german of Jesus called James and Jose. We find, moreover, a Simon, son of Clopas, whom Hegesippus and all those who have transmitted to us the memories of the primitive Church of Jerusalem, represented as the second Bishop of Jerusalem, and as having been martyred under Trajan. Finally, there are traces of a fourth member of the family of Clopas in that Jude, son of James, who appears to have succeeded Simeon in the See of Jerusalem. The family of Clopas appearing to have retained in an all but hereditary manner the government of the Church of Jerusalem from Titus to Hadrian, it is not too bold to assume that the James, the brother of this Jude, was James the Less, son of Mary Cleophas.

We have thus three sons of Clopas called James, Jose, Simeon, exactly like the brothers of Jesus mentioned by the synoptics, without speaking of a hypothetical grandson in whom was revived the same identical name. Two sisters bearing the same name is indeed a very singular fact. What is to be said of a case in which these two sisters should have had at least three sons bearing the same name? No criticism can admit the possibility of such a coincidence. It is evident that we shall have to seek some solution which shall dispose of that anomaly.

The orthodox doctors, since St Jerome, thought to remove the difficulty by taking it for granted that the four personages enumerated by Mark and Matthew as brothers of Jesus were, in reality, his cousins-german, sons of Mary Cleophas. But this is inadmissible. Many other passages assume that Jesus had full brothers and sisters. The arrangement of the little scene recounted by Matthew (xiii. 54, et seq., and Mark vi. 2, et seq.) is very significant. There the "brothers" are immediately related to the "mother." The anecdote (Mark iii. 31, et seq.; Matt. xii. 46, et seq.) gives rise to still less ambiguity. Finally the whole of the Jerusalemitish tradition distinguishes clearly the "brothers of the Lord" from the family of Clopas. Simeon, son of Clopas, the second Bishop of Jerusalem, is called ἀνεψιὸς τοῦ σωτῆρος. Not a single one of the ἀδελφοὶ τοῦ Κυρίου bears after his name the addition of tou Klopa. Notoriously James, brother of the Lord, was not the son of Clopas; if he had been, he would have also been the brother of Simeon, his successor. Now Hegesippus does not believe this. When we read chapters xi. and xxxii. of the third book of Eusebius' Ecclesiastical History, we are convinced of it. The chronology will no longer permit of such a supposition. Simeon died at a very old age, in the reign of Trajan. James died in the year 62, also very old. The difference between the ages of the two brothers might thus have been forty years or thereabout. Hence the theory which sees the ἀδελφοὶ τοῦ Κυρίου in the sons of Clopas is inadmissible. Let it be added that in the Gospel of the Hebrews, which is often so superior to the other synoptic texts, Jesus directly calls James "my brother," an expression altogether exceptional, and which people would certainly never employ to a cousin-german.

Jesus had full brothers and sisters. Only it is possible that these brothers and sisters were but half-brothers and half-sisters. Were these brothers and sisters likewise sons and daughters of Mary? This is improbable. In fact, the brothers appear to have been much older than Jesus. Now Jesus was, as it would appear, the first-born of his mother. Jesus, moreover, was, in his youth, designated at Nazareth by the name of "Son of Mary." For this we have the most undoubted testimony of the Gospels. This assumes that he was known for a long time as the only son of a widow. In fact, such appellations were only employed where the father was dead, and when the widow had no other son. Let us instance the case of Piero dells Francesca, the celebrated painter. In fine, the myth of the virginity of Mary, without excluding absolutely the idea that Mary may have had afterwards other children by Joseph, or have been remarried, fits in better with the hypothesis that she had only one son.

No doubt, the legend is so constructed as to do the greatest violence to truth. Nevertheless, we must remember that the legend now in question was elaborated by the brothers and cousins of Jesus themselves. Jesus, the sole and tardy progeny of the union of a young woman and a man already reached maturity, offered perfect opportunity for the opinions according to which his conception had been supernatural. In such a case, the divine action appeared so much the more striking in proportion as nature seemed the more impotent. People take a pleasure in representing children, predestined to great prophetic vocations, as being born to old men or of women who have been for a long time sterile-- Samuel, John the Baptist, and Mary herself are conspicuous instances. The author, also, of the Protovangile of James, St Epiphanes, etc., ardently insists upon the great age of Joseph, induced thereto, no doubt, by à priori motives, yet guided also in this latter by a just opinion as to the circumstances in which Jesus was born.

These difficulties could be readily enough removed, if we were to assume that Joseph had before been married, and had, by this marriage, sons and daughters, in particular, James and Jude. These two personages, and James, at least, appear to have been older than Jesus. The hostile disposition which was attributed at first to the brothers of Jesus by the Gospels, the singular contrast which the principles and the species of life led by James and Jude, and those of Jesus presents, is, in such a hypothesis, somewhat less unaccountable than on the other suppositions that have been made to get rid of these contradictions.

How could the sons of Clopas be cousins-german of Jesus? They may have been by the same mother, Mary Cleophas, as the fourth Gospel would have us believe, or by the same father, Clopas, who is made out by Hegisippus to be a brother of Joseph, or on both sides at once; for it was actually possible that the two brothers may have married two sisters. Between these three hypotheses, the second is much the more probable. The hypothesis as to two sisters bearing the same name, is extremely problematical. The passage in the fourth Gospel (xix. 25) may contain an error. Let no add that, according to one interpretation, a laborious one, it is true, yet, nevertheless, admissible, the expression ἡ ἀδελφὴ τῆς μητρός αὐτοῦ does not refer to Maria he tou Klopa, but to a distinct nameless personage, such as was the mother of Jesus herself. The aged Hegisippus, so preoccupied with everything touching the family of Jesus, appears to have known quite well the truth upon this point. But bow can we admit that the two brothers Joseph and Clopas had three or even four sons bearing the same names? Let us examine the list of the four brothers of Jesus given by the synoptics--James, Jude, Simon, Jose. The first two have a well-authenticated title to be styled brothers of the Lord; the two last, outside the two Synoptic passages, have no valid claim to it. Just as in the case of the two names Simon and Simeon, Jose or Joseph, which are to be found elsewhere in the list of the sons of Clopas, we are led to adopt the following hypothesis: that the passages in Mark and in Matthew, in which are enumerated the four brothers of Jesus, contain an inadvertence; that as regards the four personages named by the synoptics, James and Jude were indeed brothers of Jesus and sons of Joseph, but that Simon and Jose have been placed there by mistake. The compiler of that little writing, like all the agadists, lays little store by exactness of material details, and, like all the evangelical narrators (except the fourth), was dominated by the cadence of Semitic parallelism. The necessities of locution may have drawn them into making an enumeration, the turn of which required four proper names. As he only knew two full brothers of Jesus, he was, perforce, compelled to associate with them two of their cousins-german. In fact, it seems that Jesus had indeed more than two brothers. "Have I not the right to have a wife," says St Paul, "like the other Apostles, like the brothers of the Lord, like Cephas?" According to all tradition, James, the brother of the Lord, was not married. Jude was married, but that was not sufficient to justify the plural used by St Paul. There would need to have been a good many of these brothers, seeing that the exception in the case of James did not hinder St Paul from regarding generally the brothers of the Lord as married.

Clopas seems to have been younger than Joseph, and his eldest son must have been younger than the eldest son of the latter. It is natural that, if his name was James, a custom might exist in the family of calling him ὁ μιχρός, in order to distinguish him from his cousin-german of the same name. Simeon may have been fifteen years younger than Jesus, and, strictly speaking, died in the reign of Trajan. Nevertheless, we prefer to believe that the member of the Cleophas family martyred under Trajan belonged to another generation. Mere data regarding the age of James and Simeon are, moreover, very uncertain. James must have died at ninety-six, and Simeon at a hundred-and-twenty. This last assumption is, on the face of it, inadmissible. On the other hand, if James had been ninety-six, as it is pretended, in 62, he must have been born thirty-four years before Jesus, which is a thing very unlikely.

It remains to inquire whether any of these brothers of cousins-german of Jesus did not figure in the lists of the Apostles which have been conserved to us in the synoptics and by the author of the Acts. Although the college of the Apostles and that of the brothers of the Lord were two distinct groups, it has nevertheless been considered as possible that a few of the personages may have constituted a part of both. Indeed the names of James, Jude, and Simeon are to be found in the lists of the Apostles. James, the son of Zebedee, has nothing to do with this discussion, no more than has Judas Iscariot. But what are we to think of this James, son of Alpheus, whom the four lists of the Apostles (Matt. x. 2, et seq.; Mark iii. 14, et seq.; Luke v. 13, et seq.; Acts i. 13, et seq.) include in the number of the Twelve? People have often identified the name of Ἀλφαῖος with that of Κλεοπᾶς, by means of chlphy. This is indeed a reconcilement which is altogether false. Ἀλφαῖος is the Hebrew name chlphy, and Κλωπᾶς or Κλεοπᾶς is an abbreviation of Κλεόπατρος. James, the son of Alpheus, has not then the least title to being one of the cousins-german of Jesus. The evangelical personnel possessed in reality four Jameses, one the son of Joseph and brother of Jesus; another, son of Clopas; another, son of Zebedee; another, son of Alpheus.

The list of the Apostles given by Luke in his Gospel and in the Acts contains one Ἰούδα Ἰάχωβου, whom it has been attempted to identify with Jude, brother of the Lord, by assuming that it was necessary to understand ἀδελφός between the two names. Nothing could be more arbitrary. This Judas was the son of James, otherwise unknown. The same must also be said of Simon the Zealot, whom people have tried, without a shadow of reason, to identify with the Simon that we find classed (Matt. xiii. 55; Mark vi. 3) among the brothers of Jesus.

To sum up, it does not appear that a single member of the family of Jesus formed a part of the college of the Twelve. James himself was not of that number. The only two brothers of the Lord whose names we are sure of knowing were James and Jude. James was not married, but Jude had children and grandchildren; the latter appeared before Domitian as descendants of David, and were presidents of churches in Syria.

As for the sons of Clopas, we know three of them, one of whom appears to have had children. This family of Clopas, after the war of Titus, held the highest positions in the Church of Jerusalem. A member of the Clopas family was martyred under Trajan. After that, we hear no more of the descendants of the brothers of the Lord, nor of descendants of Clopas.

THE END

www.ingramcontent.com/pod-product-compliance
Lightning Source LLC
Chambersburg PA
CBHW021240090426
42740CB00006B/621